THE
SURE
THING

ALSO BY NICK TOWNSEND

Giving a Little Back: The Autobiography of Barney Curley
A Golden Age: Steve Redgrave, the Autobiography
You Can Win at Life with Steve Redgrave
Mark Johnston: The Authorized Biography
Close to the Wind: The Autobiography of Sir Ben Ainslie

THE
SURE
THING

NICK TOWNSEND

CENTURY

Published by Century 2014

2 4 6 8 10 9 7 5 3 1

First published in Great Britain in 2014 by
Century
Random House, 20 Vauxhall Bridge Road,
London SW1V 2SA

www.randomhouse.co.uk

Addresses for companies within The Random House Group Limited can be found
at: www.randomhouse.co.uk

The Random House Group Limited Reg. No. 954009

A CIP catalogue record for this book
is available from the British Library

ISBN 9781780890715

The Random House Group Limited supports the Forest Stewardship
Council® (FSC®), the leading international forest-certification organisation.
Our books carrying the FSC label are printed on FSC®-certified paper. FSC is
the only forest-certification scheme supported by the leading environmental
organisations, including Greenpeace. Our paper procurement policy can be found
at www.randomhouse.co.uk/environment

Typeset by Palimpsest Book Production Ltd, Falkirk, Stirlingshire
Printed and bound in Great Britain by
CPI Group (UK) Ltd, Croydon, CR0 4YY

To Louise

All good fortune is a gift of the gods. And you don't win the favour of the ancient gods by being good, but by being bold.

Anita Brookner

INTRODUCTION

In the late 1980s, an eager-to-impress member of the *Daily Mail* racing desk was dispatched to extract an interview from a racehorse trainer whose gambling adventures both sides of the Irish Sea had provoked increasing fascination.

The quest was to profile the man behind the myth created by a huge punt in Ireland and a raffle of his mansion that had made news pages worldwide.

The quarry, whose horses' names were apt to reflect his own attitudes – or sometimes those he perceived in others – had at one time had a charge called I'm Incommunicado. And that just about encapsulated him back then.

In *The Directory of the Turf*, the majority of trainers, jockeys and others in racing's fraternity readily listed full biographical details; everything from names of spouse and children to best horses trained, and contact details.

The entry for Curley, B. J. was ominously short on detail: just an address for his Exning stables, and a phone number – calls to which were never answered.

The journalist in question decided to confront the trainer one evening at a Windsor race meeting. No preamble, simply this: would he be willing to be interviewed? The laser eyes quizzically studied the questioner

1

for a second before an alternative phone number was proffered. Several days later – nothing is rushed in this man's world – a meeting in London was organised, followed by a visit to Barney Curley's Newmarket home.

A three-day newspaper serial ensued, followed by a lengthy association that resulted in *Giving a Little Back*, his autobiography. It was also to prove a career-enhancing moment for that newspaperman – the author of this book.

A quarter of a century on from that first meeting, this is the story of the nation's most successful gambler over four decades, and is centred around the betting coup that created notoriety in 1975, and its more spectacular sequel 35 years later.

This book could not have been written without Barney Curley's blessing and his cooperation. I am also grateful to racing figures who readily agreed to share their memories with me. Particular appreciation must go to Liam Brennan, Michael Furlong, Chris Grant, Tom and Declan Queally and Denis O'Regan.

This project would also not have been possible without significant contributions from Barney Curley's aides Martin Parsons and Jack Lynch and members of their team.

I am indebted to all those at Random House for their time and patience: specifically Century's publishing director Ben Dunn, who recognised the potential of this story, and his great faith in it; Julia Twaites, for her valuable assistance and forbearance; to lawyer Roger Field; and editor Mark Persad. I am also grateful to the *Racing Post*'s John Cobb, a long-time associate, for checking my manuscript, and also to my brother, Steve, for his valuable input.

My research has been by aided by the following books:

The Wayward Lad: the Autobiography of Graham Bradley (Greenwater Publishing), *The Barry Brogan Story* (Arthur Barker), *Frankie: the Autobiography of Frankie Dettori* (Collins Willow), *Silver Buck* (by Andrew Hoyle, Pelham Books), *300 Years of Racing at Bellewstown.*

But finally I must express my appreciation of Len Gould, the former *Daily Mail* sports executive, who suggested back in 1988, 'Why don't you get hold of that fellow Barney Curley . . .?'

Nick Townsend

This is a true story, though certain names and background details have been changed at the request of individuals involved.

CHAPTER 1

Newmarket, Suffolk

First light had already summoned the early shift of the town built around horsepower to the gallops of Newmarket Heath when Barney Curley arose, as usual, at 5.45. He had slept well. Invariably he did.

He knelt, as he did each morning, before a photograph of the Sacred Heart and said a short prayer: 'Lord, lay your hand on my head and see me through the day.'

In many respects, it would be an unexceptional day for the racehorse trainer and the nation's most respected professional gambler. His routine would be broken only by a visit for blood tests to Addenbrooke's Hospital, where the previous year he had lain on the operating table for ten hours. 'It had been even money on each, live or die,' recalls the man who tends to see life through the prism of odds. It is the kind of price he usually shuns.

In certain respects, however, it would be an extraordinary day.

In this town of historic equine properties – Sir Michael Stoute's Freemason Lodge and Warren Place, where Sir Henry Cecil was master until his death in June 2013, to name but two – few would have cast more than a glance at Curley's property. Cleveland House adjoined his small racing yard midway along Hamilton Road in the horse-racing town inexorably linked with thorough-breds since James I made the locale his equine play-ground.

Today it is His Highness Sheikh Mohammed, vice president and prime minister of the UAE and ruler of Dubai, who dominates. Directly opposite Curley's property was the capacious Hamilton Hill complex, part of the Sheikh's Darley organisation, a palatial base providing a pre-training set-up for his young horses.

In comparison, Curley's operation was as incongruous as a corner convenience shop – and one invariably rather low on stock at that – in the shadow of a superstore. It was amongst the smallest training establishments in this town of around 55 racing stables, though its human principal had long yielded a far more substantial degree of intrigue.

Within a few square miles, the equine population ranged from bucking, squealing youngsters to others long familiar with the routine. Some had glory in their sights and might be bound for the Classics; for others, like Curley's, there were more limited expectations.

Curley had been based in the town, known as the headquarters of racing, since he decamped with his family from Ireland a quarter of a century before, principally, he says, because he had found it near impossible to find a bookmaker there to accept decent-sized bets. We speak of a man prepared to outlay a six-figure sum on one horse – if he could get the money on.

In his day, top-class animals such as Cheltenham Gold Cup winners Silver Buck and Forgive 'N Forget had passed through his hands. On this day, Curley's equine entourage includes nothing of that quality. Indeed, early in 2010 he had barely a dozen horses capable of catching the judge's eye if the conditions were right, and even then in the most modest of contests. But Curley had long been a master at extracting the maximum from the moderate – when the money was down.

He enjoyed the early morning as he pottered around preparing porridge. This was thinking time. No one to disturb him. Just gone six, and he glanced out of the window as the first lot of his whinnying, impatient charges were prepared to clatter out to the adjacent gallops under the practised eye of his long-time assistant Andrew Stringer and Stringer's wife Alison, who organised their day-to-day work.

Three horses were the subject of special attention. They had to be groomed, shod, fed and prepared for their journey to the races. One was of specific concern, and was walked and trotted up and down under close inspection. Eventually, that horse and the yard's two other runners that day departed for the races. It was past 8 a.m.

Curley hugged his rheumy-eyed St Bernard, Arnie, his 'best friend in the world', before driving to his local church, Our Lady with St Etheldreda's. Firm in his religious convictions, despite having undergone a rare conversion from student of the Good Book to learned scholar of The Form Book early in his adult years, he always endeavoured to attend Mass.

The later delay at the hospital was not entirely unexpected, but Curley had eventually arrived back home just after four in the afternoon. He made a single phone call as he positioned himself in his beloved red chair in his office and drew contentedly on his umpteenth cigarette of the day, flicking ash into a receptacle as capacious as a crematorium urn. Mr Michael Gaunt, his consultant, wouldn't have approved but had long since given up proffering advice to quit.

The vice had never been a consequence of nerves. His consultant could at least be reassured that Curley's pulse was steady as he awaited developments in a scheme that had been maturing in his mind for years. The hard eyes would not have betrayed a scintilla of emotion, win or lose.

Curley was an intrepid explorer in an impenetrable betting jungle that had cost many reputations and livelihoods over the years, frequently those of the most cerebral and rational of men. And on this of all days, the odds could rarely have been so loaded against him. Nor the potential rewards so enormous.

London EC4

Within earshot of St Paul's Cathedral, in one of two upmarket rented apartments, sleep had not come so easily for Curley's aide, Martin Parsons. He was a man as heavily laden with responsibility as a Cairo street donkey bearing his master's market produce. He'd only got a couple of hours' shut-eye. For days he had been running on adrenalin.

During the previous week his team had begun to assemble from a host of locations, mostly in Ireland. A mix of heady anticipation and trepidation enveloped this group of willing conscripts. Few had a precise idea of what would be asked of them. This was deliberate policy.

They included those who, as civilians, would normally

have been setting off to work as doctor, accountant, estate agent, engineer, HR manager, taxi driver or primary school teacher, but who here found themselves in decidedly different guises.

They had departed from home offering a range of unlikely excuses for absence to their loved ones. 'Oh, I've some work in London . . .' one said, flirting with the truth. 'Having a behind-the-scenes look at Reading Football Club' was another, rather less plausible explanation.

Someone possessing ultra-suspicious instincts might have queried the presence of this group as they came and went. A student gathering, perhaps? Possibly political activists, only the location was too upmarket? The less charitable might have had them down as young men sobering up in the aftermath of a stag weekend.

Or, just conceivably, something more sinister.

The cleaners had shot the arriving group some suspicious glances. They couldn't be blamed. Anyone who had ventured into those apartments would have seen an array of new mobile phones on charge; bikes and folding bikes strewn throughout the rooms and corridors; a temporarily constructed network of laptops and printers; walls covered in large street maps of London and the Underground network.

As Parsons readily conceded, the cleaners could have been excused for thinking they had stumbled across the planning of a terrorist attack.

In the background, the strains of 'The Mountains of Mourne' drifted through the rooms. It is a young Irishman's perception of London sent to his love back home and became the group's theme song. It begins:

Oh, Mary, this London's a wonderful sight,
With people all working by day and by night.
Sure they don't sow potatoes, nor barley, nor
* wheat,*
But there's gangs of them digging for gold in the
* street.*
At least when I asked them that's what I was
* told,*
So I just took a hand at this digging for gold . . .

In a sense, that was what this day was about.

At least one of those present had initially pondered just what kind of scheme he had walked into. 'It didn't take a huge leap for me to speculate on the possible illegality of the enterprise . . .'

His fears were soon to be proved unfounded as events unfolded on this Monday, 10 May 2010.

Downing Street, London

A few miles away from St Paul's, the seat of government was aflame with political intrigue. Four days on from polling day, Britain awoke to a prime minister still entrenched in his bunker, still gripping on to office with those well-chewed fingernails, keeping the removal men at bay.

You don't have to be a political geek to recall those hours. Even the *Daily Star*, habitually fixated by images of voluptuous young women and the love lives and booze-fuelled shenanigans of reality TV show Z-listers, demonstrated a rare front-page fascination with political issues.

'It's Gord Riddance', proclaimed their headline in red-top-speak. For one day at least, the fate of Gordon was suddenly more pressing than the love life of Jordan.

Meanwhile, throughout the country, the factory gates of the horse-racing industry were open. Racing employs hundreds of thousands of people, and is a seven-day-a week operation inspiring a betting turnover of many billions per annum.

On Mondays, however, the sport is low-key, offering undistinguished racing and betting opportunities at what are regarded as the less heralded of the nation's 59 courses.

Early in the week, punters who view proceedings on-course, in front of their TV sets or in betting shops tend to be the hard core; amongst them the fanatical and the desperate. That day they would have been digesting their various daily sources of information: the *Racing Post* and other newspapers, and the more serious of them The Form Book.

Flat racing that afternoon was taking place around the country, at the seaside courses of Brighton in Sussex and Redcar on Teesside and at Wolverhampton, one of the less prepossessing courses on which horses race of an all-weather surface.

Later, there would be a Flat card at the ever-popular Windsor evening meeting, where you could elect to arrive by boat down the Thames if you desired a romantic conveyance, and an evening National Hunt card at Towcester in Northamptonshire, where the runners would thunder over hurdles or fences.

Just a quiet Monday, but the preparation by trainers, stable staff and jockeys was as painstaking and precise as it would have been for Royal Ascot, with all its outrageous millinery, ostentatious fashion triumphs and disasters and equine bluebloods worth millions. From first light, jockeys would have been work-riding on the gallops and contemplating their later mounts on the racecourse. Those who were not stable jockeys to prominent owners and trainers would have been booked through their agents two days previously. They would probably have already discussed tactics with the trainers concerned and reviewed the form of the horses they were due to ride.

Tom Queally was among the former group. He was retained by Sir Henry Cecil and later that season would become synonymous with the mighty Frankel. Today, however, the young Irishman would be partnering a horse from Curley's stable, one of Newmarket's decidedly lesser talents.

Queally's amateur rider brother Declan, over from the family's base in Cappagh, County Waterford, would partner another two of Curley's charges. Meanwhile, from his home in Hungerford, jump jockey Denis O'Regan prepared to make the relatively short journey to Towcester for just one ride.

As racecourse-bound horses were fed, groomed and checked to ensure they were fit and well before being loaded for travel, owners were contemplating their small piece of glory and the meagre prize money that could at least slightly offset the punitive costs of racehorse ownership.

On this day, one of those owners was Manchester United manager Sir Alex Ferguson, who in his later years had become an aficionado of the sport. He was part-owner of Rock of Gibraltar – winner of seven consecutive Group 1 events – who ran in his colours. Unwittingly – it must be stressed – Ferguson would be a bit-part player in the day's events. So, indirectly, would his football club. The previous day had been Blue Sunday, when Chelsea had secured the Premier League title by a point from Manchester United after both teams had won. Chelsea had overcome Wigan Athletic 8–0. Manchester United had beaten Stoke City 4–0.

Horse racing is a multi-tentacled beast, coiling into many associated areas, but primarily betting. That astute judge Phil Bull, who founded the authoritative publication Timeform, which since 1948 has provided analysis and ratings on every horse as an asset to backers, declared: 'Don't let anyone kid you. Racing is not about improving the breed or the supremacy of the British thoroughbred. Racing is about betting. To all intents and purposes the owners and the punters – including racegoers – foot the whole bill for the exercise.'

The off-course bookmakers are the prime beneficiaries. In their anonymous offices in Nottingham and London, the major firms would have been pricing up early odds on all known information and form in order to entice backers to part with their share of the £11 billion wagered on British horse racing each year.

The industry was once dominated by the famous Big Three – Ladbrokes, William Hill and Coral. Now there was a preponderance of online layers, virtually all with operating bases offshore, mostly in Gibraltar, a fact that will become relevant to this story in due course.

The UK was in the midst of an unseasonably cold period – in part, the meteorologists explained, a consequence of the Eyjafjallajökull volcano in Iceland belching out ash. Carried on north-easterly winds, this was still causing disruption to flights across Europe. That issue, and politics, continued to dominate the news schedules as the day progressed. The horse-trading for political power had been frenetic as the Coalition was forged from hitherto divergent interests. Before the day was out, Gordon Brown would resign the Labour leadership and make that final journey out of Downing Street.

Meanwhile, Barney Curley, the man who in 1975 had been behind the most inspired painstakingly plotted legal betting coup these islands had witnessed, awaited the outcome of a scheme that had preoccupied him for two years.

If it came to fruition, it would add a commendation to honours already won in that eternal battle between backers and bookmakers.

It was one almighty if, though. Even though this was a man who had never suffered any deficiency in self-confidence, he recognised that he would require every piece of fortune to be positively in his favour. Providence would be required to walk hand in hand with meticulous organisation.

If successful – and the route was strewn with hazards – it would represent the biggest organised gamble in racing history.

If the gods were on his side.

CHAPTER 2

Barney Curley's compact office is a mine of information. His small bookcase creaks with religious and philosophical tomes and Turf paraphernalia.

In early 2010, the room was dominated by copies of *The Racing Calendar*, the official books detailing forthcoming horse races and the conditions of entry. They had been his reading matter of consequence for months, providing the vital information that he required as he plotted and schemed with the precision and dispassion of a contract killer.

Also amongst his reading matter was a copy of Paul Mathieu's *The Druid's Lodge Confederacy*, subtitled *The Gamblers Who Made Racing Pay*. It tells of five seemingly disparate characters – a royal vet, two City financiers, a stud owner and the master of the Quorn hunt – who set up a closely guarded, remote, private training yard near Stonehenge and sent out a stream of heavily backed winners in major handicaps.

This was at the turn of the nineteenth century, mind you, an era regarded as the punter's golden age. It was a time when bookmakers would readily accept enormous wagers and their methods of communication bore no relation to those of today.

It was a story that had long fascinated Curley, for whom there were echoes of his own operation and whose presence had created a similar mystique over four decades on both sides of the Irish Sea.

Dominating this sanctum is a beige fedora. It is this iconic headwear that for years has warned bookmakers of Curley's impending approach on the racecourse. It has a rather similar effect on his adversaries to the gaze of a slavering fox on the occupants of a hen coop.

No wonder that wariness is their watchword where Curley is concerned – even today, when the bookmaking chains are possibly second only to the Bank of England as the most secure of institutions. Their shareholders won't be forming queues at food banks in the immediate future. William Hill plc, for instance, was promoted in April 2013 to the FTSE 100 index of the biggest shares on the London Stock Exchange. At that point the company had a stock market value in excess of £3.7 billion.

The age-old confrontation between punters and layers is now so one-sided that all but individuals of ingenuity and diligence such as Curley may as well run up the flag of surrender. 'They have no chance,' he says. 'The bookmakers will not allow them to win.' Which explains why he has no compunction about declaring: 'If I can hurt the big bookmakers I will.'

What the bookies don't gain from laying odds on horse racing and other sports, particularly football – enhanced considerably by their online operations – they extract from fixed-odds betting terminals, which became legal in betting shops in 2005. We used to know them as one-armed bandits. The epithet is no less apt today.

Curley is one of the few possessing the fearlessness necessary to outflank the layers. His peers have included John Patrick 'JP' McManus, the Limerick-born businessman who is now National Hunt racing's biggest owner; Terry Ramsden, whose betting won and lost him a fortune in the eighties; Phil Bull, the miner's son who taught maths before founding the iconic Timeform organisation; Alex Bird, the bookmaker's son who became renowned for betting on the outcome of photo finishes (in the days when photos were still developed by hand); and Mick O'Toole, the Irish gambler-trainer, master of the monster punt.

More recently, we can add Patrick Veitch, who claims to have taken more than £10m from the bookmakers in an eight-year period; and Gary Wiltshire, the bookie whose liabilities after Frankie Dettori's Magnificent Seven wins at Ascot in 1996 totalled over £1m, but who won it all back, and more.

Their modi operandi differ, but all have prospered over the years. However, few have cracked it significantly and consistently over such a period as Curley. As will become apparent, he stands apart.

Even the evolutionary process he underwent to become a professional gambler was unorthodox. Perhaps that is not surprising, you may say. It's not generally among the careers teacher's adviser's options for his charges ('Well, Smith, and what do you have in mind? Army officer, civil service, financial services, computer technology . . . gambler?' There can't be too many conversations like that, can there?), and few set out with that ambition.

But Curley arrived there via a particularly circuitous route. He initially studied to be a Jesuit priest, which

17

requires devotion unthinkable for the majority of us, and after surviving TB he spent a profitable period managing Irish showbands, and very successfully too.

Once he had ventured into the gambling arena, he had a spell as the teetotal owner of an Omagh pub after plundering the bookmakers' satchels at Cheltenham. He even ran betting shops until coming to the conclusion that he was a gambler, not a layer of odds. From there, he became a racehorse owner, and eventually a trainer.

There are many easier ways of making a decent living. In Curley's latter years, when the quality of his stable confined him to training in the third division, as he put it, with fewer than 20 horses, the outlay could still be £400,000 a year. Just to break even he had to win that back, purely through his training and gambling acumen.

It requires a special kind of character. Dauntlessness and self-belief bordering on arrogance.

In recent years, he has bet anywhere between £50,000 and £100,000 on a single horse. But there is a caveat. 'You also have to be comfortable losing it,' he insists. 'It's no good giving yourself stress if the horse doesn't win.'

Unlike the days when the Druid's Lodge Confederacy prospered, the elite battalions of bookmakers are armed with sophisticated intelligence networks, the capability to manipulate the betting markets, and the latest technological advances.

Ostensibly, it appears a ridiculously unequal contest – particularly as Curley is perfectly content to exist in a primarily twentieth-century world. From his comfortable red chair he maintains a watchful eye on the currency markets, on the FTSE, the Dow, and racing-related Arena Leisure and Ladbrokes shares on a computer screen, but that is about as far as the technophobe's activity stretches. All it requires of him is to operate an on-off switch. Occasionally he speculates in the money markets – by phone.

A television is invariably tuned in to the satellite racing channels. He watches certain races, analyses jockeys and horses. He may occasionally demand your opinion, though how far he assimilates the response is difficult to discern.

Here is a man whose mind the best psychologists would find it difficult to penetrate. Brough Scott, the former Channel 4 horse-racing presenter, journalist and author, once reflected: 'Let's be clear. Barney Curley can be very hard to read. Down the years punters and bookmakers have battled with the poker face and those cryptic, pause-ridden statements.' Consequently he is frequently defined by myth and erroneous perceptions.

So just who is this multifaceted character who excels in performing his mysterious arts so adeptly out of reach of the bookmakers' sphere of influence; this man who constantly searches for value and is only liable to accept paying over the odds when he accompanies his wife Maureen to his local Waitrose?

When those seemingly hard eyes lock on to yours, unblinking, the look can range from inquisitive to accusatory. First appearances can be deceptive. His demeanour can appear cold, unapproachable. Sinister, some would say. When he regards you, it's like having an MRI scan of the soul, and initially it is an unnerving process, particularly as, unlike in the consultant's room, you're never quite certain of the diagnosis.

Even one of his principal associates on 10 May, a
man who had met him intermittently over the years,
confesses he found him 'intimidating' and admits, 'I
would be afraid to cross him.' But he has also concluded
that 'his moral compass is better directed than most.
He thinks big and is not afraid to follow a vision. He
may scare a lot of people, but essentially he is a good
man.'

Physically Curley cannot fail to make an impact.
Shaven-headed, with a toothbrush moustache, he has
been likened to 'Scrooge' and St Trinian's actor Alastair
Sim, though his (usually) measured tones originate in
County Fermanagh. The soft vowels are almost soporific
once the words begin to stream. And there can be a flood
of them when his blood is up. Opinions flow from him,
often tangentially. It doesn't take much for a diatribe on
the cramped odds of a winner at Hereford to progress to
a debate on the hereafter.

He has little time for those he deems 'light thinkers'.
He is dogmatic on certain subjects, notably religion, and
his ire can readily be inflamed by the wrongs he perceives
in racing.

Few are inclined to confront him. One particular
nemesis of Curley's was the former jump jockey Graham
Bradley. He locked verbal longstaffs with the Ulsterman
and ended up on the receiving end after Curley's questioning of his riding of a horse named Robin Goodfellow
at Ascot erupted into a major conflagration. It led to
Curley being warned off for two years by the all-powerful
Jockey Club for bringing racing into disrepute. That
organisation ran racing and its authority simply wasn't
questioned. A lesser character would have capitulated,

but fired by the defiant nature that has long personified him, Curley, bloodied, clambered out of his corner, took on the Jockey Club and won.

Bradley, infuriated by the sequence of events, reflects in his life story that his adversary is 'the kind of man you never forget once you've met him. And once you cross him, he never forgets you. The billiard-ball smooth head often covered by a fedora belongs to a single-minded man who is used to getting his own way. His eyes are emotionless and give nothing away. It is a look that could cut steel.'

It is true that he can remind you at times of a cheroot-chewin' Clint Eastwood surveying a band of gun-toting desperados in a spaghetti western – although Curley has always opted for Silk Cut. Until relatively recently he smoked like Bogart. Now he is an occasional user, having turned to electronic cigarettes in an attempt to quit the habit.

Mostly reluctant to disclose the finer details of his betting activities, at times Curley takes a loudhailer to voice his displeasure with the bookmakers organisations which, he insists, do not make anything like the contribution to racing that they should, given their profits – a view shared by many in the industry.

On occasion he can be utterly scornful, scathing even, of those with whom he collides. Amongst those who have experienced his abrasive side is the former Channel 4 racing pundit and TV's *Big Brother* contestant John McCririck, with whom he has been involved in two celebrated contretemps.

Fish the waters of news and features for adjectives over the years in Ireland and the UK, and you will hook all manner of catches: Curley is said to be overflowing with self-esteem; he is obstinate and dogmatic. He can be verbose, laconic, world-weary, irascible, inscrutable – and just simply bolshie.

Simon Barnes, chief sportswriter of *The Times*, described him in 1998 as the 'legendary gambler, legendary trainer, legendary legend . . . it was simply clear right from the start that he moves to a different rhythm from the rest of us. Perfectly bald, a moustache that looks like an uncharacteristic lapse of attention when face and head were last shaved and an air of utterly challenging self-possession. His life seems to be driven by the urge to stand up and be counted. The opposite of a rebel without a cause: a man perpetually in search of a cause to fight for.'

The same year, columnist Paul Haigh opined in the *Racing Post* that Curley was 'not a man who encourages indifference. Only a few years ago Barney was the bogeyman of British racing. The Jockey Club seemed both mesmerised and horrified. Bookies' wives no doubt showed their children photographs of the ogre and told them: "Go to sleep or Barney Curley will get you."'

Curley harbours contempt for anyone he believes is guilty of naked self-interest. They include some fellow racehorse trainers. Broach certain names and he will simply denounce them with the words *me fein* – Gaelic for 'myself'. He even named one of his horses Me Fein after a characteristic that he views as one of life's great sins. In fact, glance at the names of some of the horses he has owned and trained over the years and they give an insight into his character . . .

No Pain No Gain
No Complaining
No Explaining
My Word Is My Bond
Ipay Isay
All Talk No Action
Live Your Own Dream
Keep Hope Alive
Speak No Evil

Yet he is also thoughtful, a listener; a man who readily
seeks and accepts wise counsel and will act upon it. His
observations are tempered by a dry, self-deprecating
humour. He is not blighted by pretension. Essentially,
unlike the majority of us, he cares little for self-image; in
part because he answers to no one but himself, his family
and his God. To those he adjudges have bestowed kindness upon himself or others he can be generous in the
extreme.

In the lounge of his house, photographs and trophies
from races won compete for attention with pictures of
Curley with his grandchildren and memorabilia from his
charity visits to Africa.

In a world of so many 'heroes', many with little justi-
fication, the people he admires are unconnected with
the racing world. Indeed, they are unconnected with
the material world most of us operate in. They are the
priests doing work, predominantly in Zambia, in the
name of DAFA, the charity that Curley established in
the mid-nineties and which is supported by many in
racing.

His betting forays have divided opinion. To some,
notably those who regard the bookies as a collective

Beelzebub for whom eternal hellfire is too good, he is one of the few capable of giving the layers their comeuppance.

Some years ago, after the angst he suffered over the Robin Goodfellow affair, Curley gave a typically tart response to friends and associates who suggested that he should give up training and concentrate on betting. He took on several bookmakers who readily offered odds against him sending out ten winners in the final three months of that year with his then modest string, and did it with days to spare. His tenth winner, at Folkestone, won him £275,000 and the generous acclaim of race-goers genuinely pleased at witnessing Curley turn over the bookies.

When he announced his retirement as a trainer – though one suspects we have not seen the last of him quite yet – just after the turn of the year in 2013, the *Racing Post*'s Steve Dennis pronounced: 'That sound you hear is bookmakers cheering. It's not a nice sound.' He added: 'The bookmakers didn't like Curley. That was alright. Curley didn't like them either. They waged a war fuelled by mutual disdain.' He reflected that plenty of punters got a vicarious thrill from Curley's assaults on the bookmakers, that he was 'their proxy, their knight valiant who fought and won their battles'.

And yet for others, any admiration is at best grudging. As one of his associates says: 'A lot of people think that every time Barney Curley has a winner it's no different from the fella playing the fruit machine and he's got the reels rigged.'

It is a view that is fundamentally flawed. It is true that any trainer has a built-in advantage. He can observe his horses at close quarters, know when they are flourishing, know when conditions are right for them, and suspect that they will run well (or, indeed, badly). But there will always be that element of doubt. Even a horse that is 'expected', a certainty, an odds-on shot, can get turned over.

As this story unfolds, that fact becomes all too apparent.

CHAPTER 3

In the eternal conflict between layers and players, survival is the primary quest. Glory is a rare bonus.

'There is no secret,' Barney Curley declared when I first intruded on his world, 'other than the fact that successful professional backers don't get carried away by emotion or attempt to chase losses. That's why I have survived. You have to know when to hold and when to fold, as they say.'

He added: 'To succeed as a professional, you've got to be out of the ordinary. I've seen too many people go broke. It's a dog-eat-dog world where there are no rules. Unless I am as tough as the toughest individuals who frequent the tracks, especially those in the bookmaking business, I will not survive.'

Curley's education began in childhood, gleaned from the experience of witnessing his father Charlie's fall from grace, and its effect on the family, who were nearly brought to ruin, all as a consequence of gambling. The lesson has been reinforced ever since and has helped mould a particular type of character: one who would be bold when necessary but who soon came to regard his betting environment as a world 'where there are lions, tigers and crocodiles ready to strike'.

The swashbuckler of gambling added: 'The way I look at it, I have this thick protective armour that I wear and carry an imaginary shield to stop them savaging me. It makes me a completely different person from the one I would be otherwise. If you do not go in prepared, with your eyes and ears open, they'll eat you alive. I've seen it happen so often – Terry Ramsden, to name but one.'

In the eighties, the name Ramsden became a byword for a successful businessman. He personified what could be achieved by risk-takers and entrepreneurs in Thatcher's Britain. 'My name's Terry. I'm a stockbroker from Enfield. I've got long hair, and I like a bet' was his minimal self-portrait.

For a time, Ramsden enjoyed the trappings of fabulous wealth and a lifestyle of vibrant colour after he bought a company in Edinburgh called Glen International in 1984. It had a turnover of £18,000. Three years later, that figure had risen to £3.5bn. The venture was based on his knowledge of the specialised and volatile market in Japanese warrants.

Ramsden was at one time reputedly Britain's 57th wealthiest individual, with assets said to be in the region of £100m. He had all the obligatory ostentatious accoutrements of such wealth: a swimming pool with hologram shark fins beamed on to the water at his neo-Georgian home in Blackheath; a helicopter in which he flew to Walsall Football Club, of which he was both owner and chairman. He also had more than 75 horses in training, including Katies, who won the 1984 Irish 1,000 Guineas, and Motivator, the 1986 Coral Golden Hurdle Final winner at Cheltenham and the subject of a massive punt. He rarely bet less than £100,000.

But then came the Black Monday crash of 1987. Glen

International collapsed with debts of £100m. Ramsden later served 10 months of a 21-month jail sentence for fraud, and was made bankrupt. Ramsden's betting prowess didn't transfer from the financial markets. According to Curley, everybody wanted to lay Ramsden bets – clear evidence of a loser, in contrast to Curley himself, who in the same era was having his accounts closed by the bookmakers, who banish consistent winners as undesirables.

Ramsden's story was a salutary warning to all those who believed that a sharp financial brain, allied to betting big and bold, would bring automatic reward. 'He made mega-bucks on the financial markets and blew it on the betting markets,' says Curley, who added: 'I told him repeatedly that he was burning his money, that he was a madman, and that the bookies would get him, without fail. He wouldn't listen.'

Ramsden was not entirely unaware of his own flaws. He once famously quipped: 'I like the Flat best; it's a quicker death.' Destroyed by the financial markets and the bookmakers, he lost £57m in three years. He was warned off by the Jockey Club after Ladbrokes reported him to Tattersalls Committee – which settles on-course horse-racing betting disputes – over his £2m gambling debts.

It was a piquant irony and a metaphor for their respective fates that the first property Curley bought in the Newmarket area, in Stetchworth, was the seven-bedroom White House stables owned by Ramsden until the latter was forced into a dispersal of his assets. The weeds growing over the unused helicopter landing pad in the back garden were a stark symbol of Ramsden's rise – and spectacular fall.

Though ultimately Ramsden brought his demise on

himself, it riled Curley that the bookmakers, so swift to effectively outlaw winners, were quite content to bleed him dry. Curley believed that he himself prospered because he did 'the knowledge', as a London taxi driver does before he can take to the road as a fully qualified cabbie. Ramsden didn't. The Irishman laments his fellow traveller's downfall thus: 'You see, he didn't obey the rules and the bookmakers cleaned him out just as the vultures pick the bones of a dead body under a hot desert sun.'

Ramsden was not alone. 'I've seen gamblers, over the years, who've put thousands on, but there had to be a whip-round to bury them,' says Curley, an indomitable figure who survived in one of the toughest business environments of them all. He achieved it with a gambling and training model that was unique. All the horses were his own, except a number owned by his close friend and compatriot Patsy Byrne, who persuaded him to train them.

I once erroneously alluded to Byrne as 'a builder'. Curley regarded me with those hard eyes that can conceal a myriad of attitudes, ranging from outright contempt to dry wit. On this occasion, it was the latter. 'I'd say Mr Byrne was a bit more than that,' he declared of a character who was certainly involved in rather more than knocking up the odd conservatory or extension. The projects in which his company participated include Canary Wharf and the Emirates Stadium.

Even Byrne's knowledge of his horses' progress was restricted. The agreement was that Curley only told him if a particular animal was fancied. In fact, he'd run them, . . . and there'd be silence, regardless. So reticent was Curley about revealing anything that Byrne would ring up and ask sarcastically: 'Did we have any runners last week?'

Curley was not enough of a diplomat to have owners. 'I'd have to tell people "your horse is useless" he used to explain. I'm not prepared to play the game and deceive people. I train for myself, and say what I believe. If I didn't, I couldn't sleep at nights.' He added: 'I'm my own man and can say what I think.' And oh, he does. 'I have no wish to prostitute myself, and you have to do that even if you're a top trainer. You're just a lackey.'

Curley insists that training is less about horsemanship, and more about salesmanship: selling horses to a gullible public. He believes it should come with a government warning: RACEHORSE OWNERSHIP CAN SERIOUSLY HARM YOUR HEALTH.

Today Newmarket is home to around 3,000 racehorses. It is a fluctuating number. Unwanted horses were amongst the detritus created by the global financial collapse. When incomes suffer, racehorses, which cost more to keep stabled, fed, watered, trained and entered for races than sending a child to some public schools – with only a limited chance of recovering the costs, let alone making a profit – are amongst the first casualties. Off to the sales they go.

There are exceptions, such as the oil-rich Maktoum family, who, with their vast number of horses and employees, make a significant contribution to the racing industry in Britain. The same applies in Ireland, where the Coolmore operation, founded by John Magnier in Fethard, South Tipperary, is the world's largest breeding concern of thoroughbreds.

Significantly, at Newmarket's 2012 yearling sale, the sport's major jousters invested 68,102,500 guineas (£71,507,625) in equine bluebloods, a record for any yearling auction in Europe. The highlight was a three-parts brother to 2007 Derby victor Authorized, which resulted in competition between Coolmore's John Magnier and a representative of Sheikh Fahad Al Thani, a member of Qatar's royal family. The Sheikh won the duel, with a bid of 2,500,000 guineas (£2,625,000), the third most expensive yearling colt ever sold in Europe. The colt, sired by Galileo, the Epsom and Irish Derby and King George VI and Queen Elizabeth Diamond Stakes victor, was named Hydrogen. He went into training with Authorized's trainer, Peter Chapple-Hyam.

At the other end of the spectrum, though, many trainers struggle. Ownership is hardly an attractive financial investment. Effectively you're inviting prospective patrons to burn money. On average you'd have to lay out over £20,000 a year to have a horse in training. For owners with Newmarket trainers that figure rises to over £25,000. That's without the initial outlay at the sales. Owners can expect to get back £21 for every £100 they spend, unless they exist in a parallel universe and are successfully involved in the elite breeding side of the industry.

Fortunately, racing retains a unique appeal. There are few more satisfying examples of one-upmanship than inviting friends to watch a horse run in your silks, and win. It is regarded as evidence that you have made it.

Curley cannot comprehend such a rationale. For the Irishman, ownership should always be regarded as a potentially profitable venture. Otherwise why bother? Owners, with a few exceptions, he contends, are simply subsidising the bookmakers with free – or remarkably cheap – sport for them to lay odds and reap their not inconsiderable rewards.

In 2010, around half of the 34 boxes at Curley's stables were empty. It was a deceptive statistic. As a racehorse trainer, he could probably have filled them with owners' horses if he'd chosen to encourage patronage. Patsy Byrne apart, he never considered that on a commercial scale, principally because he believes that owners, perhaps understandably, cannot be depended upon to keep to themselves the knowledge that is essential to crack the bookmakers' defences. This attitude separated him from (virtually) all other trainers. He needed the liberation of being his own man. The concept of working for someone else was anathema to him; he would stalk such an exist-ence like a caged lion.

Curley is fond of quoting the late chairman of Fiat, Gianni Agnelli, who reflected that, to be effective, a board of directors needed an odd number of people. And three was too many. The same applies to the professional gambler. In his rarified world, knowledge correlates with profit – but only as long as it is confined to as few people as possible. As Curley says: 'That's the reason I survived as a trainer since I set up here, while many have fallen by the wayside.'

He ran his training operation as he does his betting. To be consistently successful requires surreptitiousness beyond most men. He was no more liable to let slip his plans than a priest would betray a parishioner in the confessional. For all you know, he may have had a bet worth many thousands running on one of his horses that afternoon. He wore a mask of detachment.

This day would be no exception. Other than two close associates, not one person he would encounter on 10 May, or during the preceding months, would have been even faintly conscious that he had set in motion a plan of such byzantine complexity and, potentially, such eye-wateringly high rewards.

But then no one else would have attempted it. He hadn't become the bane of bookmakers in a career spanning four decades by broadcasting his intentions – to anyone. This was how he had always operated: stealthily and covertly. Even his closest family were not fully aware of the scheme that had preoccupied him for months, and had been percolating in his mind for years. Maureen, his wife of 45 years, and mother of their two grown-up daughters, Catherine and Maria-Louise, and son Charlie who had died in a car accident aged 18, would have known virtually nothing about what was afoot. That was always the custom in the Curley household. Maureen had never been involved in – and had only limited knowledge of – any of her husband's betting schemes.

'Oh, I might have said to her in passing, "I'm trying something big here", or "I'm going to work the horses – it's important",' Curley recalls. 'But it would have passed her by – I was always trying something big. But that was about it.'

Maureen, who gained a law degree as a mature student, spent much of the day, as always, in her office upstairs, preoccupied with her work as a lawyer for the consumer magazine *Which?* advising consumers on their issues.

Curley adds: 'She wasn't interested in the horse racing. But anyway, I didn't want to be telling her all my ups and downs. I always tried to keep her away from that. I didn't want her worrying that we'd end up in a caravan by the side of the road.'

Maureen's only doubts concerned the number of his equine charges at that time. 'She thought it was absolutely crazy. Could not figure it out at all, the cost of keeping the horses . . . thought it was madness with a capital M.' On this day, in 2010, she was not to know there was a method in that madness.

The couple first met, appropriately enough, at Killarney Races in 1968, when Maureen was on holiday. They married six months later. Nowadays, a successful professional gambler has a bit of prestige: he is admired as a risk-taker and an adventurer; a kind of Indiana Jones of the racing world. He (they are mostly men) has acquired an almost celebrity persona. That image has altered significantly since Curley started out, when the term 'professional gambler' had rather more dubious overtones. Even if you weren't regarded as a hoodlum, you were considered a pretty risky prospect as a marriage partner. This, it must be recalled, was an era long before the National Lottery and high street betting shops brazenly offered their services. The public's perception of gambling tended to involve organised crime and razor gangs at racecourses – despite the fact that, so they say, the last such battle was waged in 1937, at Lewes.

Some partners might have been deterred by such an occupation. During the days before they married, Maureen got chatting to Curley's eldest sister, Anne, who warned the young bride-to-be to be very wary. 'Barney has only one interest in life – and that's gambling,' she said.

Despite some misgivings – she believed that all gamblers went bust at some point and insisted he ploughed his winnings into buying their first house – Maureen Curley soon recognised the reality. She swiftly understood that Barney was a serious player, an investor, if you like, on the gambling exchange; not a hopeful amateur.

From those nascent days, Maureen Curley has always adopted the attitude that her husband was no different from any other breadwinner who got up and went about their business. Except that his business meant a potential profit or loss of £100,000 in a day, and possibly more.

'She questioned me about it, of course, and I just tried to reassure her, "Look, I'll always keep you once I really get going." I don't think she ever really worried since those early days. When I went to the racecourse she just thought of me as going off to work like any other professional man. Except I didn't wear a suit and carry a copy of *The Times*; just binoculars and a *Racing Post*.'

He adds: 'You'd never know if I'd won or lost. I could walk into a room and you'd have absolutely no idea whether I'd won £100,000 or lost £50,000. If I lose today, no matter. My philosophy is that I'll win tomorrow.' There was the occasion when Curley lost £250,000 when betting against Golden Fleece, the victorious favourite in the 1982 Derby, and in the same week lost another £100,000. He has also won £300,000 in a day.

'In my younger days, she just let me flow,' Curley says of Maureen's attitude towards his betting. 'She didn't get much sense out of me. Just took a back seat. Let me carry on. She was happy enough, as long as we weren't thrown out on the street.'

After some teething difficulties in the infancy of his career, destitution was never been a threat in four decades as a gambling man. Flick through diaries of his early days and Curley lists profits and losses like other young men would scribble the names of conquests in love. Even then, his bets were in thousands. Over the course of his career, his investments have gone into many millions.

Now into his eighth decade, Curley may have been slowed by the legacy of the operation that followed that serious illness in late 2009, but he lacked none of the cerebral dexterity required to set up his concerted attack on the old adversary. His latest attempt to outflank the bookmakers was the ultimate in audacity. What can be said with some certainty is that he is the only man in racing who could have succeeded on a day that turned into Black Monday. And not just for the outgoing prime minister.

The most curious aspect was that he had arrived here, guided by a compass of fate which should have acted as a powerful deterrent to any gambling instincts.

CHAPTER 4

Barney Curley's father, Charlie, was one of several voices of reason who chorused their opposition to his son's ambition to become a professional gambler.

'Oh, he always said there was going to be a bad end to me,' Curley recalls. 'Because nobody had ever done what I was trying to do. Nobody has ever made this punting game pay. He had seen it all, and warned me: "People have lost shops, businesses, farms, land . . . and yet here's my boy. He thinks he knows more than anyone else."'

It was an understandable and heartfelt concern. Curley's father spoke from bitter experience.

Charlie Curley, a charismatic, if flawed, character, had been something of a playboy in his bachelor twenties, being one of the first men in County Fermanagh to own a motor car, a Model T Ford. He was also a chancer.

In his youth he had been a promising footballer, considered talented enough to be offered a trial with Glasgow Celtic, though his mother wouldn't allow him to travel. He played Gaelic football too, for his county. But in common with others on the male side of the family – one of Barney's uncles, John, drank himself to death – he had a taste for liquor.

It's one of the reasons why Barney Curley rarely touches alcohol. 'I've seen what it can do to you,' he says. 'Anyway, in the business I pursued, a befuddled brain would only further tilt the balance in the bookmakers' favour. You always need a clear head. I've seen so many people gambling and drinking at the same time make serious mistakes.'

There was a religious explanation for his temperance, too, as a child brought up in a staunch Catholic household. 'When we were young you had to make a sort of pledge, an offering to God,' explains Curley. 'Mine was to say I wouldn't drink. It was a kind of sacrifice in reparation for the sins of those who had offended God by their intemperance. I've kept to that, by and large, which is not the easiest thing to do in Ireland, where everybody enjoys a drink. But it's been a big help in life. Some people drink to instil themselves with confidence, or maybe because they're unhappy, but I have never needed that crutch.'

Curley has never attempted to inflict his religious beliefs on others. He will seek your opinion on, say, the hereafter, the existence of which he has the utmost faith in. 'If I didn't, I couldn't see the point of it all,' he says. 'Life would be meaningless to me if I didn't believe in a God, and there was no afterlife.' If you respond that you're an agnostic, he betrays a little sadness and disappointment, but he is never disapproving; never attempts to persuade you.

'I would never claim to be a saint,' he says. 'If the just man falls ten times a day, I fall thirty times. But I don't like to be portrayed as some kind of Holy Joe, trying to convert people to my way of thinking. My father instilled in us to put our trust in God. His words made a great impression on me. I've had good days and bad days on the racecourse but nothing's ever worried me. I have faith in Him and self-confidence in myself.'

He takes a broader perspective than many on the Troubles, and bears no antipathy towards those on the opposite side of the religious divide. He enjoys relating the story of how the family's house was directly on the main route of the annual 12 July Orange march, celebrating the day in 1690 when King William of Orange defeated James II at the Battle of the Boyne. Thousands of people used to line the route as the procession of marchers and bands passed.

'My brother Cahal and I set up a little stall selling bottles of mineral water, together with sandwiches and cakes my mother had made, and sold them out of the window. Then, such marches were just part of the local calendar and there was no hint of violence. But the fact that ours was a Catholic house would not deter us from making a profit from the day. You got the occasional bigoted attitude. "That Barney Curley," muttered voice. "He's some bastard, giving refreshments to the Orange Men." There was about two hundred per cent mark-up, but we sold out.'

Bernard Joseph Curley – soon shortened to Barney – was born a month after the onset of the Second World War, the eldest child of Charlie and Kathleen Curley. He was one of two sons and four daughters raised in the village of Irvinestown, a 20-minute drive from Enniskillen in County Fermanagh.

Curley and his siblings were raised in a three-bedroom cottage on a farm perched above the Irvinestown to Dromore road. It was an area of bleak farmland, with the Brougher Mountains dominating the horizon towards the south-east.

His early childhood, coinciding with the deprivations of the war years, was happy, if tough. One of his first recollections was, as a child of four, walking to school, which was over two miles away, in his bare feet. His shoes were kept for best, like church on Sundays.

The family grazed about 30 cattle and reared pigs. They also grew corn and cut peat, an essential part of winter life in Ireland in those days, years before central heating became commonplace.

His father had a flair for business. If only he had restricted himself to that. Towards the end of the war, Charlie Curley bought a Ford truck and began a highly profitable business driving around the country to farms, buying six chickens here and ten rabbits there, maybe a few dozen eggs. These he would sell on to the wholesalers, who would then export them to the British market.

Together with the proceeds of smuggling – there was a black market in sugar and butter coming in from the South – he made at least £1,500 when he sold up all his stock, and in 1946 he moved the family into town. The venture had made him one of the wealthiest men in the area and enabled him to concentrate on his first loves: owning and training greyhounds, and betting in earnest.

Even with the innocence of youth, it didn't take Curley Jnr long to discover how crooked greyhound racing was in those immediate post-war years. His father, he concedes, was one of the worst offenders, although he stresses: 'It never occurred to him that it was morally wrong. As far as my father was concerned, he fed, watered and trained the dogs and he was entitled to run them how he wanted.' Curley adds: 'He used to stop them regularly at that time. There were no dope tests then and he gave them tablets which didn't appear to do any permanent harm, but slowed them by a second, which was worth several lengths. That was comfortably enough to get them beaten.' They would be downgraded and then win when the money was down.

Curley recalls a particular occasion when one of his father's dogs, called The Fag, lost at Belfast's Celtic Park when odds on favourite. The crowd responded to this obvious cheating with a rhythmic stamping of feet and a chorus of 'out, out, out', rather like a football crowd whose team are 5–0 down. His father faced the management's wrath, and was told: 'As long as your name is what it is, you will never run a dog here again.' Celtic Park was a prestige track, and it was a grave dishonour to be warned off it. Charlie Curley never went back.

His son, however, would return in the seventies, with a greyhound named Portumna Wonder, which won the Ulster Sprint at the track. 'The prize money can't have been more than £500, but I backed it heavily ante-post and won something like £5,000,' he recalls. The event was sponsored by bookmaker Sean Graham, with whom Curley was to develop a long, if not always harmonious, relationship.

In Curley's teens, his father began to embroil him in his chicanery. 'Once, when I was about 14 and on holiday from college, he sent me with one of his greyhounds to the Lifford greyhound track, a mile or two the other side of the River Foyle from Strabane. I was driven by Ernest McCaffrey, a taxi driver, who regularly took his dogs and knew the score.

'Just before we set off, my father, who was off to Belfast with another dog, handed me a little ball of mincemeat. "Now," he instructed me firmly, "when you get to Strabane, give this to the dog." I didn't need telling that there was a tablet in the meat.

'Irvinestown to Lifford is a fair ride, and on the way I got thinking to myself. My analysis of the situation was this. "If I don't give the dog the meat, he'll almost definitely win – and probably at a good price." I was already calculating my winnings.

'The taxi-driver was keeping a close eye on me in his rear-view mirror. He knew the instructions, too. When we got to Strabane, I just motioned with my hand and pretended to give my canine travelling companion the meat. If Ernest had been looking, my sleight of hand was enough to deceive him.

'I had £2 on the dog at 6–1 and he duly left his rivals trailing and I won £12. Both my father and I arrived back about midnight and he demanded to know how we'd got on. "We won," I said.

'My father looked flabbergasted. "He couldn't have won," he declared defiantly; he obviously had a big betting scheme planned for the dog. "Oh yes. Five or six lengths," I shrugged, trying to conceal my guilt.

'He thought about it for a moment. Now, these tablets had been supplied, perhaps unwittingly, by Gerry Magee, the local chemist. He was used to people taking their problems to him. But not the one he was confronted with that night. And not at that hour.

'Suddenly my father sprang up from his chair and exclaimed, "The fool's given me the wrong pills." He was inclined to be very hot-tempered at times. He strode down the street and I followed at a discreet distance.

'Despite the late hour, he started to rap on the chemist's door. Eventually someone stuck their head out of the window and there was a right commotion, with my father

42

accusing him of being stupid. All I could do was just watch and keep out of it and feel slightly ashamed. Eventually it blew over. I never let on to him either, even when I got older.

'I felt pretty pleased with myself. Going back to school £12 the richer was like having hundreds in your back pocket today.'

Father and son continued to have some beneficial nights with the greyhounds. But increasingly there were too many losing ones.

'It takes some doing to lose a fortune and fail to profit from running and betting on your own greyhounds,' recalls Curley. 'But my father made an excellent job of losing everything.'

It coincided with the time Curley Snr was having a new home built for the family until he ran out of money. He owed around £2,000, most of it to the local garage for petrol and to the builder and decorator who had been working on the house. He needed a get-out-of-jail pass, and plunged all he had left on to one dog.

This was not just any dog, however. He had stopped this particular animal for about six months to get him in the worst possible grade, and then placed a bet of £300 at 7–1. Winning £2,100 would have solved all his problems at a stroke.

The race was a sprint, and despite the dog getting left at the start, he was in front again by the first bend, only to stumble, roll over and break his back. Instead of collecting the proceeds, Charlie Curley had to trudge down the track to pick up the animal's lifeless form.

That vivid image of his father is indelibly imprinted on Barney's memory as though it was yesterday. As he carried the dog back through the stadium, his father's eyes were moist. 'The party's over, Barney. I've played my joker and lost.'

It was a wretched piece of ill fortune – though it would instil in his son the realisation that there is no such thing as a cert – and Charlie Curley knew it was the end of the line. 'Inside he was weeping from his shattered hopes,' says Barney.

Kathleen Curley didn't have to enquire what had happened when the pair arrived home. Charlie's demeanour said it all. That was his last serious bet. He couldn't even borrow money to try and recoup his losses, and things went from bad to worse. There followed an ignominious few months in which he and Kathleen were confronted with creditors at the door, looking for money they were owed – debts that simply couldn't be paid. 'It was a terrible blow to the family's pride,' Barney concedes. He vowed never to inflict such misery on his own family.

At the time, Curley Jnr was at boarding school, St Macartan's College in Monaghan Town, alma mater of some distinguished Irishmen, including entrepreneurs, inventors, politicians and men of the cloth. It was there that he would encounter Eugene O'Reilly – later to become Father O'Reilly – who would become a major influence in his life.

One of Curley's uncles, Tommy, had chided him when he was home from school. 'Your father's letting the family down. He should be ashamed of himself. He owes half the district, while we hardly owed a penny in our lives,' Curley recalls him saying. 'It's a wonder he doesn't do something about it. And it's a wonder you don't either, you big loaf, instead of going about studying. A big strapping lad like you should go to England and try to earn some money, get this debt paid. You're disgracing the family name, both of you.'

Even as a callow youth, Curley had sensed in his own mind that drastic measures would be required. Settling the family debts was a matter of honour.

The situation became so grim that father and son travelled over to Britain to work in a factory near Manchester in order to raise funds. 'It must have been very tough on my father, because he had been used to all the comforts of life, just as it was a cultural shock for me coming out of boarding school with the realisation that I had several months of hard work in front of me,' recalls Barney.

The pair were aware that they could earn four times in Britain what they could at home – and there would be work available. They found jobs in a factory in Urmston that made plastic moulds. Urmston is a town close to the River Mersey, about three miles west of Manchester United's Old Trafford ground. In the mid fifties, it was a bleak landscape, dominated by factory chimneys, but the mission was simple: to repay their creditors back home. It was not a cultural tour.

Curley Snr mixed dyes. His son, then still only a 16-year-old schoolboy, was initially employed sweeping the factory floor, but once it became known that he'd attended a prestigious boarding school and had a fair science grounding, he was promoted to the laboratory area, where he was employed testing plastic for strength.

They started out working double shifts. This meant getting up at 4.30 to catch the 5 a.m. bus, and not returning home until 11.30 p.m. It was an onerous regime. 'I could hardly make it back to our digs, such was my fatigue. But there was no way we would go back until we could walk through Irvinestown with our heads held high and debts paid off,' says Curley.

Very occasionally, to break the monotony, father and son would go to the White City greyhound track in Manchester – not to bet, just to watch. They also visited Manchester racecourse – it closed in 1963 – and took a trip to Haydock Park, where Pat Taaffe rode some winners. The Dubliner would later become the principal partner of Arkle, the finest steeplechaser to grace these islands 'I had a ten-shilling double or treble on his mounts, which allowed me to go home in rather more style than I departed,' recalls Curley.

They permitted themselves just one other indulgence. Every other Saturday, they'd catch the bus to Old Trafford to stand on the terraces and watch Manchester United play. They were fortunate enough to catch a glimpse of one of the finest group of players in the club's history, the 'Busby Babes' – many of whom would perish two years later in the Munich air disaster.

Yet overall it was a tedious existence. To obtain coal for the small fire in their digs, Curley Snr, with the help of his son, filled sacks at the depot and humped them home on his back all of half a mile. They probably weighed a couple of hundredweight. 'He wouldn't let me help carry them,' says Curley. 'In many ways, my father still treated me as a child. We'd have to make two trips and it was a filthy job. To my eternal discredit,' he adds, 'although I put it down to the immaturity of my years, I felt humiliated and was terribly ashamed of my father. I'd walk well behind him in case anybody associated me with this dirty little man heaving coal.'

Curley admits, however, that it was during this

episode that he appreciated the strength of his father's religious faith and how it helped him cope with these tough times. It would have a profound effect on his own attitudes.

'In many ways, it was a miserable year,' he said. 'Yet if I lived my life over again, I would want to experience that time once more. It was strangely fulfilling and gave me an appreciation of life outside my own community. It made me realise how much I'd been pampered until then. It was a very tough existence, and transformed me from a boy into a man.'

Virtually everything they earned, some £20 a week each, was sent back to Ireland, and within a year the family's debts were paid. Charlie Curley returned home chastened by the episode. So humiliated was he that he couldn't face the prospect of walking through the town, and arranged for a friend, the chemist Gerry Magee, to deliver him to his front door. 'He had been taught a brutal lesson that betting was not an easy game in which to be a winner,' reflects Barney.

That sorry period should have been a salutary warning to Curley Jnr,. For many men, such an experience would have ensured that any inclination to enter that precarious world would be stillborn.

But Curley was heedless. After returning home from Britain, he worked at Ulster Creameries in Belfast for ten weeks, but admits he gambled all his earnings away on the greyhounds at Celtic Park and Dunmore Park and on horse racing. He concedes: 'I was the original mug punter, backing tips in the newspapers.'

When he returned to the family home, his appearance was less one of good cheer and more Chaplinesque. Curley adds: 'My soles were worn through and I'd had to stuff my shoes with thick paper in order to fill in the holes. I didn't have the money to get them repaired, let alone buy new ones. I could barely pay for my digs and I didn't even have the price of a bus or train fare home from Belfast.

'As I walked up our street to the house, my mother's face was a vision of annoyance and shame. Her mood brightened considerably, however, when I told her how I saw my future. I intended to study for the priesthood.'

CHAPTER 5

Curley had recognised for some time that he wanted to become a priest. A Jesuit priest. That decision encapsulates his life. If you're going to do something, go for broke. And anyone who sets out with plans to don the Jesuit priest's cassock cannot be anything but utterly dedicated. 'By even contemplating this step, you can be assured that I was taking the priesthood seriously,' he says.

The Society of Jesus is an order founded in Paris in 1534 by Ignatius Loyola, Francis Xavier and others to defend and propagate the Roman Catholic faith. Whereas the normal duration of study for the priesthood is six years, it takes around thirteen years to become ordained as a Jesuit priest; hence the saying attributed to the order: 'Give me the boy and I'll show you the man.' It is a rigorous and daunting training process which produces what are known as the 'storm-troopers' of the Catholic Church. These are men who eschew all possessions and wealth and dedicate their lives to improving the existence of the poor throughout the world.

'It was a combination of factors that influenced my thinking,' recalls Curley. 'But most important were my parents' faith and my experience of deprivation, working all those hours in Manchester.'

He applied to, and was accepted by, Mungret College in Limerick. He believes his experience at the seminary taught him important values. 'It gave me confidence to stand up against anyone, head to head.'

It was a harsh regime, a complete rejection of the self-indulgent lifestyle and luxuries he had left behind. 'But that is all part of the training – to put you through the mill, to really test out your commitment to the faith. I would recommend any young man who wants to be properly equipped for life to go to a Jesuit school regardless of how he sees his future.'

He adds: 'The atmosphere was very authoritarian from the moment the college bell tolled every morning at six o'clock to wake us in our dormitories. The whole ideology of the place was different from an ordinary boarding school. The accent was more on chastisement for failure in class or misbehaving rather than the approval of achievement and good conduct.'

Curley knew the training would require extraordinary dedication; its demands would be beyond most men. At the time, that appealed greatly to him. 'We were all preparing to go on to places where there would be none of the pleasures of the secular world. You were completely in – or you were out. With this place there were no half measures,' he says.

He recalls a typical day's routine: 'After washing and dressing, there was an hour's meditation in chapel, a time when you thought about your life and God, and how you could make yourself better. We prayed in silence. Then it was on to Mass for another half-hour, followed by a simple breakfast. None of our meal portions were very substantial and it wouldn't have been much; some porridge and toast maybe. We ate nothing fried, except on Sunday mornings when, as a treat, we might get a sausage and one slice of bacon.'

For a man who has always had, shall we say, a healthy appetite, it was a decidedly meagre diet. 'But I accepted it because sacrifice was a significant part of the Jesuit philosophy. You offered that up to God as part of your efforts to try and be a Premier League player in His league of sinners.'

He adds: 'The priests were pleased with my progress. I had pretty good marks in my exams and I had made up my mind to dedicate my life to God.' He describes that time as 'amongst the happiest years of my life', and adds: 'Despite the hardships, it was amazing how happy a place it was. They were halcyon days. There was a great spirit of comradeship.'

Mungret College, Curley maintains, also altered his outlook on money and wealth. 'Yes, you need money to get by,' he accepts. 'But it's not really that important. I can say that despite having spent much of my life winning and losing hundreds of thousands a year. The happiest people I have ever met are some of those Jesuit priests. They lived a very strict lifestyle, but they were wonderfully content. They seemed to have the secret of life.'

Significantly, he adds: 'That training taught me never to be afraid to speak up if I was aware of a wrong. Those priests gave me the strength to stand up and be counted. It greatly aided my thinking, and helped me distinguish between right and wrong. I was also thankful that it gave me the opportunity to study philosophy.

'It taught me that it is wrong that the wealth of the world is in so few people's hands; the rest possessing next to nothing. The happiest people I've met in life are the ones whose belongings fit in a suitcase, like Father Eugene O'Reilly, one of my closest friends, who spent most of his adult life in Africa helping other people until his untimely death in 2011.' Coincidentally, Curley would also forge friendships that would have a significant impact on his subsequent career choice. Horse racing was a common thread.

The college was divided into two institutions: one strictly theological, for the scholastics, like Curley; the other much larger, for lay pupils, who would primarily be going on to university. One of those latter pupils was Bobby Barry, whose father Jim trained horses in County Limerick. Bobby was allowed out to ride for his father at nearby Limerick Junction racecourse, and Curley would accompany them.

It was his introduction to racing. Curley recalls that 'The sheer exhilaration of actually being on the race-track, with the brilliance of the jockeys' colours, the thud of the horses' hooves and the cries of the bookies, was like nothing I'd ever experienced before.' He concedes: 'The direction I took in later years was undoubtedly heavily influenced by those days out with Jim and Bobby Barry.'

Two other lay pupils were also to feature prominently in his life. One was Barry Brogan, whose father Jimmy, a fine jockey in his day, had trained Gold Legend to win the 1958 Irish Grand National. There was also a character some six years Curley's junior, an excellent rugby player and athlete by the name of Tommy Stack, who would become a distinguished National Hunt champion jockey. In 1977, he partnered a 12-year-old Red Rum to his third Grand National victory. Later he became a top-flight trainer on the Flat, winning the 1994 1,000 Guineas with Robert Sangster's Las Meninas, and over jumps. More than fifty years on, he is Curley's closest friend. Barry Brogan would also become an excellent jump jockey, though his riding career would be mottled with scandal, including the fixing of races.

There came a hiatus in Curley's godly intentions when sickness intervened. He had begun to suffer fatigue when playing football and 'slipped down from the A team to those who could hardly kick a ball'. He also suffered from night sweats. One day he went out to play and felt an intense pain across his chest.

He was only 20 at the time, but was taken to hospital in Limerick on the assumption that it was a heart attack. An X-ray quickly established the real cause. He had tuberculosis, or TB, as 'the great white plague' was more commonly known. The infectious disease, which attacks the lungs, was then still a killer.

The cure, if there was to be one, was complete rest, combined with fresh air. The regime would help his body's immune system to confront the disease. Medication called streptomycin had also by now been developed to combat the TB bacillus, which was no respecter of age, wealth, status – or literary genius. D. H. Lawrence, John Keats, the Brontë sisters and Franz Kafka all succumbed to the disease.

Curley survived after many months in a sanatorium at Killadeas, located above Lough Erne, aided by the restorative breezes whipping in off the lough. 'On some days, the wind would cut through you like a frozen lance,' he says. He also remembers, with feeling, the injections in the backside at five every morning. It was not an enviable cure, but it was definitely preferable to the alternative. 'They were dying like flies around me,' he drily recalls.

That fleeting acquaintance with death, though spared the full welcoming handshake, taught Curley to appreciate and savour what life he had left. 'I thought the Good Lord had called a halt, but I had a touch and got better,' he says. 'There's not much to feel scared of after that. I said to myself then that if I ever got out of there I'd never worry again. That's why, later, I was never afraid of a losing bet. You wouldn't have much regard for money, you know, if you went through an experience like that.'

There were no long-term effects. He still turned out for the Newmarket trainers' football team in matches against the jockeys until he was into his fifties.

After leaving the sanatorium, however, he required another year's convalescence. The illness had drained him. He had been at the seminary for four years, and had been determined to return. But during this lengthy period for reflection, he decided he could not cope with the gruelling demands of that vocation.

Ask him today whether he would have become a priest had fate not intervened, and after a lengthy pause he retorts: 'It's hard to say, but I don't think I was good enough to have lasted the course, to be honest. But you never know. If I had to live my life all over again, I'd want to do all that.'

Neither his parents nor the priests attempted to persuade him to return. 'They said to think about it, pray about it, and leave it in God's hands,' he recalls. 'I left and said there might be something else in life for me. I always thought the Fellow Above would give me a nod in some way – although He probably had second thoughts about nodding me towards what I ended up doing . . .'

But he has always been a fatalist. 'Whatever I've got in life, or lost, that was my destiny,' he says. 'I believe there's a programme mapped out for all of us all the way through to the end. If the Lord had wanted me to be a priest, that's what I would have been.'

His faith still provides a solid bulwark to his life. 'I try to go to Mass every day,' he says. 'That's my perfect day. Say hello to the Boss man. It's not at regular times around here. Nine fifteen, ten. It sets me up for the day. I come out of Mass with good intentions, try to be charitable to other people, be thoughtful. But sometimes it all goes haywire and I break them, and then start again.'

He would not be alone in failing to stay the course at Mungret College, though few made the polar change in direction that he did.

During his holidays from college, he had a commission-only job selling lime to farmers in Fermanagh and Tyrone. His business skills had been negligible. This enhanced them. After leaving Mungret, he obtained a job selling oil to farmers. Those six months would be the only time in his life that he was an employee and had a full-time occupation.

He bought his first car, a large red Zephyr, through a friend of his father named John James McManus, with whom he would later own his first horse. It was acquired on hire purchase and Curley failed to keep up the payments. He required fast, easy money and decided the solution was smuggling. There was a market for certain goods in the South that could be bought cheaper and of better quality in the North, and he hit upon the scheme of 'exporting' Gillette razor blades across the border.

He removed the door covers from the car and packed the space with blades, purchased wholesale from a large store in Enniskillen. He and his accomplice, Herbie McElholm, crossed the border at various locations, so as to avoid suspicion. Curley had done his homework, just as he would later with his betting exploits, and crossed when there were many other vehicles. On occasions, the pair adopted the guise of football fans travelling to or from a match at Clones; or maybe a couple of young lads going to a dance at Swanlinbar. Sometimes they'd cross at Belleek with holidaymakers heading for the seaside resort of Bundoran.

They sold the blades down the west coast and Limerick; Curley estimated that he did around 100 trips during the course of a year, if possible stopping off at a race meeting en route.

It was around this time that he began to study The Form Book, the bible of the Turf, and radically redirect his energies. Forewarned about the perils of gambling, he knew he had to be forearmed.

By now, he was betting in a small way, at least by the standards of his later career – nothing more than £50 – and initially not with conspicuous success. A friend organised a credit account for him with a bookmaker called Davy Meehan. Curley had a limit of £300, and soon hit that.

He possibly learnt more about the business and sharpened his latent gambling reflexes when he joined the opposition and became a bookmaker, believing it would be the source of easy money. Ironically, his first venture was at Celtic Park, the scene of his father's final fall from grace. He was allocated a pitch on an area that carried the wonderfully evocative name of 'Murder Mile'. He was amongst a dozen bookies up the hill, separated from the reputable, big-money bookmakers, who operated alongside the track. Amongst the latter was Sean Graham, a figure with whom he would duel on many occasions down the years.

Murder Mile derived its epithet from the fact that, according to Curley, 'It was reckoned every hoodlum in the country was there making a book, and any unsuspecting punter would get murdered – metaphorically at least.' He described his companions as 'pot-less and chancers'. He was in good company. Curley had to borrow money to make a book from his cousin Angela, who ran a hairdressing salon and was sister of his smuggling accomplice, Herbie McElholm.

But it was an education. One of his fellow bookmakers was Jimmy Nelson, a gambler at heart and a fine operator, who simply enjoyed the company. 'He'd keep an eye on the prices being chalked up by the serious bookmakers next to the track, and if he liked a particular dog, and the odds available, he'd send one of his three or four runners down with as much as £1,000, with the instruction "leave no price on the board",' recalls Curley. 'I loved to hear that phrase, and yearned for the day when I could do likewise.'

That time would not be too far distant. But not before he became that rarity, a penniless bookmaker. Too often Curley, the greenhorn, would lay far too generous prices on the favourite and end up wiped out. He admits: 'Ninety per cent of the time I was ending up with an empty satchel.'

It took a bookie named Danny McGarry, with a paternalistic interest, to have a word with him and advise him: 'You are not a bookmaker. All you want to do is gamble.'

Curley took McGarry's advice and packed in his brief and inglorious career as an on-course bookmaker.

What he turned to next, however, was just about as incongruous, given his somewhat sheltered background and the fact that, by his own admission, he had no interest in, and certainly no knowledge of, modern popular music.

He was asked to manage a showband.

CHAPTER 6

He was perplexed by the request. Barney Curley had no music background whatsoever, unless you counted playing the triangle in his grandfather Tommy's 20-strong brass band, which toured pubs in outlying villages. He had never even been to a dance or a disco in his life.

A guitarist-singer Pio (named because of his initials, P. O.) McCann, who lived in a neighbouring village, had heard that Curley had a knack for salesmanship and persuaded him to get involved. He then began a new life as a manager and promoter of McCann's band the Claxton.

He was an unlikely entrant into the world of showbiz, and, though he would lay no claim to being a Simon Cowell of his day, that episode exemplified his life: he never allowed lack of knowledge or expertise – or, indeed, grounding – in a particular sphere to deter him. This would be a guiding principle.

Showbands were a uniquely Irish phenomenon in the fifties and sixties; the counterpart of British pop groups. They had a fuller sound than their British equivalents and tended to consist of seven or eight musicians: a drummer, lead singer, two guitarists, and maybe a tenor saxophone, trombone, trumpet or piano player.

The schedule was exhausting: often six nights a week, playing until the early hours of the next morning. Most of the musicians had day jobs as well. They had been performing mostly in village halls in the vicinity of Irvinestown and Omagh; their ambition was to play the major venues in towns and cities. Curley's role was to arrange dates and negotiate payment.

Initially he enjoyed qualified success. He ventured into the Republic, promoting his band as 'the latest sensation from Northern Ireland', and booked a gig at a 3,000-capacity ballroom at Dromkeen, outside Limerick City, for which he negotiated a fee of £50, a considerable sum in 1963.

Unfortunately, neither he nor the band had considered the implications of the transition from village halls to a large auditorium like this. Their amplification system was not up to it, and afterwards the venue's management was besieged with complaints.

Curley learned fast. He swiftly realised that he had to inject more professionalism into the band, and culled some of the lesser performers. In 1966, the best musicians from the Claxton were amalgamated with those from another band, the Polka Dots. Lead singer of the new band which retained the name, the Polka Dots, was Frankie McBride, who also recorded the solo single 'Five Little Fingers'.

Curley was there in the studio when the disc was recorded. The engineer gave a nod of satisfaction and told him: 'This will be a winner.' The record reached number 19 in the British singles chart in the summer of 1967.

Despite some changes of personnel, McBride stayed with the band until 1970. The Polka Dots made quite a name for themselves, performing throughout Ireland, as well as touring Britain.

Curley travelled with the band, anxious to get feedback from their fans. He might not have had a particularly musical ear, but he listened to what others had to say, and he was unstinting in his promotion and placing of the band in the face of competition from several other top acts. He was also a shrewd negotiator. (It was during this time that Curley became friendly with Albert Reynolds, who owned a number of successful dance halls and who would later become Taoiseach of Ireland.)

When he started out, he arranged a straight fee with the owner of the hall, but he soon realised it would prove far more beneficial to demand a cut – as much as 50 per cent – of the night's takings. With attendances of 2,000 at times, it was an astute strategy.

For a time, Curley recalls, he and the band enjoyed the lifestyle of Arab princes. They were all driving around in new cars, and if one was damaged they'd take it back to the garage and buy another. 'It was easy come, easy go, all cash in the back pocket, and nothing as irritating as tax . . .' Curley himself bought a Caravelle, the first Renault sports car. He soon crashed it – one of three write-offs in as many months.

His success with the Dots built him a reputation, and the Curley stable of talent would later include such exotically named outfits as Brian McCall and the Buckaroos, and Hugo Duncan and the Tall Men. Duncan's 'Dear God' reached number 1 in the Irish charts, and remained there for 22 weeks. Promoters were eager to buy his contract. 'I wouldn't have accepted £50,000,' says Curley. Duncan would become a radio presenter in Ireland.

In their heyday, the showbands went on tours of Britain. Venues included the Gresham in London's Holloway Road, the Galtymore in Cricklewood and the Buffalo in Camden Town, all popular with the big Irish community in the capital.

The world of popular music, and its attendant vices, was something of a shock for a man who only a few years previously had been immersed in philosophy and the classics in the tranquillity of the seminary at Mungret. There were inevitably some wild nights on the road, with too much drink, as well as drugs. Curley discovered that Dexamyl, known as 'purple hearts', was being taken. It was regarded as a 'soft' drug, and he turned a blind eye to it.

Being on the road was an ideal cover for his smuggling enterprises, which had continued during his period managing the bands. By now, he had a new ruse. The contraband was tyres. He bought Michelins for up to £4 in Omagh and sold them for £10 in the South, where they were unavailable. They were secreted in the Ford Transit vans used to transport the bands' instruments and equipment.

On one occasion, he and his accomplice, Herbie McElholm, who was also a driver for one of the bands, were stopped by the Garda at a checkpoint. Curley managed to bluster his way out of it, but realised the folly of his ways and ceased dealing in contraband shortly afterwards.

By now, he was a married man. He had been down at Killarney with one of his bands, and nipped away to the town's racecourse to back a horse named Herring Gull, trained by Georgie Wells and ridden by Tommy Carberry, in a maiden hurdle. He had £100 on to win £110, and collected. (Herring Gull, incidentally, would progress to win the 1968 Irish Grand National.) If the horse had been beaten that day, he would probably have departed immediately. Instead, fate decreed that he would hang around to watch subsequent races, and he got talking to Maureen, who hailed from St Helen's, Lancashire, but was of Irish extraction.

He handed her a promotional card offering her and her friends free admission to one of the band's shows. When she spotted the name of the manager on the card, it amused her no end. Curley was her surname too. They arranged to meet at a dance that night and hit it off immediately. Barney was 28 at the time, and Maureen was around eight years his junior, but he admired her intelligence and outlook, despite her relatively tender years. They were married soon afterwards, on 18 April 1968. Their first child, Catherine, who was born the following year, would accompany her parents to many gigs. Curley would look after the band, while Maureen would check the money on the door to ensure that they were not underpaid.

Increasingly Curley was dividing his time between the bands and betting. He didn't bet big. It was more of an education. He evaluated the condition and conformation of a horse, and scrutinised races for pointers to the future. He looked for horses that had been unlucky in running or possibly had been run over the wrong trip.

It was boom time for the showbands. This coincided with the period when the Beatles were making an extraordinary impact in the national psyche in Britain and, after the austerity of the post-war fifties, the sixties were swinging wildly. Curley's bands featured on TV programmes like *The Late Late Show*, presented by Gay Byrne.

However, in the end, the avarice of those concerned killed the bands. They demanded too much from promoters to allow for their considerable overheads, and self-destructed. 'Looking back, we took too much money out, and the bubble burst,' Curley conceded.

One morning Curley awoke and decided to quit the music scene. He planned to go into gambling, seriously. He recalls fondly how Gerry Magee, the local chemist in his home town of Irvinestown – the man who had, coincidentally, supplied his father with all the tablets that had 'slowed' his greyhounds – tried to deter him. Magee, regarded as the best-educated man around, warned him: 'Barney, please. Don't be mad. Don't be a fool,' when Curley told him he was setting out to be a professional gambler. 'You're crazy. Nobody has done it, and you're not going to be the first. Forget about it.'

The words went unheard, and Curley reflects: 'Gerry Magee's long dead now, and despite those words, I think he would have been proud of what I've achieved overall. In a sense, though, Gerry was right. Winning at this game in the long term is virtually impossible. I've always believed that the Man Above has sent me down with a very good brain. To be a success you have to be out of the ordinary, and I knew I was. I had an ego which told me I could crack the system – and I was right, but only by keeping myself under strict control.'

By the early seventies, Curley was staking between £1,000 and £2,000 at the major tracks in Ireland: the Curragh, Leopardstown, Naas. His strategy was to build up a reserve of funds, his 'tank', as he called it. Even in those early years, he was a bold operator. In 1971, he ventured to the Cheltenham Festival with £700 in his pocket. He came away with £50,000.

His first major successful gamble at the Festival was on Fred Winter's Crisp, partnered by Paul Kelleway. The Australian-bred had won his prep race carrying a formidable burden of 12st 7lb in a handicap chase at Wincanton five days previously. Curley placed him amongst his bankers at the Festival. Crisp won the Champion Chase (now called the Queen Mother Champion Chase) easily, by 25 lengths. At 3–1 and better, Curley regarded it as extraordinarily good value.

Curley was 'red hot' at the time in terms of his betting, and from that period he exposed the belief that when you're on a winning run, you should kick on. When you're cold, ease back.

He returned to Omagh, where he and Maureen were living. Though a teetotaller, he was persuaded to spend £30,000 on a pub, which he renamed the Cheltenham Arms. He went racing as frequently as possible, but was a lone wolf from the start. 'I made up my mind early on that there was one way to ruin and that was to listen to people in racing.'

His parents' expressions told him everything about their displeasure. They'd assumed that with his decent education he'd enter one of the professions, 'rather than driving around betting and running a pub'. His father's fate was also a spectre that had long hung over the family. Curley Snr constantly quoted stories of relations or friends who had lost everything.

Their mood was scarcely brightened when Barney ventured into owning betting shops. His first was in Kevlin Road, Omagh. That was followed by a larger premises in Market Street, Enniskillen. He paid for it by backing a winner. At one time he owned six offices, adding to his empire one in Forthill Street, Enniskillen, two in Lisnaskea, and another in Omagh.

Eventually he decided to sell up. Taking odds, not laying them, was his game. He'd confirmed the instincts he'd first harboured back on Murder Mile at Celtic Park. 'I wasn't born to be a layer. I'm not a layer at heart. They require a different mentality, and you can't do both,' he explains. However, those experiences, on and off course, were an important part of his education, giving him an intimate understanding of the other side of the business.

Curley's determination to stand no nonsense from anyone shone through when he offloaded a shop in Armagh to Billy Charlton, an acquaintance who had helped him acquire his first house. When Charlton was a little tardy in his payment, Curley stood outside and picketed the premises, informing customers who entered: 'This man has not paid me for this betting office.' Charlton happened to be a friend of his mother Kathleen, and according to Curley, he got 'some serious abuse' from her about the incident.

One legacy of disposing of the betting offices was that it allowed Curley to plunge head first into that mire of unpredictability and expense called racehorse ownership. The potential benefit of owning horses to back them had always fascinated him, though his first experience could well have quelled his enthusiasm.

Curley paid £500 for a half-share in Charge Straight, which he owned jointly with John James McManus, who had sold him his first car. The horse was trained by Christy Grassick, who was based at Phoenix Park. Curley arranged for Barry Brogan, who he knew from his Mungret days, to ride him out. Brogan was amateur rider for Tom Dreaper at that time and among other duties rode Arkle on the training gallops.

Charge Straight was not exactly in that league, but Brogan told Curley that he was flying during his home work. Charge Straight was entered for a bumper at Ballinrobe and arrived there accompanied by high expectations. He was pulled up halfway.*

Though it was not an auspicious start, Curley would have numerous successes in bumpers over the years ahead; many as an owner with trainer Liam Brennan, whom he met at Tramore races through McManus. Brennan, formerly a jockey, was based at the Curragh and trained around 40 horses, mostly jumpers.

It would turn out to be a highly remunerative, if at times tempestuous, relationship.

---

* 'Bumper' is the common term for a National Hunt Flat race. They are intended as preparatory events for horses with a jumping career ahead.

CHAPTER 7

Liam Brennan was unaware initially that he was to be involved with such a serious punter. 'I had no real idea at the beginning,' he recalls. 'I knew Barney liked to have a bet. He started off betting steady, then he got a little bit bigger as we went along and had a bit of success. Fair Rambler, now, he was a lovely horse. I bought him for Barney. He won five or six races. He got a fair few quid out of him; then he put it into more.' Brennan adds: 'I was very light on betting . . . I was more into the training. I did have a bet now and again when I thought one would win – but the minimum in comparison to Barney.'

Brennan had a ferocious temper, as Curley discovered when he failed to settle the invoice for his first horse on time, but eventually they became very close. Curley regarded Brennan as an excellent judge of thoroughbreds. 'As we say in Ireland, he wouldn't count his sheep as lambs,' he says. 'Liam wasn't a trainer who'd ever make the big time, but I had total faith in him. He was a very good teacher. I learnt a lot from him. He always made maximum use of the horses he had. He had the knack of producing them fit to win first time out.' Brennan also taught Curley the importance of 'tight lips' if gambles were to succeed.

For Curley, it was an excellent, if belated, apprentice-ship. By then aged 37, he was still in the infancy of his gambling career and he had much to learn about race-horses. He watched and listened to those in the Brennan circle. 'I was a late starter and had to work harder than most to understand it,' he concedes.

Brennan brought his horses along quietly, patiently, refusing to rush them. It was the strategy that gave Curley his first victory as an owner, with a horse named Little Tim, partnered by Bobby Barry, another friend of his from their Mungret days. The horse was the subject of a spec-tacular and superbly executed gamble in 1972 when he ran in a bumper at Mallow, a country track around ten miles north of Cork. It was the first time his owner had laid out serious money on one of his horses and in many respects it was a precursor of what would follow, even more spectacularly, three years later.

Knowing that Brennan had Little Tim spot on for the race, Curley called a meeting of trusted collaborators to a meeting room at the Cheltenham Arms the night before the event. They each had their own group of 'putters-on', the expression he employed to describe the men placing bets anonymously on his behalf. They all departed into the night clutching £100 in cash and with instructions to back the horse the following day throughout the country from the moment the betting shops opened.

Up to 40 people were involved in total – from showband members to his shop and pub staff. In those days, there were fewer chains and there weren't the same conduits of information between shops. Little Tim was backed down to 8–1 from 20–1, but the horse's comfortable win earned Curley at least £40,000 for an outlay of £4,000. His men collected the winnings, and 'weighed in' back at the Cheltenham Arms. That room became known thereafter as the Weighing Room.

On this one occasion, Maureen was involved. Curley told her to have £100 on the Tote at Mallow. The Tote girl correctly accepted the bet on number 17, Little Tim, but when Maureen decided to add her own £10, she was mistakenly given a ticket for number 7. She hasn't had a bet since.

For Curley, though, it was a valuable dress rehearsal.

Another early success was the aforementioned Fair Rambler. Curley bought him as a yearling, and he developed into a multiple winner, starting with the big meeting at Punchestown in 1973.

Curley had swiftly learned that if you could pitch a horse unfancied by anyone but you against a highly regarded animal from a major stable, 'you'd be laughing at the bookmakers' expense'. It would guarantee him rewarding odds. Fair Rambler was a case in point. At Punchestown, the horse was up against Grand Lachine, an ex-Vincent O'Brien Flat horse, then with Mick O'Toole, who was considered to be the business. Grand Lachine ensured that Fair Rambler's odds remained long. The Curley horse won at 20–1.

By now, Curley and his family were based in the Republic. The situation in Northern Ireland had deteriorated and he feared he could become a target because of his perceived wealth, his increasing notoriety and his religious background. After his experience in the sanatorium, death did not trouble him. His primary concern was that his family could be caught up in the violence when he was away racing in the Republic.

He had twice experienced that jeopardy first hand. One

night, he was trapped in crossfire between the IRA and the British army on the Monaghan–Tyrone border as he travelled back to Northern Ireland. He was saved by a British Army officer who told him to keep his head down and turn his lights out. Later, he would reflect on the officer's courage: 'He risked his life and showed great bravery.' In another incident, a bomb detonated as he was walking out of the house in Omagh.

Curley once said: 'If I have a winner, I hope and believe it's cheered as loudly in the Shankill as it is in the Falls.' He maintains, 'I can see both sides' point of view. I am not a bigot, and I see everybody, be they Nationalists or Unionists, as equal. I want fair play for all.' Curley lived in Northern Ireland for 30 years and freely admits that many of the people who helped him on the way were Protestants. 'It has been the politicians and leaders of factions who have had no interest in anything but their own narrow cause that led our country close to destruction. Too many of my countrymen just listened to all these fanatics and would not utter a word.'

He is acutely aware, though, of the discrimination against Catholics. 'The Protestant population didn't want Catholics in the best jobs. They wanted to keep the professions for themselves. That's why many of us from my part of the world ended up as club-owners, publicans, bookmakers, running or playing in showbands – or became tricksters of one sort or another.' It is significant that, despite being well educated, he ended up being involved in all of these areas.

Today, Curley reminisces about his smuggling enterprises between Northern Ireland and the Republic as a young man and concedes: 'If I hadn't got out when I did, I would have ended up in jail.'

In 1972, Curley sold up everything as he prepared to leave Ulster. (He was particularly grateful to dispense with the Cheltenham Arms pub, which had made him a loss of around £100,000.) He moved the family to Ashford, County Wicklow (close to where *Ballykissangel* was filmed) and bought the 80-acre Boswell Stud. For a while he developed an interest in eventing. He stabled a team of 20, who were trained and ridden by Sue Sinclair, a keen English horsewoman. She took the horses to the Dublin Show and Ballsbridge, and won a few events. But there was no money in it. As Curley explains: 'The show-jumpers were fine, but you couldn't back them. Even if you won, all you got was a rosette – and rosettes don't pay bills.'

He had other business interests at that time, without conspicuous success. He ran a large piggery, until being informed by his bank manager that the enterprise was £20,000 in debt. He also had an involvement in cattle, but that proved a failure too. He launched a newspaper called the *Northern Advertiser*, one of the first free publications. It was run from Omagh and delivered throughout Fermanagh. It was breaking even, he believed, but there were problems with distribution and after a year he closed it down. On advice, he invested £160,000 in silver shares – and was wiped out when the market collapsed.

One visitor to the stud was Paddy Broderick, who rode Night Nurse early in the career of this prolific winner who would come to be regarded as one of the greatest hurdlers of all time. Broderick's daughter Alison married the man who would become Curley's assistant, Andrew Stringer.

Curley also had a number of store horses – National Hunt horses that are put out to grass to strengthen up and mature, with the aim of sending them jumping at five or six years old, in contrast with their more precocious Flat equivalent. One of these cost £1,000 and he named it Yellow Sam. It was to change his life irrevocably.

Curley's early years as a professional gambler produced many stumbles. He concedes there have been some occasions when he came close to ruination – when he just couldn't pay, barring a miracle. Invariably he was blessed with one to get him out of trouble.

One such occasion was in 1972, when he owed £30,000 to various major bookmakers: Sean Graham, David Power (whose firm would became Paddy Power) and the Mulligan Brothers. It was not an enormous sum to win even then, but, as he put it, it was a considerable amount when you couldn't get your hands on it: 'Once you say you can't pay, you get a bad name, and there's no more efficient bush telegraph than the betting fraternity. Your credit may be curtailed for good.'

He had a strong fancy for Roberto in the Derby, and scraped together £10,000 and headed off to Epsom for his first bet on a British racecourse. The eventual starting price was 3–1 but, as has been stressed before, Curley always sought value. He managed to place the £10,000 to win £35,000, at odds of 7–2.

The race has long been the subject of debate – the fact that the horse's original partner, Australian Bill Williamson, had lost the ride to Lester Piggott for one; Piggott's staccato use of the whip in the final few strides for another. As the *Racing Post* columnist Ian Carnaby recalls of Piggott: 'The way he sways back, almost like a rodeo rider, while maintaining perfect balance and using his whip in a rat-a-tat, quick-fire fashion, is astonishing.'

Curley confesses that if it hadn't been for Piggott galvanising Vincent O'Brien's colt near the line to get up by a short head from the Barry Hills-trained runner-up Rheingold, his gambling career would have probably come to a premature and ignominious end. As he put it drily, 'Roberto barely stayed the 12-furlong trip and if the maestro Lester hadn't got Roberto's head up on the line, mine would have been on the block. If Lester had got beaten, there would be no way back. I would have been cleaned out. I'd go as far to say that I wouldn't be here today, at least not in racing . . .'

It was one of the few occasions when he sweated on a result. It required a photo finish to confirm the outcome, and even then the victor had to survive a stewards' inquiry. Curley sat slumped on the steps in the sun, oblivious of the crowd around him, as he awaited the stewards' deliberations. Eventually it was announced: 'The result stands.'

In the infancy of his owner-gambling, Curley's fortunes fluctuated. By February 1975, he had 13 horses with Brennan and he owed £8,058.68. 'Cheque would oblige' (underlined), his latest invoice read – and not for the first time. But it was principally his gambling that, in the early summer of 1975, led to him striking the rocks once again and putting out a distress call after a particularly bad sequence of losing bets. This time there would be no such lifebelt as that provided by Roberto and Piggott; no such obliging reprieve.

From such desperation, however, an imaginative scheme was born. It involved a horse of unexceptional ability, yet one that was to stamp Curley as one of the most imaginative and astute gamblers in racing history.

What took place would establish his name in gambling folklore, not just in Ireland, but across the Irish Sea.

CHAPTER 8

Make one of a party whose spirits are hearty
Get a seat on a trap that is safe not to spill
In its well, pack a hamper – then off for a
*   scamper –*
And hurroo! For the glories of Bellewstown Hill.
        From *300 Years of Racing at Bellewstown*

On a sun-griddled afternoon at Bellewstown racecourse in the summer of 1975, a swooping hawk
would have spied two figures crouched amongst the gorse
bushes in the centre of the track. They were adjacent to
the second-last hurdle, watching the hindquarters of a
field of unexceptional runners disappear towards the finish
post.

Barney Curley was accompanied by Ann Brogan,
daughter of trainer Jimmy and sister of Barry, the National
Hunt jockey who had been a lay pupil when Curley had
got to know him at Mungret College. She was an excellent point-to-point rider, and later also had several
winners as an amateur under rules (the world of professional racing). On this day, though, it wasn't her racing
expertise that Curley sought but her company and her
wheels. Curley himself owned 'a big, flashy red Jaguar',

as he recalls it, which would have attracted even more unwanted interest than normal.

So surreptitious had he been that few would be aware, other than those managing the betting shops of Ireland, both sides of the border, of the outcome of the enterprise until the following day. At that stage, even many of those involved had no notion of its true significance.

Bellewstown, on the main Belfast to Dublin road, is an idyllic venue, laid out high up on the Hill of Crockafotha, against a backdrop of the Mourne Mountains, the River Boyne and the Irish Sea. It is one of Ireland's oldest racecourses, with records going back to 1726. At one time it had a royal connection. King George III was persuaded by George Tandy, former mayor of nearby Drogheda, to sponsor a prestigious race there in 1780. It was named His Majesty's Plate and was worth £100 to the winner. Every monarch continued to support the race until 1980, when the present Queen discontinued the practice.

Informality and a classlessness has been key, stretching back to the eighteenth century, when the *Drogheda Conservative Journal* described 'the numerous and elegant assemblage of beauty and fashion' mingling with the 'peasantry, whose peaceful and unoffending demeanour was gratifying'. These days, the track has an outside running rail. At one time, a makeshift barrier was provided by horse boxes and trailers to prevent the horses colliding with picnic parties just out to enjoy a day's racing.

Today there are five days of racing a year at Bellewstown. In 1975, there were three days in total: a two-day meeting in June, and another day's racing in August. On all occasions, the attendance is swelled by holidaymakers. You'd visit the track for the splendid scenery alone, and the bracing, invigorating air.

But on this day Curley wasn't at Bellewstown for the benefit of his health. He was there to seek a restorative for his financial plight. He knew he had to pull off a masterstroke.

This scheme had been born of desperation. It was organised to settle debts incurred during the early years of his gambling career; principally what he owed the bookmakers. Liam Brennan adds wryly: 'It wasn't just the bookies he owed – he owed me a few quid, too. That was more important to me.'

At first Curley had attempted to take remedial action, and sold the eventers he had stabled at Wicklow in an attempt to make ends meet, but it was not sufficient. 'I badly need to pull off a touch,' he told Brennan. 'Let's go through these horses and see which one is capable of doing it.'

Not that there was too much choice at that time of year. Being summer, the plan required a horse that would appreciate the prevailing firm or good ground. Most of Curley's better horses were resting, awaiting softer going in the autumn, or were away on their holidays at grass. Jump horses – hurdlers and steeple-chasers – are generally at their best, and certainly prefer it, when there is give underfoot. Firmer ground can jar them up.

But as Curley would demonstrate on so many occasions, a major gamble doesn't have to involve outstanding horses or major racecourses. After a couple of days' consideration, Brennan told him: 'You know, Barney, this horse Yellow Sam – I think he's improved a bit.'

Curley had named the horse after his father. Apparently

Curley Snr was known as 'Yellow Sam' because he had a sallow, almost jaundiced, complexion – though his son has no idea where the 'Sam' originated from.

The brown gelding was described by Curley as 'unexceptional-looking and never very good'. He hadn't much pace. But his redeeming quality was that he was an excellent jumper who could make two or three lengths at every hurdle. Though he might have been slightly overstating his ability, in Curley's regard he was 'as good a jumper as Persian War' – a horse that had won three Champion Hurdles at the end of the sixties and beginning of the seventies.

In his nine runs over two seasons Yellow Sam had been unplaced – although, admittedly, some of his races had been at the major tracks like Fairyhouse and Punchestown, where competition would have been relatively strong. His best placing was eighth. This was his record:

Season 1973–74
8 December 1973 Fairyhouse (soft) 1m 6f 3-y-o hurdle, unplaced, not in first 9 of 20
26 December 1973 Leopardstown (soft) 1m 5f 3-y-o hurdle, 9th of 15
26 January 1974 Naas (heavy) 2m 1f maiden hurdle, 8th of 17
17 April 1974 Fairyhouse (firm) 1m 6f maiden hurdle, 9th of 17
Season 1974–75
28 December 1974 Punchestown (heavy) 2m handicap hurdle, not in first 9 of 14
17 March 1975 Limerick (heavy) 2m 5f handicap hurdle, 9th of 16

29 March 1975 Mallow (good) 2m 5f handicap
hurdle, not in first 9 of 20
14 May1975 Navan (soft) 2m 5f handicap hurdle,
not in first 9 of 29

Those mostly modest performances meant that at least he was well handicapped. Horses are allotted a handicap rating based on their first three runs, or when they have won, whichever is the sooner. That determines the weight they carry in any particular race. Unless they're so good they race in non-handicaps, they then move up and down the weights, dependent on their performances, as decreed by the handicapper. If he has done his job well, the participants in a handicap race should finish close together. Serious backers try to identify blots on the handicap.

There are many ways of getting a horse's handicap mark down. They include racing it over an unsuitable distance, running it on going that doesn't suit it, or employing unsuitable riding tactics. Some cynics might suggest that Yellow Sam hadn't been seriously asked a question before, or, as the euphemism goes, given 'educational' runs; that he had been set up specifically for this race for a long time.

Curley recalls: 'It was true to say that I had set horses up with Liam in the past. But there was no truth in it now. We just needed a horse to do a job, and Yellow Sam was the only possibility. He was a big horse who would always be likely to require time to develop and come to his best and he just suddenly began to show that he was sparkling.'

Yellow Sam produced enough on the gallops at the Curragh to demonstrate that he was capable of winning a moderate race with everything in his favour: namely the going, the jockey and the quality of the opposition. Brennan identified a suitable target: a hurdle race for amateur riders at Bellewstown three weeks hence – assuming the ground stayed firm.

For all its charm, Bellewstown has tended to stage low-quality Flat and National Hunt cards, though there have been exceptions. Thomond II, a Bellewstown steeple-chase winner in 1931, went on to finish runner-up to Golden Miller in the Cheltenham Gold Cup two years later; other victors at the Hill included Hatton's Grace, who progressed to win the Champion Hurdle at Cheltenham three times for Vincent O'Brien in successive years from 1949, and Pollardstown, successful in a Flat handicap for Kevin Prendergast. He went on to win the Triumph Hurdle and be placed second to Sea Pigeon in the 1981 Champion Hurdle.

The Mount Hanover Handicap Hurdle for amateur riders, however, over two and a half miles, in which Liam had entered Yellow Sam, did not attract anything resembling that quality. 'This would be the equivalent of a horse turning out at Sandown, then being sent to a country course like Fakenham,' says Curley. 'It was a different class altogether, a significant step down.'

Today, Brennan, in his early eighties, still recalls selecting the event. 'I picked it simply because it wasn't a good race, and I knew my horse would be a lot better on firm ground. He'd had one good run at Naas in heavy ground (finishing eighth), in good company. I had always kept that in my mind. I thought, well if I can get him into lower company now on fast ground, he could do a job for us.' He adds: 'I thought he'd win. But I went up the day before and walked the track, to check the ground.'

There was no way that an innocent spectator could have looked at Yellow Sam and what he had achieved and imagined he would ever pull off a 'job'. But that suited Curley, who hoped that his likely starting price would be around 20–1. That would not be overgenerous. It was the price represented on all known form.

To guarantee that, it was essential that this was a clandestine operation. In Curley's mind, there was one man who threatened to breach that secrecy: Barry Brogan. The Mungret old boy had developed into a highly successful jump jockey on both sides of the Irish Sea, and for a few months rode work on the training gallops for Brennan and partnered a couple of winners for him. In early 1975 he rode Yellow Sam on the gallops and was convinced the horse had a race in him. 'He was moving exceptionally well,' Brogan was to comment later.

However, his old school pal's association with the horse troubled Curley. Brogan was the antithesis of the rest of his family, for whom Curley had always had the highest regard. By his own admission the jockey was a heavy gambler and drinker, and, as he later revealed in his life story, he fixed races to pay his betting debts. Worse, where Yellow Sam was concerned, as Brennan says bluntly, 'He had too big a mouth.'

Brogan recalls in his autobiography that Brennan 'was renowned for his tight lips and secrecy'. If he ever asked the trainer if a horse was fancied, 'the reply would have been the usual rude glare and absolute silence'. Curley says: 'Barry was exceptionally talented, possibly as gifted a rider as Richard Dunwoody or Graham Bradley, but he went off the rails in a major way. Initially, I tried to make excuses for him and tried to sympathise with him. Being charitable, I can only put it down to him witnessing the death of his trainer father Jimmy at only 44, when he dropped dead with a heart attack in front of him. It was a terrible thing for a young man to experience. Both Liam Brennan and I tried to help him by giving him rides, when others were rejecting him.'

He adds: 'What happened to him was a tragedy. He was an alcoholic. I tried to help him. He should have been on the favourite for the 1973 Gold Cup, Fulke Walwyn's The Dikler, but instead ended up in John O'Gods, where the alcoholics and drug addicts go, in Dublin. He was drying out. I went in to visit him. It was like *One Flew Over the Cuckoo's Nest* in there.' You can imagine Brogan's chagrin as he watched on TV as The Dikler overcame Fred Winter's Pendil by a a short head under his replacement, Ron Barry.

'He was a strange fellow, a liability,' says Curley. 'You simply could not trust him. He was too close to several other professional gamblers and bookmakers and he had loose lips, even more so when the drink was flowing.' Not surprisingly, Brogan would be the last to know about what was brewing here.

Brennan had consulted Curley about a jockey well in advance. Michael Furlong, one of the best amateur jockeys in Ireland, who would later ride professionally in Britain, was booked. Furlong, who was attached to trainer Padge Berry's yard but would also ride out for Brennan, was competing for the amateur riders' championship with Ted Walsh. He recalls how, several days beforehand, Brennan requested him not to take another ride in the race.

'At the time, when I was still an amateur, I used to get a few spare rides from Liam and I rode in a few points for him as well. Usually myself and Ted Walsh, we got a ride offered the day before. It was "If you're not riding tomorrow will you ride mine?" That was usually the arrangement. But on this occasion, several days before the event, Liam said to me, "Don't take a ride in the amateur riders' race at Bellewstown on Wednesday, 25 June."'

Furlong was left feeling somewhat perplexed. He recalls, 'Liam never said any more about it. I had a ride or two in between for him. But still no word about that race.' He adds: 'Ted Walsh and I were having a cracking little race for the amateurs' championship at that time. We were neck and neck. So most times you'd be grateful to get any ride. Eventually, I saw the entries and noticed Liam had entered a horse named Yellow Sam. I'm thinking, "Why the hell does he want me riding this?" His form was terrible.'

Even Furlong's knowledge of what had been planned was kept to a minimum. 'Once or twice I went to sit on horses of Liam's at the Curragh. One of the lads, making a list of horses to ride out, said: "What about that horse there?" He was pointing to Yellow Sam. Liam said to leave him in.' He adds: 'The rest of the lads in the yard thought he was having an easy time, but apparently Liam and one other chap in the yard were coming in real early and riding him out, and getting him fit.'

Because of his previous moderate displays, when the declarations were made Yellow Sam was allotted a weight of 10st 6lb in a field of nine runners. The top weight carried 12st. Yellow Sam was third lowest in the weights. It was hardly a great burden given the unexceptional standard of his opponents. One of them had won a maiden hurdle, and another had been placed, but both had been in low-grade summer events.

Curley could not have asked for a more ideal set of circumstances in which to execute his scheme. He had the race. He had the horse. The horse had the fast going he required. But it was the starting price that concerned Curley as he formulated a plan to plunder betting shops in every large town in Ireland.

Though bookmakers were already highly circumspect where his horses were concerned, Yellow Sam's form was so uninspiring he would be likely to open at a long price. But how could Curley ensure that he stayed that way, and didn't shorten up as he lumped on the kind of money he had in mind?

That required a scheme only this most ingenious of backers could have contemplated.

CHAPTER 9

Curley overcame the predicament he faced by capitalising on a specific feature of Bellewstown racecourse, and an intimidating accomplice.

In British and Irish racing, it is the on-course bookmakers' pricing of a horse, dependent on weight of money, that determines its all-important starting price (SP). Official SPs are formed by the average odds on offer at the 'off'. If there was negligible money for Curley's horse in the betting ring at the track, where the on-course bookmakers operate, his SP odds would be big. There would be no particular reason for anyone not in the know at the track to back him.

Normally, off-course bookmakers transfer their liabilities to the on-course market, which would have the effect of bringing down a particular horse's odds. With today's communications technology, this is a straightforward matter. Even then, all it should have taken was a series of phone calls from the betting shops. But Curley's strategy was that the calls would never get through – until it was too late. His tactics involved no law-breaking and nothing contrary to the rules of racing. He simply took advantage of a particular set of circumstances.

The course in County Meath was selected for a crucial

reason other than the moderate quality of its races: its lack of communication with the outside world. In 1975, there was only one public telephone box there. For a course in use only three days a year, that was considered sufficient. In general, people didn't hang around in phone boxes. They tended to be used for emergencies or quick calls. The machines' voracious demand for more coins to be fed in if conversation became too protracted ensured that. You formed an orderly queue and waited your turn. This afternoon, it would be a long wait.

Remember, this was well before the arrival of even the most primitive mobile telephone the size of a house brick – and certainly before modern computer communications. In the summer of 1975, that single course telephone at Bellewstown was the only means the on-course book-makers had of receiving intelligence of market moves from the betting shops around Ireland. Curley planned to ensure that this one line of communication was, shall we say, continually busy.

The most vital member of his team of associates in this strategy would be a character named Benny O'Hanlon, who was allocated a rather different duty to the remainder of his team. Curley describes O'Hanlon as 'a balding, heavily built fellow – a tough sort that you wouldn't want to get into an argument with'. He had worked for Curley in his betting offices and at the time was manager at his shop in Lisnaskea, County Fermanagh. However, his physique and demeanour belied an essentially decent nature. 'No man could have possessed more integrity than Benny,' Curley says. 'If you told him to do something, that was it. He'd obey you implicitly. As for his honesty, he wouldn't take a pound if you left it in front of him for a year.'

O'Hanlon was charged with one simple but vital task: to block the racecourse telephone – and to employ a plausible reason for doing so. If he didn't do his job properly, the whole thing would be blown wide open. 'He was a man I could trust with my life. He would let no one pass. To get him off the phone it would need a man to take out a gun and shoot him,' says Curley. 'And the important thing was, he was a great talker. He wouldn't have dreamt of stealing £20 from my shop – but he didn't think twice about blocking that phone box because he trusted and believed in me without question.'

O'Hanlon hailed from a respectable family that ran a clothing shop in Curley's home town of Irvinestown. He had held down every sort of job in his time, from buying and selling jute bags to working as a barman in London. He was once so short of cash – so the bizarre story goes – that he confessed to being the Notting Hill serial killer John Christie to get a police cell for the night.

Curley adds: 'He was a born worrier. He was always going on about how the day had gone against him; how so and so had taken a lot of money off us. To listen to him, you'd think we'd never come out on top. He forgot all the times when the punters had gone down. For that reason I never explained how big this operation was, and how major his part would be. He would have been quaking in his boots. But I had no hesitation nominating Benny as my "phone man" without any reservations.'

The plan Curley had formulated was for a team of men to place bets on Yellow Sam in about 300 betting shops in total. The idea was that it should be a concerted action, with the bets going down roughly at the same time, just before the race, and all in such small quantities that it would conceal the true magnitude of the plan.

It was still a far from straightforward logistical task. It was not a question of his team quietly going round and placing bundles of tens or twenties without question. At that time, Curley's name had already become notorious on- and off the course. 'Over three years I'd built up a bit of a reputation,' he says. 'When the money was down they'd fear my horses.' He was determined that the book-makers collectively would have no idea that the money was down – until it was too late.

Curley likes to quote an old adage, 'Loose lips can sink ships', and that was in his mind constantly as he sat and plotted. One word out of place could scupper the oper-ation, or at the very least drastically reduce its effectiveness.

For weeks, Curley didn't leave his home at Wicklow. He sat in his office and prepared everything down to the last detail; as he puts it, 'like a general massing his troops before going into battle – only the enemy, on this occa-sion, were the bookmakers'. The timing had to be right and he had to be certain of his collaborators.

'I was like a recluse as I sat in my little room at the Boswell Stud with my maps and my lists,' he recalls. 'Maureen had a fair idea about what was going on, but this was something I had to plan alone.' He adds, 'I spent hour upon hour, over many weeks, poring over my lists and maps, striking names out if I wasn't sure about them, to make sure I had the best possible team. It was not that I feared they would be traitors; just that too many men cannot be charged with keeping a secret. It was vital that no one broke the line. It was a massive operation and I put a lot of thought into it.'

The team leaders were paid around £1,000 each; the ground force around £200. Yet the majority got involved just for the sheer exhilaration of being part of a scheme.

Long before Twitter, Curley had followers. 'Money wouldn't have been the main object for most of them,' he insists. It would not be the last time that he was the beneficiary of this element of human nature. 'I like to think I'm a good judge of people and I chose people I believed I could trust. Eventually I had compiled a list of a hundred men.

He organised five or six key figures, men in whom he had absolute faith. They were responsible for teams of punters, who would receive a call to action on the day. Eamon and Bernard Bradley, who had run one of his first betting shops, in Enniskillen, were typical of those involved. Another key figure was one of his nearest neighbours in Wicklow, who owned a meat business in Dublin. Many of the ground force would have been punters in the betting shops all over the country whom he'd known down the years since his days with the showbands. They regularly backed horses and would not provoke any undue suspicion.

No one close to him was aware of his plans. 'Even Liam Brennan didn't know precisely what I was going to do, or the extent of it,' says Curley. 'Everything was kept as low key as possible. Just one whisper from anyone could have jeopardised the whole operation.' This made it all the more remarkable that one of the limited number in the know should be Ireland's biggest bookmaker, Sean Graham. The family bookmaking business in his name still flourishes today.

The two men had been friends for 15 years, ever since those nights at Celtic Park when both made books. Now, in the summer of 1975, Curley owed Graham alone around £20,000. He also owed other bookmakers, including David Power. He was allowed credit, but knew that he required a major hit to pay off those debts. 'I've hit a brick wall, Sean,' he told Graham about a week before the big day. 'I need your help. I could do this without you, but I'd rather I had your help. You'll have to give me your word you'll not tell a soul.' Graham agreed – with the crucial proviso that Curley didn't go anywhere near his betting shops.

'I didn't go into details straight away; just that I was going to back a horse,' explains Curley. 'I could have blocked the phone without telling him, but it would have aroused his suspicions anyway. Normally one of Graham's men would be on the phone in question to make sure that money came back to the course, so I thought it best to put him in the picture. I knew I could trust him to keep quiet and he told no one. The knowledge that my horse was fancied and was a 20–1 chance was very useful to him . . .'

One obvious question is this: why didn't Curley's men take a price before the off and avoid all the subsequent subterfuge at the racecourse?

The simple answer is that the betting shops would not give a price on one of his horses. Normally punters can take a price once the first show of odds comes in a few minutes before a race. However, caution was the layers' byword when it came to Curley-owned runners and bets on his horses could only be struck at SP.

If liabilities started mounting up, they would send the money back to the track. In theory, anyway, there would be a balanced market. If the money went down, so would the SP. They could live with that.

With his organisation complete, Curley set out to drive the 50 miles from Wicklow to Bellewstown on the morning of the race. He had done all he could and felt confident and composed; yet strangely, he felt compelled to talk to someone whom he knew he could trust.

He called in to the Brogan family home at Gilliamstown Cottage, Rathfeigh – though it was not Barry he wanted to see, but his sister Ann. It was a bleak outpost of a location on top of a hill, about four miles from the course at Bellewstown, but Curley recalls: 'It was a nice, welcoming house, and they'd sit you down with tea and cake.'

He adds: 'The whole family were involved in some way with horses, and Ann, who was a lovely girl and a joy to talk to, though she was a lot younger than me, became a particular friend. I always admired Ann. I had a great lot of respect for her. She was a wonderful woman.

'I suppose I felt a tinge of excitement and just needed someone to talk to. Ann was a great listener. We had a lot in common, sharing a religious faith and a love of horses. She wasn't into betting or anything. She knew I was a punter, but would have had no idea of the massive scale that this was on. She probably thought I was talking about a few thousand.'

In reality, he had around £15,000 to play with, calling in one or two debts of his own. He hadn't dared calculate what success could mean financially. He was just looking to clamber out of an ever-deepening financial abyss. 'All I knew was that if all went to plan and my men did their job, it would be the equivalent of, today, my six numbers up – and the bonus ball.'

For all his planning, there were many unpredictable factors. He couldn't guarantee Yellow Sam's starting price, or know precisely what his men could get on. Was he being seriously over-optimistic in assuming they could place the bets without causing a ripple of interest in those betting shops? As for Yellow Sam himself, while Curley was confident of victory, racehorses, he knew, did not always perform to expectations.

'I could barely contain myself about what was planned when I met up with Ann. I couldn't help just throwing into the conversation casually, "I'm pulling off a big coup today, and if it comes off I might end up in *The Guinness Book of Records.*"'

He didn't add that, if it didn't, he'd probably end up in the poorhouse.

CHAPTER 10

An unquestioning Ann Brogan did precisely as she was bidden. 'I'd said to her, "Now listen, Ann, I can't afford to be seen",' recalls Curley. 'She agreed to drive me up to the racecourse, but, under my instructions, kept well away from the hurly-burly of the public enclosure. I knew the meeting would be well attended, with maybe a couple of thousand people packing the place.'

If it sounds absurdly surreptitious on his part, a whiff of his presence would have had the bookies quivering like startled deer stirring in the proximity of a hunter. 'People would have been looking out for me because my horse was running. And that could have been construed as a sign that it was fancied,' he says. 'So I got Ann to drive me up to the races, but we kept well away from the stand. I never went near the entrance until afterwards.'

The home straight of the track at Bellewstown runs parallel to the road, so Ann Brogan stopped halfway along and the pair scurried over the course itself to the centre of the racetrack. As they positioned themselves out of sight, Curley had his hat pushed down as far as it would go. He must have resembled George Cole playing the gambling spiv Flash Harry in the St Trinian's films.

Meanwhile, all over Ireland, his troops were preparing to move into action. At 1.45 Curley alerted his team leaders. But it wasn't until 15 minutes before the race, due off at three o'clock, that they passed on the word to their own contacts. Each man placed anything from £50 to £300, depending on the size of the shop. The total outlay was £15,300.

Curley had deliberately selected many independent bookies so that there would be less of an intelligence network. The offices were happy to accept the bets 15 minutes before the race. Most assumed that a 20–1 outsider would be beaten anyway – even one of Curley's. If there was significant support for Yellow Sam, the SP would be considerably shorter as the money went back to the course. They'd have no trouble in laying off their liabilities. All they would have to do was pick up the phone and have it back on course. Or so they believed. 'Of course, they would be pickled, come five to three when they couldn't get through and no other off-course bookmakers wanted any money for the horse,' recalls Curley. 'They would have to sweat it out and hope Yellow Sam got beaten.'

But whether his scheme went to plan presumed a lot; specifically that Benny O'Hanlon played the role that Curley had cast him in. Curley's instructions had been emphatic: O'Hanlon was to occupy that phone box 25 minutes before the race start. 'No matter who comes to the phone, do not leave it under any circumstances until the commentator announces "They're off",' he was told.

It was a huge obligation. Such was the crowd that day that to keep the phone occupied for up to half an hour required some imaginative tactics, and a garrulous nature. O'Hanlon got talking to a non-existent hospital in nearby Drogheda, where he supposedly had an aunt who was at death's door. Every few minutes he would announce his relative's state of health: 'Oh, all right, then, that's not so bad . . . Oh dear, she's taken a turn for the worse.'

It was the mundane kind of thing people say when they're enquiring about someone in hospital, but it did the trick. Never has a patient gone through so much recovery and relapse in half an hour. She was about to pass away and then she recovered. She was about to expire again and then she rallied. According to Curley, O'Hanlon carried it off brilliantly.

Just as insurance, Curley arranged for another character to be on hand nearby – 'in case it turned nasty'. Benny picked him up on the way and told him to be first in the queue and not budge for anyone. He was there as a kind of minder, to keep a bit of control outside the phone box.

There were plenty of people wanting to use the phone, especially the agents for the off-course bookmakers. It was their job to get through to see if there was money off course for any horses. Alternatively the people off course should be ringing in to this one phone.

Curley's strategy had the desired effect. With no money to speak of on course and no word from the layers off course, the price of Yellow Sam, the outsider, remained static on the bookmakers' boards as the field set off on their 18-furlong journey. The officially returned SP was 20–1. The fact that Yellow Sam returned £31.54 (to £1) on the Tote only served to confirm the dearth of interest in the horse on course.

'The phone would have been hot with people trying to get through as the money went on in the shops,' says Curley. 'Once Benny relinquished his position, it had the effect of a dam bursting.'

Meanwhile, out in the parade ring, Michael Furlong, who had assumed he was on an unfancied horse, had arrived and was preparing for Yellow Sam's race, which was second on the card.

The tropical heat had brought the crowds out in force. The carefree mood was enhanced by the fact that there were eight winning favourites during the meeting. Whatever else occurred over those two days, Yellow Sam would be a long-priced exception.

'For me, there was nothing unusual about the day,' says Furlong. 'I arrived at the course, got in my gear and weighed out. No owner was there, but Barney didn't always turn up anyway.' His rivals in the race included some decent amateurs: Sam Morshead, Willie Mullins, who would become a Grand National-winning trainer, and Ted Walsh, who would also become a trainer and TV pundit as well as father of the jockeys Ruby and Katy. Others were John Fowler and Mrs Ann Ferris, who in 1984 would become the first female jockey to win the Irish Grand National.

Furlong was given simple instructions by Brennan, who basically told him to bide his time and hit the front when he thought it was the right moment. He was still oblivious to what had been plotted off course, and had no great expectations. 'When I went into the ring, Liam said, as he legged me into the saddle: "This fella will win." I thought to myself: "He can't." It may have been a bad race, but he was about the worst horse in it – on paper, anyway.' However, as Curley says: 'Knowing my reputation, and Liam's, he would have understood the message without need of repetition.'

Furlong didn't take long to reconsider his view as he headed for the start of the sharp-left-handed oval of nine furlongs, with a run-in of three furlongs and an uphill finish. 'He'd never be a superstar, but the horse gave me a great sense of his well-being. I used to enjoy getting the feel of a horse going down and jumping the first. I used to like that period of a race. You get to know your animal, despite what the trainer or lad has said to you.'

According to Curley, on course there'd have probably been barely a pound taken on Yellow Sam before the start. In running, though, as news began filtering through, some punters who had become aware that something was afoot were rushing to take the price still on offer. The race lasted nearly five minutes, so there was plenty of time to do so.

Yellow Sam's price quickly tumbled to 2–1, and some more cautious souls among the bookmakers' ranks even wiped his name off their boards. Ann Brogan's mother Betty, who was at the races, reported that there was a real buzz about the place as it was whispered that there was a 'job' on.

Curley himself, behind that gorse bush in the middle of the track, a couple of hurdles up from the finish post, could only view the runners as they galloped up the straight. He could see precious little of the finish, but insists he suffered no apprehension; no doubts or anxiety.

He adds: 'I knew that all it would take would be a fall or a bad mistake at any one of the 13 flights of hurdles and I'd kiss the money, all £15,300 of it, goodbye. You couldn't read me when I went betting, and there was nothing different that day. Once I got to the course I was ice cold, even though defeat would have wiped me out.'

There was never any chance of that. Curley had complete faith in his horse's jumping ability and the prowess of his rider. Neither let him down. Spectators witnessed Yellow Sam make progress from midfield to assert his authority after four flights, assuming a lead on the inside from Satlan and Philipine Hill.

Furlong recalls: 'Liam was right. He told me to ride him handy and said, "If you're not happy it's a decent, true pace, you can squeeze him on." That's what happened. It was a two-and-a-half-mile race and I took it up around half a mile, six furlongs, out. He won easily enough.'

From their vantage point Curley and Ann Brogan only got a rapidly disappearing view of the horses' hindquarters, the backs of jockeys and whips being waved like conductors' batons. 'I couldn't actually see who had won. I thought we had done it, but, only getting a rear view, you can never be certain what has won and we couldn't hear the commentary,' says Curley. 'I wasn't absolutely sure so we dashed across the racetrack, back into the car and drove round to the entrance.'

He adds: 'I did not know quite what to do or say. I just stood there, lost for words; then somebody said, "Well done, Barney," and I knew I could relax. As you can imagine, at that price and with his form, the majority of the crowd, who would have been ignorant of what had been going on, weren't exactly ecstatic.'

The bookmakers certainly weren't as Furlong returned to unsaddle. He recalls: 'We pulled up in the parade ring, which is right beside the track. Angry-looking bookies [representing the major off-course firms] were coming in to the parade ring, and were beginning to scream a bit. They weren't too happy. Liam said to me: "You'd better weigh in and go. Don't hang around getting changed." That's what I did. That was my one ride.' He adds: 'Of course, we knew, everybody knew, that Barney would always have a shot at the bookies. It wasn't rocket science to work out, when he did appear in the ring afterwards, that something had gone on here.'

Curley recalls: 'There was a bit of a hullabaloo going on. I hung around for about ten minutes to watch the effect of his win and I saw at least one bookmaker kicking up a right fuss. All hell broke loose. All the shops were at last getting through on the phone in the box which Benny had now long vacated, and the men at the course were realising that the off-course offices had been caught, although even then I don't think at that moment they realised the gravity of the situation.'

It was an appropriate moment to make a diplomatic departure.

This was how they finished:

Mount Hanover Amateur Riders' Handicap Hurdle, 2m 5f

1st Yellow Sam M. J. Furlong
2nd Glenallen H. C. Morshead
3rd Silver Road W. Mullins
4th Satlan A. Tyrrell
Portballintrae Mrs P. Ferris
High and Mighty T. M. Walsh
Philipine Hill E. Woods

Gerties Beauty T. McCartan
Deadlock J. R. Fowler
Distances: 2½ lengths, 2½, 2½
Time: 4 mins 51.20 secs. Tote: win paid £31.54

Brennan still has vivid memories of the day: 'I'd given him a couple of runs in the winter on soft ground, and he hated it. I waited until the ground got faster in the summer. When it came good, I really got stuck into him and he showed me quite a bit – enough to win the kind of race he won. He wasn't a great horse, no, but he was good in his own company.'

News of the coup took a while to become apparent. So discreet had Curley been that it was not until the following day that even Furlong became fully aware of his plan. 'The next day I was going to Dublin to collect a load of oats for my boss Padge Berry. On the road, I bought myself the *Sporting Life*, and there it was on the front page. I thought, "So, there *was* something going on."'

Many years on, Furlong still admires the audacity of the coup. 'I felt proud [to have played a part], because they'd picked me as the jockey to do the job. There were a lot of half-decent amateurs in the country at the time.' He adds: 'Being an amateur, I received no payment for a win, but sometimes you got a present. A week or two later, Barney drove me to a garage somewhere in Dublin, and gave me the keys to this car. I got a car, a BMW.'

Curley says: 'Michael gave him an excellent, confident ride. He was always a great jockey at getting horses to jump, and he always looked to be going better than anything else. He held on with something in hand.'

Ann Brogan drove Curley back to her house for a cup of tea. Ann's mother Betty was there, as well as Jim Dreaper, who'd trained Betty's horses for many years, and Liam Brennan. Then Barry Brogan arrived, still none the wiser about what had gone on.

Apparently he had strolled into the racecourse after the race and been told by the gateman that Brennan had had a big winner. Brennan perpetuated the deception by declaring, when Barry congratulated him, 'Oh, don't talk to me, I'm sick. Michael came through on him and we didn't expect him to win. Barney is furious.' It was nonsense, of course. But even afterwards, it was felt imprudent to immediately reveal the truth to Barry. Nor was anything said next morning at the stables after Barry had ridden out. Indeed, it was not until the following evening that he finally bought an evening paper and saw the headline emblazoned: 'Biggest SP job ever landed in Ireland – Yellow Sam at 20–1!'

In his autobiography, Brogan admits he nearly collapsed with the shock of it all. However, he also applauded the covert nature of the operation. 'Curley and Liam had excelled themselves as masters of the art of secrecy. Not once did they offer the tiniest clue that a penny had been won,' he wrote, adding, 'Even now they hadn't let the secret slip. It was the bookmakers who were screaming. Curley had slayed them. They had been caught with their trousers down, and I didn't feel a bit sorry for them. I was delighted for Liam and Curley.'

As for the instigator of one of racing's great schemes, Curley regarded the day simply as one of financial salvation, not as an excuse for celebration. 'I simply drove home and went to bed, feeling quietly satisfied at a job well done,' he says. Mind you, he was so short of cash, he had to borrow five pounds from Betty Brogan to buy petrol for his journey back to Wicklow.

Before he fell asleep, Curley just mentioned to Maureen: 'We've had a touch.'

CHAPTER 11

The following morning, a sense of relief as much as exhilaration flooded through Curley's brain. 'It was still on my mind that if the bet had gone down I'd have been in serious trouble. The tank would then really have been empty.'

He still had no precise idea of how much had been won. 'It took a few days to collect it all and I didn't dare get my men to bring it to the stud,' he says. 'It would have been too dangerous. I feared the boys with shooters might hear about it. So we rented a room at a hotel in Wicklow – said it was for a game of poker.

'The boys brought the money there in big bags. Some bookmakers paid out in those big green single punt notes. That amount in one-punt notes, that takes a lot of space, and we had to put it into one-hundredweight bags before we moved it to the bank.'

It turned out that Curley had liberated Irish bookmakers of at least IR£306,000, the equivalent of over £2.5m in 2013, though he concedes impassively: 'You know, it could have been more. I gave up counting by then . . .' What he does know is that, at the time, it was the most valuable betting scheme organised in these islands in which the bookmakers paid out.

He says today: 'It was a massive touch at the time. Very few people would have had more than a quarter of a million cash then, thirty-odd years ago. You have this business of "Oh, you can't beat the bookmakers." Mostly that's true. But I proved you can. You always like to do things that nobody else can do. But it was only a one-off.' Or so he believed.

According to the newspapers, some bookmakers were refusing to pay. 'There was a desperate hullabaloo, but my initial fears proved unfounded,' says Curley. 'My men had gone round to collect and most had paid out. Just a few prevaricated.' Certainly some blustered and made threatening noises about withholding payment, but there was a grudging acceptance of their fate. Yellow Sam had won. Bookmakers had accepted bets on him.

'I had no qualms whatsoever about the scheme,' says Curley. 'It was there to be done – and it worked. There was nothing illegal about it, and I never considered there was anything immoral about it.' As he stressed, it was quite simply one man's brains against the bookmakers. 'I'd outwitted the system and taken advantage of unique circumstances,' he says. 'Because we thwarted them; prevented them getting a scent of the plan as we went for the kill, they moaned afterwards. Naturally, they would. They always do when you go for the jugular and leave them gasping.'

Gambling debts are not recoverable by law, but the layers probably realised that if they hadn't paid, Curley would have refused to let the matter rest. 'I'd have kicked up a real commotion,' he says. 'Had they continued to withhold payment, my recourse would have been to object to their licence next time they tried to renew it.'

Ultimately there was not one defaulter.

'Bookmakers as a breed are a lot more honourable than people imagine,' says Curley. 'At least, they were then. I don't remember anyone that didn't pay eventually. There were a lot of cracks about me afterwards from the bookies, but it was mostly in good humour. I think it was their pride, which had been dreadfully wounded, that got to them more than any financial loss.'

One of the bookmakers who was particularly sore was Terry Rogers, who for three decades was an institution at Irish racecourses. He would make a book on anything within reason and normally paid out with remarkable stoicism. Rogers was aggrieved not by Yellow Sam's success but by Curley's collusion with another bookmaker. 'What annoyed me was the revelation that Curley and Sean Graham were in cahoots, which is a bit rich for a guy who is always going on about bookies rigging the market,' Rogers was to observe later.

Curley, with typical candour, says: 'I can't say I really blame him. I could understand his frustration, although I could never see the rationale of his argument; the simple fact was that the scheme would probably not have worked without Sean's cooperation.' He adds: 'Having said that, Terry's was the first cheque in the post. He's always respected me for paying my debts on time and never welching.'

The final tally was certainly a lot more than Curley had originally estimated, but it was spread relatively thinly. No individual shop had to pay out more than £6,000. A sizeable payout like that might have reduced their profits for the next couple of months, but wouldn't have threatened their livelihoods. There wouldn't have been much other betting on that race; not on an amateur riders' handicap hurdle on a Wednesday afternoon.

However, it had not been Curley's aim to put anyone out of business. Whether they appreciated this kindness is debatable.

Intriguingly, he would later say: 'You couldn't do it today. If they'd been able to, the bookies would have driven the price of that horse into the ground. If those calls had got through and they'd got the money back to the track, they would have made that horse 6–4 favourite, but that was not their divine right.'

He could not have dared hope it would all go so obligingly to plan, without a single hitch. His strategy worked because not a whisper got back to the track until it was too late. 'To do something like that, to kid everybody, and for it all to go so smoothly, gives you a great sense of achievement,' Curley admits.

To this day, he acknowledges the key part played by his phone-blocker. 'Benny, God rest his soul, played a starring role in the success of that day. He was a great actor. They ought to have given him an Oscar for his performance. He was absolutely brilliant. He picked exactly the right theme,' says Curley. 'When he stuck his head out of the door and said he had a relative dying it would have silenced them, at least for a few minutes. Who's going to berate a man with that to contend with? There was mostly sympathy, not aggravation. They gave him a little bit of hassle, but nothing like if he'd been ringing for racing results or something. A stick of dynamite couldn't have moved Benny that afternoon.

'He didn't do it for the money, either. He just liked to be in the thick of anything going on, although he did admit to me later. "Barney, I wouldn't want to have to go through that again . . . Still, it can't have deterred him too much – a few years later he would become involved in another scheme of mine that was nearly as lucrative."'

Curley's parents had only discovered what had been going on by reading about it in the papers. He recalls his father calling him up a few days later.

'"I see you had a touch," he said.

'I replied, "I did."

'He said, "Did you get paid?"

'I said, "I did."

'All he said was, "That's what matters."

'Those were the only words we ever exchanged on the subject.'

When you suggest the coup was, in part, driven by a need to somehow avenge his father's downfall, all he will say is: 'A small part of me regarded the success of the scheme as some kind of retribution for what had happened to my father nearly twenty years before.'

The plan required qualities that few possess: boldness, an almost obsessive attention to detail, and a charismatic character that inspires absolute loyalty. Barry Brogan discerned those qualities in Curley, describing him as 'a man whose whole life has revolved around horses, dogs, cards and every other means of gambling. He's known as the "Silent Man" of racing . . . with his bald head, dangling cigarette and his pale, cream raincoat. He had a string of good horses in training with Liam. Whenever he was up for a killing, Curley was always incredibly patient. He was methodical, meticulous, patient and arrogant. Nothing flustered him.'

Brogan and Curley's paths would cross again shortly afterwards, and although Brogan views certain events in that period from a somewhat different perspective than Curley, he concedes: 'He is the most professional gambler I have ever known, and I respect and applaud his skills.'

Wednesday, 25, June 1975 was to become a defining moment in Barney Curley's life. It may have earned him a metaphorical badge of honour, but events that day also bestowed upon him an unwanted notoriety. 'Never again would B. J. Curley ever be allowed to run a horse in Ireland or Britain without the bookies treating it with the utmost caution,' he says.

As for the fate of the other participants in the story, Curley recalls: 'Ann Brogan died a few years later. But I am sure she found peace. She was always too good for this world. Ann was never a very worldly sort of girl and I always thought she was destined to be a nun.'

Liam Brennan is retired and lives in Newbridge, near Dublin. His affinity with bloodstock has been passed on to his sons Niall and Ian. Both are trainers in the United States. Niall runs a thriving training centre in Florida, concentrating on juveniles. Orb, winner of the 2013 Kentucky Derby, was one of his 'graduates'. Oxbow, the 2013 Preakness Stakes victor, was trained by Ian.

Michael Furlong, despite Yellow Sam's win, finished runner-up that season in the amateur jockeys' championship. Ted Walsh beat him to the title by just one. Two years later, however, he achieved greater prominence when he partnered the Padge Berry-trained heavily backed favourite Bannow Rambler in the 1977 Cheltenham Gold Cup, only to be brought down by the fatal fall of Lanzarote. The Michael O'Toole-trained Davy Lad went on to win.

Furlong moved to Britain in the eighties and rode for Captain Tim Forster in Wantage for one season, but had to compete for rides with the likes of Steve Smith Eccles, Hywel

Davies and Anthony Webber. 'If I got twenty rides I was doing well,' he recalls. Later he went to ride for Bobby Beasley at Lewes, Sussex. 'They were mostly moderate horses, nothing to get excited about, but I got a bit of a reputation for giving a horse a ride,' he says. 'I rode for Barney a couple of times again, while in England. I remember Urbi Et Orbi at Plumpton beat one of John Jenkins' that was considered unbeatable. But the one who won most for me – four – was Silver Cannon, a Fontwell specialist.'

Furlong broke his leg in a fall in 1991 and quit the saddle aged 37. Returning to Ireland, he trained for a season and a half on his brother's farm at Enniscorthy, County Wexford. 'But it didn't work out. The most horses I had was seven and I never trained a winner. My few owners started to cry because they were losing their businesses, money, everything that went wrong here around 2008.'

Recently, though, he discovered his ideal role, 'doing what I should have been doing for quite a few years'. Furlong has worked as an exercise rider at the County Tipperary stables of Ballydoyle where Aidan O'Brien sends out big-race winners throughout Europe, North America and the United Arab Emirates as private trainer to John Magnier and his Coolmore operation. He went to the Breeders' Cup in Kentucky with Homecoming Queen, the filly who went on to win the 2012 1,000 Guineas. 'It's a great job to have and a great man to work for.'

Barry Brogan eventually emerged from his apparent quest for self-destruction to become a leading trainer in the Far East. In between, he fought alcoholism – 'the amount I drank was staggering and would have made George Best look like a teetotaller' – an addiction to gambling, and had to contend with four separate jail sentences.

And the horse that will always be associated with the classic sting? Yellow Sam ran twice more for Curley. Taking advance of his lenient handicap mark, he won a three-mile event at Wexford under a 7lb penalty before finishing ninth of 17 at Galway in an amateur riders' hurdle.

By then, the handicapper had caught up with him. Curley knew he was unlikely to win in Ireland again. Yellow Sam was sent to Doncaster Sales and bought by Ken Oliver for 4,900 guineas. He had a chasing career planned but never took to it, and, after being placed a few times, was killed in a fall.

Inevitably, Curley's initiative inspired other equally ambitious, though unsuccessful, schemes. In October 1978, a friend of Curley's, Con Murphy – at the time a part-time bookmaker from Abbeyfeale, County Limerick – attempted to do something similar at Mullingar greyhound track. The plan had all the hallmarks of 'Yellow Sam'.

Murphy invited along around 40 associates – teachers, accountants, civil servants, shopkeepers, even a Garda officer – who were instructed to block up all the Tote windows for as long as possible, on the pretext of being confused about which dog they wanted to back, or what number it was. When they eventually put their money down, they were instructed to place money on every dog *except* Murphy's.

Murphy's dog, Ballydonnell Sam, an absolute cert, duly won the Midlands Cesarewitch at 2–1 on. Because of the manipulation, the Tote paid 956–1. It was an inventive scheme, but the winning bets were not honoured. When Murphy's team went to collect at the betting shops, having asked for the Tote price rather than the SP, they were refused. Indeed, the Garda were called to investigate this blatant manipulation of the Tote operation.

Curley later named a horse in honour of the unsuccessful coup; its name was Mullingar Con.

CHAPTER 12

As Curley's successful major gambles continued to create headlines, he was about as welcome as a whining mosquito on a humid night where the layers were concerned. They reacted as anyone would when confronted by a blood-sucking pest: they erected a net. They changed the rules to try and make sure they didn't get caught out again by a similar scheme, including setting a limit of £25 that could be bet just before the off. Curley's success also hastened improvements in bookmakers' communications.

Undaunted and unabashed, he had another tilt at his adversaries. 'After Yellow Sam, the bookmakers were all determined not to let it happen again. I thought, "Right, I'll teach them."' And he would have, had it not been for a judge's verdict that cost him nearly as much as Yellow Sam had won him.

The origins of the episode can be traced back to 1973, well before Yellow Sam, when, on a visit to Las Vegas, Curley came away not with a jackpot from the slot machines, but with a racehorse, Dr Hines, apparently named after Dr Mike Hines, a Las Vegas divorce attorney whose clients included many stars of stage and screen.

Curley paid around £5,000 and had the horse shipped home. Initially he was trained by Liam Brennan, but was then sent to Ray Peacock's small yard at Tarporley in Cheshire. Peacock had the reputation of being a thoroughly decent, hard-working and – crucially – non-gambling trainer. When he had winners, they invariably went in at long prices.

In the March before the Yellow Sam coup, Dr Hines, having failed to instil any fear in the bookies in five runs that season, was entered to run in a hurdle at Bangor. Barry Brogan had been asked to ride, but had already accepted a booking to ride a well-regarded horse named Topping, trained by John Edwards, in the same race.

This was all part of the plan. In the race card Brogan was named to ride Topping. Dr Hines (down to run in the ownership of Mrs Mary Kelly, though Curley paid the bills) had no jockey next to his name. That was not unusual. Jockeys then did not need to be declared overnight and could be switched almost at will. Today, there has to be a good reason – usually injury.

As Brogan recalled: 'We bamboozled the public even more by deliberately delaying the announcement of my switch to Dr Hines until barely an hour before the race.' Dr Hines started at 16–1, but Curley had him backed at 20–1 and 25–1 in Britain and Ireland. Potential winnings were £300,000.

The horse needed to be held up and produced late. Brogan, in Curley's estimation, manifestly failed in that task. 'It needed a man with patience and courage to play the waiting game . . . but Brogan lost his bottle and probably wasn't fit enough to settle the horse anyway because of the effect of all his drinking binges,' says a man who doesn't pull his verbal punches when he is affronted.

Dr Hines struck the front too soon, and was headed on the run-in, finishing third. Curley was furious at what he deemed to be Brogan's incompetence, and strode to the weighing room to confront the jockey. He accused Brogan of making too much use of Dr Hines, leaving him in front for too long. It culminated in a heated exchange, with the pair doing an excellent impression of rutting stags.

Dr Hines reappeared again in the August of 1975, following the Yellow Sam coup. Curley and Liam Brennan, to whom he had now returned, identified another opportunity for the good doctor, and he was declared to run at Downpatrick in a maiden hurdle. Curley had two horses entered in the race. Dr Hines was the supposedly unfancied 16–1 outsider of the pair. His other horse, Cannon Gun, partnered by Brennan's stable jockey Ben Hannon, would start at 5–4 on favourite.

Employing similar tactics to the Yellow Sam coup, Curley recruited a team to place small bets of £10 or £20, which wouldn't arouse suspicion, around the country – not on the favourite, but on Dr Hines. He also had £6,000 on in Dublin betting shops, using credit accounts, which were not affected by the new rules.

It was a desperately close finish. Curley believed that Dr Hines had just got the better of a horse named Caroline's Dream. He was so certain of the result that he left the track, convinced the horse had won. Today the photo-finish camera would have confirmed it, but then Downpatrick didn't have that facility. It was left to the opinion of the judge, and he made the winner Caroline's Dream by a short head. Cannon Gun was unplaced. 'I got into my car, and the first I heard of it was when I turned on the radio and discovered I'd lost. I couldn't believe it.'

A bizarre theory subsequently circulated that the judge had assumed Curley had backed Cannon Gun, and his bet had gone down. His somewhat perverse reasoning was that he was somehow doing Curley a favour by naming Caroline's Dream the victor to ensure that Dr Hines remained a novice (and hence wouldn't incur a penalty the next time he ran). Today, as he relates the story, Curley shakes his head, and takes a draw of an e-cigarette. At the time, he was incandescent.

Some consolation was gained six weeks later when he took Dr Hines over to Sedgefield. With his pal Tommy Stack in the saddle, the partnership won a seller – though a price of 11–8 on was never going to yield riches.

The policy of sending horses to Britain became a regular and profitable feature of Curley's strategy. In November that year, he dispatched another of his former store horses, Tommy Joe, to Britain to secure a handicap hurdle at Doncaster at 9–2, with winnings estimated at £30,000.

The previously mentioned Fair Rambler, a fine servant to Curley, was entered for a long-distance hurdle at Hereford in 1976 after his owner realised the horse was too exposed in Ireland. He scarcely looked primed for the task, having contested novice chases that season, finishing fifth and fourth at Limerick and Leopardstown respectively.

The field was only four strong, and it was effectively a match with a horse of Stan Mellor's, named Cartwright, which was sufficiently well thought of to ensure Curley could benefit from rewarding enough odds of 5–2. Jockey Ben Hannon just got Fair Rambler home.

CURLEY ALTERED HIS tactics for a period, arranging for unraced two-year-olds to be based with trainers in Britain not known for winning with juveniles. These horses had been honed to peak fitness by Paddy Norris, the Curragh-based trainer who had won with Mark Royal in 1967 Royal Ascot's Coventry Stakes. 'If Paddy said they were ready to win, you didn't ignore him,' says Curley, who bought the horses from Norris and sold them on to British owners, thus keeping his name – so toxic where bookmakers were concerned – neatly out of the equation.

In they went, first time out, at big prices. His strike rate was seven out of eight, with winnings on each occasion between £50,000 and £70,000. One success was Cathmaria, a combination of his two daughters' names – the Curley family had now been extended to four, with the birth of a second child, Maria-Louise, on New Year's Day 1975. His son Charlie would arrive in 1977.

Curley sent Cathmaria to Ray Peacock and, running in the name of the trainer's wife, the horse was entered for a seller at Haydock under Willie Carson. Curley and his accomplices backed her down from 14–1 to 13–2 and won £50,000.

Another unraced raider was a three-year-old named Tralee Falcon. Curley sent him to Jimmy FitzGerald's Malton yard in early 1977. The chestnut filly, running in

FitzGerald's wife's colours, was declared in a five-furlong seller at Thirsk. Curley was anxious that none of the money his men were placing around Britain and Ireland got back to the track. He tells how a telephone engineer, for a consideration of £1,000, offered to 'knock out' the phone lines in the Thirsk area for a few minutes before the off, thus causing a break in the bookmakers' lines to the major firms.

Tralee Falcon got left at the start, but made up ground under Edward Hide, and won by half a length. Curley backed the horse at 14–1 and collected around £80,000. The horse won her next race, too, a non-seller.

Curley admits to a degree of duplicity about running the horse under another trainer's charge and owner's silks, but contends there was nothing illegal; nor did the strategy transgress the rules of the Jockey Club, which then administered racing's affairs. If the horse had run under his name, he contends, it would have started at 6–4.

Meanwhile, away from the racecourse, there had been another ramification of the Yellow Sam coup. The scheme was responsible for a new-found lifestyle for Curley and his family; not only did it allow Curley to make good some serious debts, but it yielded a substantial windfall too. He had always worked on the basis that Yellow Sam's price would be around 20–1 but never imagined his men would be successful in placing so much money at the 150 betting shops he'd targeted. He had around £250,000 to play with from the proceeds of Yellow Sam after expenses and debts were cleared. He had also sold Boswell Stud.

In an impulsive act which was in conflict with much of the rest of his life – he has rarely been intoxicated by wealth or its trappings – he splurged most of the money on Middleton Park House, in Castletown Geoghegan, County Westmeath.

The Georgian mansion was quite a pile, and was imbued with history. It was the ancestral home of the Boyd-Rochforts, who were major landowners in Ireland. It was also said that T. E. Lawrence – 'Lawrence of Arabia' – had been conceived there. There remains some debate about that fact, but it all added to the allure of the house, which was located 9 miles from Mullingar and just over 50 miles from Dublin.

When Curley first saw the 40-room property, standing on 377 acres of land bordering the shores of Lough Ennell, he was understandably smitten. Its horse-racing and sporting heritage also appealed to him. A noted stud had been established on the estate and many valuable horses had been bred there, including Airborne, the 1946 Derby winner. That horse was bred by Harold Boyd-Rochfort, and trained by his brother Cecil, who had been a captain in the Scots Guards during the First World War.

Born and raised at Middleton before being educated at Eton, Cecil Boyd-Rochfort developed into an illustrious trainer, winning all five English Classics. He won the St Leger no fewer than six times, amongst 13 Classics in total, and was the royal trainer between 1943 and 1968, for both King George VI and Queen Elizabeth II. Boyd-Rochfort was also stepfather to Henry Cecil, who took over his string on the captain's retirement in 1968. The estate was also the venue for point-to-points, and a starting or finishing point for the Westmeath Hunt.

Curley particularly enjoyed frequenting the library, with its roaring log fire. He would sit there studying The Form

Book, as he recalls, 'like the squire of the manor'. Visitors would laugh and say: 'Would you look at him – monarch of all he surveys', alluding to the piece of verse relating to the castaway who inspired *Robinson Crusoe*.

They had a housekeeper, but no servants. Curley could have afforded it, but would have felt distinctly uncomfortable. This was no Irish Downton Abbey. The concept of 'Upstairs, Downstairs' was not really him.

Middleton's lush, verdant acreage was ideal for cattle. 'Beef to the knees, like a Mullingar heifer,' Curley remembers the saying. He ventured into cattle farming himself, with the operation under the care of his brother-in-law Frank – married to Maureen's sister Marie – but farming was never his forte. Like his previous farming ventures, it failed.

He made better use of the land to raise the National Hunt store horses that he began to accumulate. At one time he had around 40, and was a substantial owner. There was only a small gallop at Middleton – he took the horses to racecourses like Thurles to get them fit – but he cantered horses in front of the house. One of these was named Silver Buck.

Silver Buck's pedigree wasn't exceptional. He was the son of Silver Cloud, winner of the Chester Vase, Ascot's Cumberland Lodge Stakes and Newmarket's Princess of Wales's Stakes, and a mare named Choice Archlesse, whose only win was a moderate hurdle race at Cartmel. He had appeared to be rather small for a potential steeplechaser. Initially, he was temperamental and difficult to handle; his first owner found him 'headstrong and unmanageable'. But the brown gelding evidently possessed talent. Curley bought him for 8,000 guineas from Paul Doyle, son of Jack 'JT' Doyle, head of the great racing and bloodstock family, after Silver Buck won a bumper, his first race under rules, at Clonmel by eight lengths.

After a brief 'holiday' at Middleton Park, Curley sold him on as a four-year-old to the Dickinsons, that great triumvirate of National Hunt racing, Michael and his parents Tony and Monica.

Tony Dickinson had been a fine amateur jockey and champion point-to-point rider in 1954. He trained under permit before taking out a full licence in 1968. His wife Monica – 'Mrs D', as she was universally known – had also ridden in points and had been Britain's ladies' national champion in the show ring at Blackpool in 1950. Their talents complemented each other superbly. When Monica died in 2008, Sir Peter O'Sullevan, that doyen of commentators, described her as 'a stalwart and a driving force in one of the most efficient National Hunt racing production teams in the last half-century'.

Michael Dickinson, a former champion amateur rider who became a professional jockey, took over his parents' training operation in 1980. In his formative years, he had enjoyed the tutelage of Vincent O'Brien, the most successful trainer in the history of the Turf, and co-founder of the Coolmore empire. Dickinson was three times champion National Hunt trainer, but most famously sent out the first five home in the 1983 Cheltenham Gold Cup. He would later enjoy a successful career in the United States.

Curley, introduced to the Dickinsons by Tommy Stack, admired them for their honesty and great wealth of knowledge. It resulted in a flow of equine talent arriving from Ireland to their Gisburn yard, with the proviso that Curley would make no profit from the sales. 'Sometimes they were cheaper than I should have let them go for, as a return for information – secret information,' he explains. The deal was that the Dickinsons would pass those horses on to owners not interested in backing them. Curley just wanted to be the first to know if they were fancied. Many won first time out.

Christine Feather, who became owner of Silver Buck, once described the Dickinsons as 'fairly secretive', adding: 'You could ask them a thousand questions and they'll only tell you what they want you to know.' This explained why Curley viewed them as 'my sort of people'.

Once his horses had won a bumper in Ireland, and Curley had backed them, they were sent over to the Dickinsons to be trained for a hurdling campaign. He had either raised them himself from yearlings or spotted them in running. The first of these was Tommy Joe, who would win 13 races, including the Mandarin Chase at Newbury in 1978. Others were I'm A Driver and Buck Me Off, the horse that ended Michael Dickinson's career and nearly his life at Cartmel when the horse slipped and propelled his partner into the rock-hard turf. Dickinson badly damaged his liver and spleen and was in intensive care for seven days. He retired from riding, after 328 winners, to concentrate on training.

The Dickinsons' expertise exorcised Silver Buck's demons and transformed him into a champion. He finished eighth at Carlisle in his first race in Britain, partnered by Michael Dickinson, over two miles two

furlongs – a distance too short for the gelding. As Curley
recalls: 'That was a sighter on the practice range. Next
time, the ammunition would be live.'

His next race was over a more suitable three miles. It
was an amateur riders' hurdle at Catterick, and this time
he was partnered by Michael Dickinson's brother-in-law,
Tom Tate. Curley received the message from Dickinson:
'He's a good horse and has done one or two nice gallops.
He will win, provided he doesn't do anything stupid.' The
horse was still liable to become easily spooked, and Tate
was told that under no circumstances should he lead
before the last flight, and that he should keep away from
the rails.

That race, on a chill December day in 1977, was an
ideal event from Curley's perspective. The favourite,
Yellow Fire, was warming the bookies' hands (he started
at 2–1 on), and that served only to enhance the price of
Silver Buck, who had exhibited nothing to stimulate
punter interest. He started at 5–1, which was rather skin-
nier than Curley would have desired. With no form in
Britain, he had hoped it to be 25–1 or more.

Victory was by no means a foregone conclusion, and
in the closing stages of the race Silver Buck began to
look about and idled in front, but at the line he prevailed
by a length. The bookmakers were particularly badly hit
in Ireland. Curley can only remember that he 'did very
nicely out of it'. But the story did not end there.

Curley was perplexed by the relatively short price, and
refused to let it rest. Eventually he came to the conclusion that an operator at the local exchange had been
listening in to his conversations with Michael Dickinson,
and, together with friends, had cashed in on the information, thus affecting the price.

Curley gained his revenge. He let slip some deliberate false information – suggesting, in future conversations with the Dickinsons, that horses without a hope would be certain winners. Before the eavesdropper got wise, he would probably have lost more than he and his cohorts won from Silver Buck's first triumph.

To discuss authentic information securely, Curley made the 90-minute drive over the Fermanagh–Cavan border to use a remote public telephone box. From there, he could dial direct. It was a perilous journey, one that he made twice a week; it wasn't the cleverest thing to do to be driving alone near the border during the early years of the Troubles.

As for Silver Buck, he gave a stern rebuke to those who initially had misgivings regarding his character. He would proceed to win four hurdle races and 30 chases, including the 1982 Cheltenham Gold Cup and two King George VI Chases. His 1979 King George triumph was another big payday for Curley.

The Dickinsons were occasional visitors at Middleton Park House. Swiftly appreciating that the upkeep of the place was not necessarily a priority in their host's life – they'd find the lights wouldn't work or the water stopped running – they compared it to Fawlty Towers, and came to refer to Curley as 'Baz', after John Cleese's character Basil Fawlty. They even named a horse after him, called Basil's Choice – a winner, incidentally.

There was mutual regard, and information and advice passed between the camps. Curley recommended Tommy Carmody to them; one of many leading riders to whom he was to become a mentor over the years.

One jockey troubled him, though. Later, the affection and respect that had always existed between Curley and the Dickinsons would be compromised following Graham Bradley's riding of a horse named Robin Goodfellow, culminating in a sensational legal case that transcended horse racing.

CHAPTER 13

Ironically, given what ensued, Graham Bradley's first winner for the Dickinsons was Talon, a horse sent to them by Barney Curley. His admiration of the Yorkshire-man's horsemanship was well-founded.

Bradley's triumphs would include the 1982 Hennessy Gold Cup and the 1983 Cheltenham Gold Cup, as well as the King George VI Chase in 1985 on Wayward Lad, an appropriately named partner, as it transpired; this would also become the title of the jockey's life story. Curley described him as 'one of the most talented riders I have ever come across. He is a beautifully balanced exponent of his art and a man who can really get his horses to jump for him.'

But there was an issue; one that niggled away at the Irishman. When the prices of horses that Curley had sent over to the Dickinsons began to plummet, and were starting at 6–4 and 5–4, he sensed that information was no longer being confined to the stable.

It had never been a betting stable, and Curley didn't harbour a scintilla of doubt about the integrity of Michael Dickinson, who by now had taken over his parents' oper-ation and moved to a new yard, Poplar House Stables, in the village of Dunkeswick, near Harewood, West Yorkshire. If Michael Dickinson had a fault, in Curley's estimation, it was his naiveté.

In contrast, Curley, whose intelligence antennae were highly sensitive, had swiftly divined the source of the bookies' information. He recalls, 'We had all got on well until suddenly the horses I had an interest in began to start at even money – and you have to back a lot of winners at even money to make it pay. There was someone marking the bookmakers' cards.'

He adds: 'I made enquiries, and became certain that it was Bradley who was the problem. I told Michael Dickinson, "There's no doubt about it. The rotten apple is Bradley." I cut back the horses I sent to the Dickinsons. I decided there was no point sending them when the newspaper seller knew on the way through the racecourse gate how they were going to run.

'I never understood what motivated him, because in other ways he's not a bad fellow.' Reflecting on what he perceived as Bradley's shortcomings, Curley concludes, 'There are some I could mention who are complete wrong 'uns. He was just flawed. I would not forget him . . .'

Bradley would later argue in his book that Curley was mistaken and he did not leak information. It was purely because of the success of the Harewood set-up that it was impossible to keep the ability of the horses secret. That said, later on he did end up being banned for five years for that very thing: passing on information for reward. But Curley allowed the matter to fester, and the subsequent fall-out, to which we will return, nearly caused his ruination.

By the early eighties, Curley had become a significant

owner of equine talent. Some had been acquired very cheaply by Frank Barry, breeder and bloodstock agent, who bought his horses for him over many years. At the November sales of 1981, Curley and Barry purchased an unbroken chestnut son of Precipice Wood for 4,000 guineas.

In those days, Curley often acted precipitously, as he readily admits, and his purchase came at a time when he had fallen out with Liam Brennan over what is now a long-forgotten grievance. The two men happened to bump into each other leaving the sales, and a rapprochement was affected when Curley asked Brennan to train the horse. In recognition of that renewed concord, he named it Forgive 'N Forget.

The quality of the purchase was soon evident. Brennan ran the horse in two bumpers at Leopardstown. In the first he was a well-beaten seventh in the hands of amateur Anthony Powell, Brennan's nephew. Ten days later, under the same jockey, he had an easy victory against several of the same runners. He was well backed by Curley, who had warned Brennan that Forgive 'N Forget's win could not fail to attract the stewards' attention, given the horse's swift improvement. It culminated with Brennan and Powell being warned off for four months and one month respectively.

Curley later sold Forgive 'N Forget for £45,000 to Tim Kilroe, a Manchester-based owner of trainer Jimmy FitzGerald's. Kilroe, a civil engineer and owner-breeder, had lost a potential Gold Cup horse with the death at Kempton of Fairy King. Forgive 'N Forget provided ample compensation.

The transaction yielded a nice profit for Curley and proved an astute purchase by his new owner. Typically,

Curley completed the deal on the condition that he should continue to 'manage' the horse, who would now be trained by Tipperary man FitzGerald, the former jockey who had become a good friend of Curley's. His target was the Coral Golden Hurdle Final at the 1983 Cheltenham Festival. It was, and still is, a fiercely competitive handicap.

At the time, Curley had been warned off by the Irish Turf Club, following a dispute with bookmaker Sean Graham over non-payment of a debt. Curley had counter-claimed, saying that Graham had been slow paying out on a winner, but the warning-off meant that Curley was not permitted to enter British racecourses either.

He had backed the horse off course, but was determined to place more money in the ring at Cheltenham. Initially he was ejected by security men, but he sneaked back in and backed Forgive 'N Forget at prices from 4–1 downwards. The gelding's SP was 5–2 favourite.

Forgive 'N Forget was in ominously good form, having won a qualifier event at Ayr by 12 lengths. Despite carrying a hefty 11st 6lb, there was never any danger of defeat. The prize money was £9,392, a pittance compared with the sum Curley, trainer FitzGerald and owner Kilroe won. Curley alone estimated that he collected £200,000; his biggest payday since Yellow Sam. It was one of the largest wholesale gambles ever seen at Cheltenham.

He subsequently settled his differences with the Belfast bookmaker, albeit reluctantly, and paid the £6,000 the latter said he owed. But he went through a phase of refusing to talk, or bet, with Graham. Curley admits: 'It was ridiculous behaviour, and the truth was that I always admired Sean for standing some exceptionally large bets. I pray for him every night.'

It has been estimated, and he doesn't dispute it, that

Curley won around £1m overall in that period. Yet he insists to this day that if Forgive 'N Forget had made a mistake and fallen or pulled up, he would have accepted it without chagrin. 'I believe I have remained successful because I have never let betting get to me,' he says.

At times there were losses. There always are. And some were of such a frightening magnitude that the majority of us would never have recovered. But Curley had learned early on to adhere to an important maxim: the secret of successful gambling is not to panic.

That explains why Alan Byrne, chief executive and editor-in-chief of the *Racing Post*, once wrote about him in the *Sunday Independent*, contrasting him with Terry Ramsden: 'Curley is different. He has lasted the pace. When it comes to serious gambling for big stakes, he is a stayer rather than a flashy sprinter . . . he has won enough to stay in the race longer than virtually anybody else.'

There are certain events he has tended to avoid, however. He generally disregards sprint handicaps ('those sprinters just keep beating each other'). He doesn't trust the form of all-weather ('it tends to be poor quality') and prefers high-quality racing ('when the form is more reliable and every horse and jockey is trying his best'). However, following that theory in the Classics has brought him despair as well as reward.

He recalls Nureyev being first past the post in the 1980 English 2,000 Guineas. Curley believed he'd won £200,000, only to discover the French invader had been disqualified because of an infringement of the rules by his rider Philippe Paquet. He won on merit and today would have kept the race. But Curley says: 'You've got to be able to take a hit occasionally without it affecting you.'

On another notable occasion, he wanted to oppose

Golden Fleece, favourite for the 1982 Derby. He didn't concur with the popular view that Vincent O'Brien's colt was a good thing for the Epsom classic. He got people to 'stand' the horse for him, laying it to lose, effectively acting like a bookmaker. By his own admission, however, he failed to take into account the fact that it wasn't a particularly brilliant year (it would be regarded as 'average' by two astute judges, Tony Morris and John Randall).

The favourite started at 3–1 (having drifted), and benefiting from the late withdrawal of his principal rival, Henry Cecil's Simply Great, surged home under Pat Eddery to win by three lengths and become Vincent O'Brien's sixth and final Derby winner. Curley pondered liabilities of £150,000 on Golden Fleece, and lost another £100,000 in other bets in that period.

In stark contrast, in 1997 he wagered £10,000 each way at 10–1 (started 11–1) on John Gosden's Benny the Dip. There was a hot favourite that year, 2,000 Guineas victor Entrepreneur, who would start at 6–4 on, but Curley was convinced that hype and home reputation had overcome rational thought and that, at his price, Benny the Dip was excellent value to at least reach a place. He decided to leave nothing to chance, and tells how, on the Thursday night before the Epsom classic, he called round to the Newmarket home of Benny the Dip's jockey in the big race.

Willie Ryan was considered a journeyman rider, better known as partner of Cecil's second-string horses. Both Olivier Peslier (riding André Fabre's Cloudings) and Frankie Dettori (riding Saeed Bin Suroor's Bold Demand), who otherwise could have got the ride, were unavailable. Curley says he told Ryan: 'Willie, I've got a big interest in Benny the Dip,' before adding, 'If this Entrepreneur is as brilliant a horse as he's made out to be, I'm a very bad judge.' He had also put £10,000 on Entrepreneur to lose.

The Irishman had a high regard for Willie Ryan as a rider. But a slight worry picked away at Curley's confidence: the jockey's dearth of big-race wins. There was a lingering thought in Curley's mind that Ryan could be negatively influenced; that he might be indoctrinated with the belief that he couldn't win the race because of the opposition. Though he was sure that wasn't the case, 'it didn't do any harm to tell him that he was going to win the Derby'. Curley adds: 'He knew me well enough to appreciate that I'm not a dreamer and not liable to platitudes. More importantly, he knew I wouldn't throw good money at a worthless cause.'

It was no race for nervous supporters of Benny the Dip, who just prevailed by a short head from Silver Patriarch. Entrepreneur was a well-beaten fourth.

According to Curley, Ryan told him that his first thought after passing the post was the Irishman's declaration that he had a big interest in the race. Whether that had steeled Ryan's resolve to win, and squeezed that vital effort out of his mount, we will never know.

Returning to Curley's Golden Fleece setback in 1982, there was a curious addendum. The day after the race, Curley took Maureen and the children off to California for a three-month sabbatical. He describes it as like convalescing from an illness. Rarely for him, he was brooding on what had happened. He thought he'd lost his touch.

The family rented a beach house at Del Mar. Their neighbour was the doyen of American racehorse trainers, Charlie Whittingham. 'The reason for going there was to try and learn something from the greatest trainer in the world,' says Curley.

Curley had plans to add another talent to his repertoire. It proved to be quite an education from the man known as 'the bald eagle' (because of his gleaming pate). 'He wasn't the kind of fella who'd pour out his soul to everybody,' says Curley. 'He just took to me, possibly because he thought I was a right ignoramus – which I was at the time. He gave me all the guidance that he could.'

Curley watched Whittingham at work most mornings, noting how patient he was with his horses. 'He had a knack of knowing when his horses were beginning to peak. It was a gift I like to think I possess in my own way. I learned one important lesson from him. People from Europe would send him horses and tell him what distance suited them. "I have learned," Charlie said, "that these fellas are mostly wrong." But he was always insistent. "Do your own thing," he'd say. He used to take the horses and start from scratch and give them time. That has always been my way, too.'

After Whittingham's Estrapade won the 1986 Arlington Million, the trainer was asked at what point he'd thought she'd win the race. 'When we entered her,' he retorted. That amused Curley no end. It would later coincide with his own approach.

Curley had three horses in training with Whittingham, notably Alianna, a horse with Classic form costing £150,000. She was intended to be an investment. She had been runner-up in the 1984 Irish 1,000 Guineas, a neck behind Terry Ramsden's Katies. The plan was to race her in the US before retiring her to the paddocks and a breeding career.

Whittingham, not one for overstatement, reckoned she

could win an Arlington Million. 'He was prepping her for the race, and she ran well in New York, but I went to Australia and got a message that she had died of a twisted gut.' Curley pauses. 'I remember that well because I lost so much.' By then, Curley had been offered, and rejected, £500,000 for her. A big loss, in every respect.

If Alianna demonstrated that ownership can be a precarious business, Prince Echo confirmed it. The colt had finished third behind King's Lake in the 1981 Irish 2,000 Guineas, and fourth in the July Cup, for Liam Browne. Curley bought him and sent him to Henry Cecil. But he didn't flourish and he was sold to go to stud in New Zealand.

CHAPTER 14

In 1983, after eight years, Barney and Maureen decided to abandon their seemingly idyllic lifestyle at Middleton Park. The house and grounds were expensive to maintain. The farming side had failed. And Curley was concerned that the Irish betting market was increasingly offering him too few opportunities. The bookies had long got wise to him. The time had come to decamp to England, where his eventual aim was to set up his own training operation.

There was much discussion about how best to market the property. There wouldn't be too many purchasers at the price Curley had in mind. Another consideration was that property values were depressed anyway in Ireland at that time. His natural instinct was always to get value for money, but how would he achieve this?

Curley was laid low with 'flu, idling scanning news-papers in the four-poster, when his eye caught adverts for raffles run by pubs and clubs. The thought occurred: 'If we raffled this house, it could be the biggest winner ever.'

He later claimed that his draw would be the forerunner of the national lotteries in the UK and Ireland. It would certainly culminate in another windfall, but not before the heavy, not to say clumsy arm of the law intervened in a bizarre fashion.

Curley reckoned Middleton was worth around £1m. If he could cover that, he'd be happy. Anything above would be a bonus. He could possibly suffer a serious hit if the raffle failed to take off, but he was prepared to accept that risk.

Large draws or raffles were only allowed if intended for charitable or philanthropic purposes. To circumvent the gaming laws – or so Curley believed – he planned that the draw would raise money for a bona fide local Gaelic football club, Ballinagore GAA. (Ballinagore is a hamlet on the N52, between Mullingar and Kilbeggan.) Once an entrant had purchased one of the maximum 9,000 tickets, costing £175 sterling, they became a member of the club. An article in *The Times* described it as 'the biggest club in the world, bigger than the New York Yacht Club or Lord's'. A donation would also be made to the Irish Wheelchair Association. The raffle was officially described as a private limited subscribers' draw. Some would-be entrants drove up to look at the place, just to ensure that it actually existed. Previous such draws and raffles had inevitably been found to be the work of fraudsters.

From the moment Curley set up the raffle early in 1983, it received national newspaper coverage both sides of the Irish Sea. To promote the draw, and confirm that the prize did indeed exist, he had a video made of the property, complete with lilting Irish string music and a seductive voiceover from that doyen of commentators, Michael O'Hehir.

There was no doubt that the hugely respected O'Hehir lent the enterprise integrity. He had been the voice of Irish sport for half a century, commentating on racing, football and hurling, and his evocative tones were amongst the most distinctive in the world – as were some of his expressions. 'And it looks like there's a bit of a schemozzle in the parallelogram' was his euphemism for a fight on the pitch.

O'Hehir had been on holiday in New York with wife Molly when John F. Kennedy was assassinated in 1963, and he stayed on to provide a five-hour commentary of the funeral for the Irish broadcaster Teilifís Éireann, for which he received much acclaim. He also commentated on racing for the BBC, and his description of the chaotic scene at the twenty-third fence in the 1967 Grand National, when 100–1 chance Foinavon took advantage to win the race, will be recalled by those of a certain age.

The commentator, referring to 'a right pile-up', identified every horse that fell at that fence, and immediately called Foinavon as he came away from the obstacle all on his own.

O'Hehir glowingly described Middleton Park thus: 'This magnificent house is a home which has heard the sound of children's laughter for generations. How much is it worth? A million, maybe two could be more realistic, but it's yours for the price of a ticket.' Few potential subscribers could have failed to be impressed as he waxed lyrical. He spoke of Lough Ennell, which once yielded a record brown trout. And inevitably he introduced T. E. Lawrence: 'Did his pursuit of glory in the deserts of Arabia begin at Middleton as he contemplated the painting of Napoleon above the globe of the world which he so nearly conquered?'

Who could not be impressed, and immediately invest in a ticket (or maybe several) after such a lavish commendation? To confirm that all was totally above board, Curley's raffle, according to O'Hehir, was 'bound by rules as solid as the forge'. He added: 'There are no leases, no catches . . . not even a ghost.'

Curley called upon three major racing names to act as trustees. They were Tommy Stack, the two-times National Hunt champion jockey, who had partnered Red Rum to his third Grand National triumph, and two great characters of Irish racing, trainers Mick O'Toole and Michael O'Brien. The last-named had been a top jump jockey in the United States until a fall confined him to a wheelchair. He returned to his homeland and trained many big-race winners. The raffle was advertised in the *The Sun*, *The Mirror* and the *Sporting Life*. Curley himself appeared on Gay Byrne's *Late Late Show* in Ireland and on the national news in the UK.

Syndicates were formed and there were several 'celebrity' entrants, including Eric Clapton, the Queen's former jockey Harry Carr, owner Robert Sangster and members of the aristocracy. The whole thing was superbly executed. Interest spread as swiftly as a forest fire in an arid summer. Curley spent four months travelling around the world promoting the raffle. His rationale was: 'I got the house by taking a chance, so I would like to pass it on to someone else prepared to have a go.'

By the time he flew to the United States, 6,000 tickets had already been sold. 'Irish betting legend comes to America' was the headline in the *New York Post*, describing Curley as 'a fine broth of a lad from County Westmeath'. He was 43 at the time.

Curley couldn't resist the opportunity to offer a critique of American betting, with its 18 per cent parimutuel takeout (which went to the government). He snorted: 'I would not last twelve months betting at those rates. The government gets all the money here.'

All appeared to be going smoothly. Back home, tickets were dispatched from the family's kitchen, with Yellow Sam phone man Benny O'Hanlon, and Paddy Griffin, who looked after Curley's horses at Middleton, in attendance. They provided an element of security. Then, a few weeks before the draw, the Garda raided the place. It was the first of several visits, during which they removed documents and tickets.

Curley claims he was not unduly troubled. Certainly there was no way he would allow such an intrusion to deflect him. There was just one aspect that did concern him. O'Hehir had readily agreed early on to conduct the draw. Curley tried to dissuade the commentator from performing the task, fearing that any further intervention by the Garda would not be good for his reputation. O'Hehir, who was receiving only expenses, retorted quietly: 'I'll be there. My word is my bond.'

The raffle took a year to come to fruition and the draw took place on Thursday, 9 February 1984. Curley had guaranteed that it would go ahead if a minimum 2,000 tickets were sold. The hype surrounding the enterprise had had its effect. In the event, 9,000 tickets had been sold, with receipts of just under £1.6m. Garda officers were in attendance on the day of the draw; Curley assumed they were there just to ensure fair play.

Media interest was huge. Even the BBC had got involved and covered the event exclusively. *The Irish Independent* described it as 'the second great mystery of Irish racing after Shergar's disappearance, except this one is about to be solved'.

Before making the draw, O'Hehir stated: 'If the government was running the country as well as this man has promoted this, we'd be living in a better country.

Barney has been doing such a good job, he should be running Bord Fáilte [Ireland's national tourism development authority] and Coras Tráchtála [the Irish export board].'

O'Hehir picked the winning ticket: number 41877. It belonged to a six-strong syndicate from Gloucestershire. The leader was Tony Ray, who ran an agricultural supplies company. The group came over to survey the property but never took up residence; they sold it on a few months later. Today the house is owned by a hotel chain and run as a wedding venue. In recognition of his part in its history, it contains the Barney Curley Bar.

Everybody appeared to emerge well from the lottery, not least the football club, which benefited from a new pitch and dressing rooms. There had been no complaints. Indeed, Curley was praised for his running of the draw. Just one person had asked for a refund after reports of the Garda raid.

The family moved out of the house and stayed for a time in the gatehouse. Maureen told the national newspapers: 'Things are always happening around Barney. I love the adrenalin and the excitement. But I still have the shopping to do . . .' Curley, fatigued, announced his retirement from running lotteries. He estimated a £1m profit after expenses.

It was not long, however, before his satisfied state imploded. He was charged with running an illegal lottery – and worse still, O'Hehir was charged with him.

Curley was outraged. His scheme had been absolutely straight – unlike some others at the time. 'Instead of charging me,' he believed, 'they should have been honouring me for services to the community.' On a bright July morning, the nation's biggest gambler and its best-known commentator, together with three members of Ballinagore GAA, stood in the dock at the village court at Ballynacargy, near Mullingar. It was an incongruous spectacle.

Curley was found guilty of unlawfully promoting a lottery, contrary to Section 21 of the Gaming and Lotteries Act 1956. His actions, according to District Justice William Tormey, had been a deliberate breach of the law. The judge sternly declared that there was only one sentence he could impose and that was the maximum: Curley received a three-month jail sentence. The three GAA members were each fined £100. To Curley's relief, however, the charge against O'Hehir, accused of unlawfully assisting him, was dismissed.

Absurdly, at one stage it looked as though even Gay Byrne and RTÉ would become implicated. The judge asked the state prosecutor if he thought the presenter and the TV station had assisted Curley by interviewing him and broadcasting the video, to which the reply was 'Yes.' Fortunately, no charges ensued.

As for Curley, he claimed that a prison sentence in itself wouldn't have unduly troubled him. 'I would have nearly volunteered for it, given half a chance. I was exhausted and wanted a rest,' he says, only partly in jest. However, his lawyers insisted he must appeal, and Curley knew they were right. A criminal record – even a suspended sentence – was not something he could afford, particularly if he wanted to apply for a licence to train in Britain. He needed the advantages of running, and backing, his own horses if he was to pursue his gambling career.

Curley's jail sentence was adjourned pending an appeal, that was eventually heard at Mullingar Circuit Court. Peter O'Malley, the circuit judge, still found the charges proved but placed Curley on probation, with no conviction recorded. The proviso – bearing in mind that the festive season was approaching – was that he should pay £5,000 to the Christmas Fund of the Society of St Vincent de Paul, the international Catholic voluntary organisation dedicated to serving the poor and disadvantaged. A relieved Curley doubled the amount. Later he would name a horse in honour of O'Hehir. He called it My Word Is My Bond.

After the draw, Curley applied for a licence to train racehorses in Ireland. He had no owners and lacked experience, so was only granted a permit to train (that allows the permit-holder to train only his own and his family's horses). 'I was forced into training my own horses because every year I was winning a large amount of money but half of it went on paying trainers (he had others apart from Brennan) who were apt to be wrong 90 per cent of the time. Even if they were right, then the crowd was likely to know when your horse was fancied. The trainers were tipping to their friends. You may as well have trailed a banner from an aircraft and buzzed the crowd,' Curley says.

As he explains, 'There's no point outlaying thousands on a horse, paying two years' keep, and finding first time out that it starts at evens favourite. If you're paying the bills it's only fair that you should get first crack of the whip.' He adds: 'I believed I could do it better myself. I'd had experience in America, with Charlie. For the first time I had control of my own destiny on the racecourse, and I didn't hang around.'

He sent out three bumper winners at major tracks. His debut victory was I'm Incommunicado, running first time out at Naas in a race won previously by such exalted individuals as Arkle, Mill House and Nicolaus Silver. Prize money was £996, but the horse, partnered by Willie Mullins, was backed at all prices from 20–1 to 5–2 to win Curley £120,000 from what was a 'massive gamble', as it was described in the press. 'Not a bad start for a rookie trainer,' he says.

A majority of that was won on-course from layers who would stand large bets: men like Sean Graham, 'The best bookmaker there's ever been – he would lay horses to lose £60,000, way back nearly 40 years ago', Terry Rogers, David Power, Jim Mulligan, Malachy Skelly and JP McManus.

It didn't take long, though, for the bookies to get wise to the novice trainer; not with The Tariahs' success for him at Naas the following month, earning Curley £100,000, and The Hacienderos following up at Fairyhouse. The same horse finished second in another Fairyhouse bumper, but Curley was not unduly bothered. He had bigger plans in mind for that individual. He also had a future mapped out for I'm Incommunicado, who was one of the horses Curley would later bring over to Newmarket, but he broke a leg on the gallops and had to be put down.

By NOW, ANY evidence of a Curley-trained horse being backed had the Irish bookmakers drastically slashing their odds. 'At the time I got the permit, I could get 12–1, 14–1 on my horses. The bookmakers were of the opinion: this fellow's obviously only playing at this training game. With all the top trainers there, they were thinking, "He has no chance." But I was winning, and then the bets got smaller and the prices got smaller. I couldn't make it pay any more – not with the number of horses I had.'

It was at that stage that Curley said to himself: 'That's the end of it. I'm getting out.' He felt that British racing had far more to offer. Initially this new adventure gave his friends and associates a laugh, albeit a good-natured one. Gambler, impresario, bookmaker, publican, and now trying to make his name as a racehorse trainer . . . what other talents was he hiding up his sleeve?

Not for the first time in a long career, Curley vowed to teach the doubters a lesson.

CHAPTER 15

Professional gamblers have long had dark associations. Fiction portrays them as shadowy figures, constantly plotting corrupt new schemes, like the sinister Meyer Wolfsheim in F. Scott Fitzgerald's *The Great Gatsby*. When Gatsby introduces the naïve narrator of the story, Nick Carraway, to Wolfsheim, Carraway assumes he is a business partner of Gatsby's.

"'Meyer Wolfsheim? No, he's a gambler.' Gatsby hesitated, then added coolly: "He's the man who fixed the World's Series back in 1919.""

Fiction maybe, but laced with fact. Wolfsheim is said to have been inspired by Arnold Rothstein, nicknamed 'the Brain', a leading figure of the New York mob, whose agents allegedly paid members of the Chicago White Sox to 'throw', or deliberately lose, the World Series. He betted against them and made a significant sum in what was known as the 'Black Sox Scandal'. He also invested in a horse-racing track at Havre de Grace, Maryland, where he was reputed to have fixed many of the races that he won. Rothstein's successes made him a millionaire by the age of 30.

Barney Curley found it difficult to escape such comparisons when he arrived in Newmarket in 1984 accompanied by over 30 horses, a dozen lads – and a young Irish jockey named Declan Murphy.

It had always been Curley's plan to have his own jockey. He wanted a man he could depend on; someone who would give good feedback on the horses. When he had horses trained by Liam Brennan, Curley insisted on riders blessed with intelligence and ability, men of honour. He found these qualities in Ted Walsh and Willie Mullins, the six-time amateur champion in Ireland who rode Curley's three big bumper winners there and has subsequently become one of the country's most illustrious trainers.

As a youngster in Ireland, Murphy had been a champion pony race rider at 12, and partnered a winner for Kevin Prendergast, the British and Irish Classic-winning trainer, with his first mount as an amateur. Yet he had no great plans to pursue a riding career. He had visions of being a vet, an accountant or a businessman. Later he would admit: 'I never really had the passion to be a rider, but racing kept getting in the way.'

Then Curley intervened and invited him up to Middleton Park. 'He was bright and well educated,' says Curley. 'I had seen him riding and though he was very promising.' It required Murphy only half an hour to decide that he wanted to join the Curley exodus to Newmarket, later claiming that it was his new boss, not racing, that had been the deciding factor.

'Most kids that age would have been a bit intimidated by going up to a place like Middleton Park to discuss a move to Newmarket,' reflects Curley. I remember I asked him whether he would be up to the job. He replied, without hesitation, "Don't worry, I'll be good enough."'

Curley was impressed by the articulate, self-confident manner of Murphy, who had an amateur licence and had originally ridden on the Flat. Curley promised that, despite his inexperience, he would partner all his horses. He rated him in the same class as he would later place Frankie Dettori.

Murphy, who hailed from Hospital, County Limerick, was an engaging if somewhat complex character. He was only 18 and had just left school when he had his first winner in Britain on 13 November 1984. His mount, a nine-year-old maiden, Who's Driving, won an eight-runner selling chase at Plumpton by no fewer than 25 lengths.

Murphy had arrived in Newmarket forewarned of the possible reception he and his guv'nor could receive. There had been a pointed parting shot for the young jockey. 'I remember Declan had asked one prominent Irish trainer for his advice. He told him: "You'll be back home within six months – and your boss'll be in jail."'

Curley chuckles at the recollection now, but at the time he bridled at such sentiments, though it merely confirmed what he already suspected. He admits wryly: 'I was aware from the moment I arrived in Newmarket that there was a general perception of me as a bandit. People were saying, "How can this man have thirty or more horses, pay for their keep, and not be fixing races? There must be some skulduggery." But ultimately, you have to live with yourself. And I can.'

Curley had notched up no fewer than 14 winners in Ireland by the time he moved to Newmarket. However, he had been on the periphery of Irish racing as a trainer. Now he wanted to train and bet at the epicentre of British racing. As he explained: 'If you want to construct a large ship, you go to where there's a lot of water.'

He rented a yard, Harraton Court in Exning, a village on the outskirts of Newmarket. He has since been based at different locations in the town, although he travels back to Ulster frequently. He retains great affection for his birthplace. 'I'm very patriotic, and owe my country a great debt. It gave me a great education and start in life.'

He had 28 full boxes at Harraton Court, and more elsewhere. Before 1988, when he had his contretemps with the Jockey Club, he built the numbers up and rarely had fewer than 50 horses. Initially, his horses were offi-cially trained by next-door neighbour Dave Thom, due to the fact that his application for a training licence in Britain had been rejected. The irony was that he could not even secure a permit (to train his own charges) because he was regarded as too professional and had too many horses.

It was an absurd contradiction. Curley says that at least one member of the licensing committee, Captain Miles Gosling, formerly chairman of Cheltenham racecourse, made clear his distaste for him. Curley, for his part, regarded Gosling as an 'arrogant and self-centred' man who 'listened to no one'.

Curley was advised to gain some experience as Thom's assistant and reapply later. In that respect, he accepts it did him no harm. Despite his irritation at not being granted a licence immediately, he appreciated the addi-tional schooling he received from Thom over the next 12 months.

Thom, who had lied about his age to become a Royal Marine during the Second World War and had taken part in the D-Day landings, took out a training licence in

1959. In 1986 he saddled Touch of Grey to win the Wokingham at Royal Ascot. Other top horses in his charge included speedy juveniles Absent Chimes, winner of the Molecomb Stakes in 1984, and Forty Winks, second in the 1976 Gimcrack Stakes. Absent Chimes was owned by Curley, who sent him over to Charlie Whittingham in the States, but after finishing second in a race the horse broke a leg.

Curley originally came over to Newmarket alone, leaving the family in Ireland, and for the first three years lived in a small flat above the stables. 'It was a lonely, spartan existence,' he recalls. And, after Middleton Park, a shocking contrast in terms of home comforts. He shared his accommodation with rats and mice, attracted by the horses' droppings. 'At about two o'clock the orchestra would start,' he recalls. 'My only protection was a pair of heavy boots, which I used to hurl at them.'

Maybe, as Curley's Jesuit philosophy had taught him, after the splendour and comfort of Middleton Park he was taking his turn at the bottom of the ladder – just as he had during that time with his father in Manchester. He had always felt somewhat uneasy in his mansion when so many lived in squalor, and as he progressed through life, he harboured no desire to accumulate money for its own sake. He stresses: 'If I needed money, I went out and won it. I was never going to have £10m in the bank. I've won millions over the years – but out of necessity, not avarice. Money doesn't do anything for me. In fact, I've always been afraid of it. I've seen how it can destroy some people. That's been my belief since I was lying in that sanatorium with TB.'

He has never coveted property, fine art or fast cars. Some of his most contented times were spent staying with his mother at her terraced house with its two small bedrooms in Irvinestown. 'I'd chit-chat with her, wander down to the betting shop to watch a few races and return to her making me bacon and eggs with some of her home-made soda bread.'

Curley's training operation was, necessarily, a closed affair. He laid down strict rules to his staff, telling his lads that he didn't own an oil well or a factory; his enterprise was not supported by Arab interests, the aristocracy, new money or 200-strong syndicates. He operated the only yard in Britain where no one outside knew its business. 'I own horses and do so solely to back them,' he advised them.

Those who worked for him had to be satisfied with their wages. There were to be no 'extras' from supplying tips or information to outsiders. He didn't even want them backing the horses themselves. Anyone who ignored his demand for confidentiality to be observed faced the sack – with no appeal. He placed the offence on a par with a supermarket worker hiding produce under his coat on the way out, with the argument that his wages were too low.

Horse racing is an industry riven with reports and gossip from many sources, but principally from within the stables. The bookmakers have their own intelligence networks. If a horse works well ahead of a major race, that know-ledge swiftly circulates. Curley couldn't succeed if his own staff were supplying information to the opposition, the bookmakers.

He made an inauspicious start of assimilating himself into the Newmarket racing community, none the less. There are 50 miles of turf gallops, and he hadn't under-stood the strict rules about when they can be used, and by whom. One morning, a character employed some choice language to bawl out the new man over his misuse of the gallops.

It turned out to be Bill O'Gorman, trainer of a number of fine two-year-olds, including Abdu, Manor Farm Boy, Sayf El Arab and Sayyaf. The two men made up, Curley apologised, and his son Charlie, known as Chuck, gained much experience working for O'Gorman for a time.

After that day, Curley became a confidant of a number of leading trainers and a mentor of several leading jockeys. On the racecourse, though, he continued to feel a marked man, and not simply because his fedora, atop those stern features, ensured that he would never be the most inconspicuous figure. Every horse he ran, even though initially it was in Thom's name, was scrutinised closely, as was the riding of his jockey, Murphy.

The young Irishman was too often before the stewards, called in for trying too hard and incurring bans for misuse of the whip, or not trying hard enough – often the consequence of his poise in the saddle; he was the ultimate stylist, who timed finishes to perfection. He was even punished for being too enthusiastic. He once falsified medical evidence so that he could ride, and was banned for four months. But his worst crime in some eyes was the man to whom he was inextricably linked.

When he entered the racecourse, Curley was convinced that he received knowing looks from officials, whose expressions clearly said that they knew he was there to fix races or dope horses. The *Daily Mail*'s then racing correspondent, Jim Stanford, reported that Curley was getting the *persona non grata* treatment from local stewards – an accusation refuted by the officials.

Initially Thom took the brunt of it, despite an unsullied

reputation during his 24-year career to date. Curley concedes it was embarrassing that the Scot was being called too frequently into the stewards' room. 'If there were any stewards' inquiries poor Dave went in, while I was outside,' he recalls with a smile. 'I remember he had a habit of blowing his cheeks with irritation. But he was always a real gentleman. Never complained. He was very good to us – the whole team.'

One particular instance involved The Tariahs, which Curley has always maintained was potentially the finest horse he ever owned and trained. He had bought him from Ted Walsh – coincidentally a jockey in the Bellewstown race won by Yellow Sam – after he had been beaten in a bumper in Ireland. 'He was the most lovable horse you've ever seen, so sweet and kind. He would nearly talk to you when you fed him mints.' If that sounds incongruous coming from a man regarded as a hard-hearted pragmatist, it is one of his endearing character-istics. He would stop at the horse's box and tell him, 'Your time has not yet come.'

The Tariahs was a hard puller and Curley knew it would require patience to extract his optimum performance. Declan Murphy was told that he must teach the horse to settle, and at Kempton in a novice hurdle he tucked him in last, and made late progress to finish eighth of 15.

The stewards weren't happy. They called in Thom and Murphy and 'recorded' the latter's explanation that the horse didn't like being held up and had sulked in the first half of the race; effectively that meant that they would be keeping a close eye on him next time. Thom was furious. 'The stewards seem to be gunning for the owner,' he declared, adding, 'My conscience is clear so I don't care how many times I am marched into the stewards room but it is beginning to get to Declan.' It transpired that the horse had been suffering from the potentially life-threatening condition of colic.

The Tariahs' target was the 1985 Coral Golden Handicap Hurdle at the Cheltenham Festival – for which he was due to carry virtual bottom weight of 10st. His prep race was at Warwick. He finished eleventh of 28, but Curley felt the horse had been taught to settle at last.

At home, The Tariahs did a serious piece of work with The Hacienderos and a decent mare called Mary Kate O'Brien, and, in Curley's words, 'absolutely laughed at them'. It was a gallop that resulted in Curley having no less than £50,000 at 14–1 on his star performer. He regarded the gelding as the biggest certainty to ever arrive at the Festival. The horse started at 10–1.

The Tariahs was travelling easily when he overjumped, turned over and buried Murphy in the turf. The horse broke his neck. For Curley, it meant the loss of the 'best and kindest horse I've ever been associated with'. There were tears, and Curley admits it was the only time he was emotional about a horse. The money, he says, was irrelevant. It was his worst moment on the racecourse.

Timeform offered a brusque epitaph: 'Moderate hurdler. Dead.' Curley, though, grieved the loss of a true equine friend.

The stewards' scrutiny continued to concentrate on Curley's horses and Murphy's riding. Thom said it didn't bother him. Both he and Curley, however, were concerned at the possible impact on young Murphy.

Thom was probably relieved when Curley was finally granted a jumps licence in November 1985. Because the yard had been stricken by a virus, it was not until the following year, 1986, that he entered the record books as a winning trainer in his own right – with an appropriate victor, too. Faaris had been bred by his friend Tommy Stack. The horse had initially been trained on the Flat by Kevin Prendergast for Hamdan Al Maktoum. Curley paid £10,000 for him, and on 17 May he won a novice hurdle under Declan Murphy at Bangor-on-Dee. Curley made 'a bundle', which can be translated into around £100,000.

Those early days were spent in relentless pursuit of reward and information. 'I did it six days a week, Declan Murphy and me, up and down the country. If you were going to punt successfully, you had to be on the road. You learnt from watching; not listening or reading. There were no TV racing channels then. You had to be there – and I was. Even if I didn't have a runner, I'd be off early in the morning, back late at night. It ensured I had an advantage and I made betting pay. You had to get out and do the work. That said, how we weren't killed, Declan and me – I never realised until later how fast he used to drive.'

As a trainer, Curley rarely got involved in the day-to-day running of the yard. Feeling joints and checking feed was not for him. His interest was when the horse was on the gallops. He brought his practised eye to bear when a horse was reaching his peak, 'when he's bouncing in his box and enthusiastic about his work'. He compares it with a football manager identifying a player relishing training and determined to show what he can do, as opposed to one who's sulking because he's been dropped or criticised by fans.

Such an example of the former was The Hacienderos, one of that early trio of Curley's winners as a trainer in Ireland. He had the son of Deep Run in a competitive novices hurdle at Newbury on Hennessy Gold Cup day (the big race was won that year by Jenny Pitman's Burrough Hill Lad, incidentally) and told his men: 'Back him – and keep backing him.' Eventually he had £50,000 on the 4–1 shot. Declan Murphy brought The Hacienderos home with relative ease.

At least one columnist pointed out the incongruity of the fact that while the stewards were apparently 'stalking' Curley, two or three of his rivals were given an 'easy' that day (were not seriously put in the race to win) without any response from officialdom as The Hacienderos dominated proceedings.

When gambling is the *raison d'être* of your operation, particular scrutiny of your team's running and associated betting is an occupational hazard. It was something Curley learned to accept during a near 30-year training career in Newmarket. It was when certain individuals read more into incidents than he believed was justified that quiet indignation turned to wrath – as John McCririck, the garrulous betting guru, discovered a number of years later.

CHAPTER 16

Whether it was the fast going, the sun on his back, or just the fact that he was fulfilling his optimum potential, Barney Curley's seven-year-old Cristoforo, a horse that had improved with age, had given his trainer and owner Patsy Byrne a rewarding three months in the summer of 2004, albeit at short-priced favouritism on every occasion. The gelding recorded a sequence of four wins on the Flat, partnered three times by Tom Queally and once by his brother, the amateur Declan Queally, all on good-to-firm going.

He was given a deserved six-month break and re-appeared early the following year in a handicap hurdle at Folkestone. His probable SP in the morning papers (frequently well clear of the mark, incidentally) was odds on. In fact he opened at 2–1 and drifted to 3–1 before being returned at 11–4. The Paul Nicholls-trained, Ruby Walsh-ridden Lord Lington who finished runner-up, started favourite.

The going was soft, and despite Paul Moloney, Curley's regular jockey in jump races, giving him some energetic encouragement, Cristoforo became tailed off and was pulled up before the last obstacle. The stewards looked into the performance, but significantly did not hold an inquiry.

That would probably have been the end of it had Curley, travelling home in the horsebox, driven by his assistant Andrew Stringer, not realised that the colour bag (containing the jockeys' silks) had been forgotten. 'I went back for it in the weighing room. As I'm coming out, I put my ear to the TV and there's John McCririck and Luke Harvey giving off about this horse that was pulled up after it had drifted in the betting. So I just charged in and told them what I thought about them.' It became the battle of the big hats: Curley in his fedora; McCririck in his trapper.

Curley pointed out, on air, that the ATR (At The Races, one of the two racing satellite channels) duo were talking 'absolute rubbish'. Almost incoherent with rage, he accused them of 'Downgrading racing . . . always pumping things up. It's a disgrace what you are saying.'

It was also a highly personalised attack. During his diatribe, Curley asked McCririck what he had contributed to racing, and referred to him as 'a takeout merchant'. Harvey, the former jockey turned TV and radio racing presenter, he opined, was 'an underachiever in life'.

Curley drove home and thought the whole matter was forgotten about. It wasn't.

'The next day, Maureen said to me: "Are you in dispute with John McCririck?"

'I said, "Ah no – just a difference of opinion."

'She said: "That's funny, because it's made all the national newspapers." Her colleagues on *Which?* had informed her, apparently.

'Maureen said to me: "You are heading a charity and to behave like that at the races is a disgrace."

157

'I said: "All right – I'll go and apologise tomorrow."'

And he was true to his word. He appeared on the channel at Lingfield and read out a statement, apologising to the presenters 'on the instructions of Mrs Maureen Curley'. His self-inflicted punishment was not attending any race meetings for the next eight weeks.

Years on, the evidence is still there on YouTube. 'I'd like to get it taken off. It's desperate,' he says with a mock-mournful expression. The bombastic McCririck's stock-in-trade is being provocative. But Curley admits he shouldn't have reacted to what he overheard. He adds: 'I admit I was in the wrong in the sense that I shouldn't have performed like that. *They* were wrong in what they were saying – but that didn't give me the power to abuse John McCririck.'

The Jockey Club looked into the running of Cristoforo but failed to detect any suspicious activity. Its spokesman Owen Byrne commented: 'Our betting analysts have completed their review of the betting patterns and nothing has come to light to warrant further investigation.' When the horse returned to a racecourse four months later, he was backed into 5–4 from 11–4 and finished a well-beaten last of seven runners at Bangor. Strangely enough, this result received hardly any media coverage at all.

Today Curley says of the contretemps with McCririck and Harvey: 'Look, no one in their sane mind would send a horse to Folkestone, which is a fair distance away from Newmarket, and arrange that it is pulled up. It achieves nothing. The handicapper disregards the run. It is an advantage to no one.'

The only conceivable benefit to him would have been if he had laid the horse to lose, but Curley retorts: 'I had nothing to do with things like that. It's stealing money. I would never have told anyone a horse of mine would not win or attempt to benefit from it.'

As for the explanation for the horse drifting in the market, Curley maintains that because his reputation invariably provoked caution amongst the layers, the price was simply too short in the first place.

The reality is that today, those who transgress the rules can be reasonably certain that the BHA's Integrity Services team will expose their wrongdoing. Among their duties are identifying and deterring breaches of the Rules of Racing and monitoring real-time betting markets for suspicious activity.

Penalties can be severe, as Flat jockey Eddie Ahern, the former Irish champion apprentice, discovered in May 2013. He was banned from racing for 10 years following a BHA disciplinary hearing that found him guilty of conspiring to commit a corrupt or fraudulent practice with former Premier League footballer Neil Clement, by communicating inside information for reward and intentionally failing to ensure that a horse was run on its merits.

Curley had been aware, from early in his training career, of those quite prepared to engage in corruption. His first experience involved The Hacienderos, who, having triumphed under Declan Murphy at Newbury, won two further novice chases at Leicester and Lingfield in 1986. At the Surrey course, it was effectively a match between The Hacienderos and the Nick Vigors-trained Cumrew. Curley was offered £10,000 to stop his horse.

He recalls: 'About 15 minutes before the start, a character shuffled up behind me and whispered: "Barney, here's ten grand if you give yours a quiet one."' To enforce the point, the man showed him four rolls of notes and added: 'Take it – if you'll block your horse.' Curley admits he had a shrewd idea of the man's identity. Without turning round, he said quietly: 'I'm going to count to ten, and if you're still here I'm going to grab you and hand you over to security.'

He says that Declan Murphy would have refused to stop the horse anyway, although he adds pointedly: 'There are jockeys about who, if the money is right, lose 15 lengths in a race without racegoers or stewards being any the wiser.' Murphy, though, was one of the straightest jockeys he had dealt with. 'Declan was too intelligent for that. Once a rider gets a name for stopping horses, it sticks.'

It was far from the only occasion in that period that Curley was approached by influential men, both punters and bookmakers, to fix a race. Without exception he gave them the withering eye of contempt.

Scrutiny continued, however. Though Curley has nothing but admiration for the vast majority of stewards, he maintains that in some quarters there was blatant discrimination against him because of his name and reputation. 'Overall, the occasions when I have been before the stewards accused of running "non-triers" have been few and far between. My disciplinary record is open to inspection.'

Curley gave a horse an educational run for a specific reason, as he did with The Tariahs. But there's a line he refused to cross. He stresses he would never have asked a jockey to 'block' a horse. He would never have said to a jockey: 'You must get beaten today.'

'I run horses to back them,' he once declared. 'That is my sole reason for ownership. But obviously I don't back them every time. They can't win every time. The secret is knowing precisely when they are at their peak of their fitness. I don't do anything that's different from anyone else – I just do it better.'

He added: 'If you have a horse, and keep something up your sleeve and then go to the well and draw at the right odds, I believe there's nothing morally wrong with that. The bookies aren't fools. They are up to every trick in the game. They have their lines into the big stables. And gambles come unstuck as often as they come off.

'I will do anything I can to beat the layers except fix races to ensure there's only one guaranteed winner. That is morally, and legally, wrong. It is corrupt. You may as well hold up the bookmaker at gunpoint.

'The secret is a knowledge of what your horse is capable of, and keeping it to yourself. I exploit the system as much as I can. I see nothing wrong in lining up a horse like The Hacienderos or The Tariahs for a race. If my judgement and preparations are right, I'll win. If not, I won't. But I won't do anything illegal. Throughout my life it's been my brains against the bookmakers'. Not a single other trainer, without the benefit of owners' fees, could achieve that and make a living.'

At one time Curley had 50 horses in training, purely financed by betting. The cost, even towards the end, when he cut back to fewer than 20, could be up to £500,000 a year. He speaks of staking £3m a year in total.

'There's an art in bringing horses along quietly, getting them ready to win first time out, or maybe after a long break. A good trainer knows when his horse is going to win.' He pauses, and adds drily: 'Some wouldn't know if it was Wednesday or Thursday.'

He once said: 'All trainers talk a good job. But with

me, the talking has to stop. Given similar weaponry, I could take on any trainer. I'd love to be there taking them on with a hundred horses because I know I'd be better than anyone else.'

Eternal hope is the opiate that pulses through all owners' veins. It's what guarantees the outlay of those monthly training fees, when good sense should prevail. Curley's particular gripe is that some trainers 'cheat their owners by keeping horses in training that will never win a race and should be put out to grass.'

Even if those owners do enjoy a visit to the winners' enclosure, the prize money for all but elite racing is relatively meagre – the consequence, he has long maintained, of the fact that the contribution of bookmakers to a sport that nourishes such healthy profits is insufficient.

He adds: 'As an owner, unless you're a John Magnier or Sheikh Mohammed, you're a cert to do your money. You're looking to go home with a grand from some of this all-weather racing, after expenses and jockey fees.'

Curley believes that owners should be told the arithmetic before they buy a horse, or a share of one. 'For every £50 they put in, they're likely to get £5 back. They may as well burn their money. At least if you buy a yacht or flash car, there's resale value.'

He also maintains that markets are too easily manipulated by the major betting firms, but there is never any discussion of this on the satellite racing channels because they have 'prostituted themselves' to the bookmakers. 'If these commentators told it as it is they'd have no jobs. That's why nobody does.'

Some have questioned the volatile effect of Curley's own horses on that betting market. Yet, put it to him that the most familiar criticism of him is that ordinary punters can be the victims of his machinations, and he retorts: 'I wouldn't deny that I always ran my horses to suit myself. I'm my own man, the horses were my property, and I had them to bet on. I captained my own ship and was never anyone's first lieutenant.' He adds: 'My only moral responsibility was for myself, my family, and those who worked for me.'

CHAPTER 17

When Barney Curley engaged with the enemy, he was, to borrow from that old menthol cigarette ad, cool as a mountain stream. He was calculating, devoid of emotion and sentiment.

He adhered to certain rules. He never chased losses. There's always another day of racing. Survival was the prelude to any thought of profit.

Curley was always circumspect about his wins – and reverses. There was a certain pride, arrogance maybe, about his success, but he tended to talk of winning 'a bundle' rather than divulging specifics. Not only would he consider that vulgar, but, as has been explained before, gambling was a business to him, one in which he had, to return an annual profit. He was the antithesis of the TV game-show contestant who gets lucky. All a big win meant was that it offset part of his significant outlay.

He may have had a dozen bets a week. Or he may have been quite content to keep a watching brief if there was no value about a potential bet. If a horse was 2–1, and he considered it should be 4–1, he was quite content to watch it win and walk out of the gate empty-handed.

But once he decided to strike, he attacked his target head on. If he really fancied something, he loaded on as much as he could. 'When Forgive 'N Forget won that 1983 Coral Hurdle Final, I had £50,000 on mostly at 4–1, but I still backed him down to 3–1 because even at that price he was still value.' The SP was 5–2 favourite.

Curley avoided trainers' pre-race prophecies, preferring his own judgement. 'Many have no idea what they're watching,' he says. 'It's a circus. There are too many dreamers and too much rubbish is talked about horses.'

He believes he was helped by the fact that he was not steeped in racing traditions and didn't come from a racing background. However, he admits that his successes were not necessarily the consequence of precise scientific analysis. 'I'm not always a logical thinker,' he says. 'A lot of my success was down to gut instinct. But I stayed the course because I was a watcher, not a listener.'

He believes that seeing certain things that most are oblivious to is a gift. Which is why, he claims, he saw something amiss with Graham Bradley's riding of Robin Goodfellow at Ascot in 1986. 'I need to have sharp eyes for the job I do, one I do successfully, and there was no doubt that day at Ascot that he was stopping his mount,' he says.

What began with a suspicion evolved into an episode that threatened to end his career, making him a 'disqualified person'. 'I had experienced that state before, when I was warned off by the Irish Turf Club over my dispute with Sean Graham, but I always knew I would get my licence back once I paid that debt. This was different. Along with my later dalliance in racing politics it was the greatest mistake I ever made.

'Maybe it was the high standards set by "Mr D" Michael Dickinson, the most honest racing man I've ever known, that concentrated my feelings against Graham Bradley. Ever since those great days in the seventies that jockey had gnawed away at the back of my mind like a tooth that needs filling.

'Maybe it's a weakness, but whenever I suspect somebody of letting me down, I keep my eye trained on them. I felt the first chance I got I'd teach him a lesson. It was wrong in a way. I should never have done it. I took it too far. I have regretted it ever since.

'From the day I realised what he was up to I always said to myself, "I'll get even with him." It was totally out of character for me and I'm not normally a vindictive man, even if someone has wronged me. But in his case I made an exception. He needed to get his comeuppance.'

When Curley arrived at Ascot on that bitterly cold November day in 1986, he was well wrapped against the elements, in a thick cashmere overcoat with luxuriant fur collar, his wide-brimmed brown fedora slightly angled. If his fashion sense didn't make him stand out from the crowd, his purpose there did. Back in those days, when Curley arrived in the betting ring it was like one of the Clanton brothers walking into Tombstone. Heads turned and he received knowing looks.

The Robin Goodfellow of Shakespeare's imagination is the alternative name for Puck in A *Midsummer Night's Dream*. He personifies the trickster or the wise knave. His equine version was due to contest the opener, the Kennel Gate Novices Hurdle, at 1 p.m.

Curley had planned this betting foray for some time. He intended to have on £25,000 in total, and started with £4,000 to win £5,500 with bookie Dougie Goldstein. Soon, however, his defensive instincts kicked in. In a later statement to the Jockey Club he said, 'I had originally intended to have around £25,000 with various book-makers, but the more I put on, the bigger the price became. After I put £12,000 on I became suspicious and stopped betting.'

Though Robin Goodfellow started at 13–8 favourite, the bookies were readily laying the horse. One was even backing him with a rival, an ominous portent. The lack of confidence was vindicated when the Toby Balding-trained gelding was beaten by eight lengths by Ron Hodges' Teletrader at level weights. Both had won their previous races.

Curley regarded Graham Bradley as probably the best jockey in Britain in that period. His only equal was Declan Murphy. There was no one better than Bradley at setting horses exactly right at their fences, which in Curley's opinion only emphasised what he was up to on this occasion. 'He was a great man for seeing a stride, but he wasn't doing that this day. He was shortening him up at his jumps, making him make mistakes. I was so angry, if he'd been riding for me I'd have taken him by the throat when he came back to unsaddle.'

He accepts that many will consider it simply a case of a man bearing a long-term grudge; a man who had seen a bet go west. It wouldn't be the first time in the history of racing. But frankly a loss of £12,000 would not normally have troubled him greatly.

The race prompted no suspicions of wrongdoing from other observers. The Form Book comment on Robin Goodfellow read simply: 'Sweating: steady headway 4th: every chance approaching two out: beaten when blundered last.' Certainly, the racecourse stewards failed to identify anything amiss. 'If they'd been doing their job properly, the problems that followed would never have

arisen,' Curley insists. Nor had the race-readers and
reporters noticed anything untoward, though as Curley
opined: 'Some of them couldn't read elephant tracks in
the snow. If the press had been doing its job there would
have been no need for me to say anything.'

THIRTEEN DAYS LATER, on Friday, 28 November, the
first two at Ascot were in opposition in the Sunley Builds
Novices' Hurdle at Sandown, also at level weights. Robin
Goodfellow won, with Teletrader third, nine lengths away.
The comment this time about the winner was: 'Held up:
lead last: driven out.'

Toby Balding was apparently satisfied with Bradley's
riding of Robin Goodfellow at Ascot. 'He's a good man,
but I suspect he just didn't know what was going on,' says
Curley. 'Very few trainers do. Of course, I had a bet at
Sandown too. I knew what I'd seen and knew he (Robin
Goodfellow) should win – if he was trying.

'In hindsight,' he admits, 'what I did next was not a
very clever thing.'

So impassive when putting the money down, yet so
impassioned when confronted with what he perceived
as a wrong, he believed that the only correct course of
action was to report Bradley to the Jockey Club, and
point out that Robin Goodfellow had been a 'non-trier'
at Ascot.

'At that time I still believed that the Jockey Club were
really concerned with the integrity of racing and would
do everything in their power to weed out cheats. Robin
Goodfellow was the favourite in a race at Ascot, and the
royal course is accepted as the pinnacle of English racing.

In a strange sort of way, I probably wouldn't have taken it so far at any other track. But to do that sort of thing at Ascot was, I thought, a disgraceful impertinence.

'I said to myself, "I must go through with this." I just could not put up with skulduggery. I had some faith in the system. But I certainly wouldn't do it today. If I saw someone doing the same, I'd keep it to myself after the mess they made of that.'

If that had been the extent of Curley's actions, it's likely that the matter would have run its course. His error was to ring the Dickinsons the day after the Ascot race, followed by a call to Bradley.

According to Mrs Dickinson, Curley informed her that Bradley had stopped Robin Goodfellow, that a bookie had paid him to do it, and that the jockey had stopped some of her horses in the past. He added that he would contact the Jockey Club, and that he would ring Bradley. The jockey, forewarned by Mrs Dickinson, taped the conversation on the advice of his solicitor. It began with Curley asking, 'How much did you get for stopping him?'

During the protracted dialogue that ensued, Bradley protested that he was 'a hundred per cent innocent'. Curley warned him that he was considering going to the Jockey Club, and put it to him that 'Maybe you were feeling sick or maybe you had money problems?' At one stage Bradley asked: 'So, you are not going to blackmail me or anything like that?' Curley replied: 'I certainly am not.' You sense that the fires of anger still smouldered within Curley, who needed this verbal hose to douse them. It was, frankly, a rambling, pointless conversation, which culminated with a stream of profanities from Bradley, directed at Curley.

169

Bradley says he then handed over the tape to the Jockey Club's security department. Meanwhile Curley also contacted the Jockey Club and reported his observations. He was told that they were investigating, but was eventually informed that, having reviewed the tape of the Ascot race, they had not identified a problem.

Two months passed, and then came the bitter upshot: the Jockey Club charged not Bradley, but Curley, under what is known as the 'catch-all' Rule 220(iii). He had, it was alleged, 'caused serious damage to the interests of British racing'.

Curley takes up the story. 'As far as Bradley was concerned, yes, I rang him, but never, as he suggested, to "blackmail" him. I rang him and told him that he was a disgrace. I'm not a spiteful person. I just wanted to tell him that he thought he was smart, but I knew what he was up to. Yes, I suggested that he should make a donation to the Injured Jockeys' Fund as a penance. Apparently he recorded our telephone conversation, but it merely substantiated all that I said. I just told him, "You stopped him." That's not abuse. That's just a statement of the facts, as far as I was concerned.

'I was so incensed I just kept on, and he said, "Are you going to do anything about it?" presumably trying to goad me into condemning myself. I didn't handle it very well and he later released the contents of a tape of the conversation – made on the advice of his lawyer – to the newspapers. It was a real coup for them, of course. The stuff of Dick Francis novels, but this time it was reality. Inevitably, it got blown up out of all proportion.

'I did not abuse anybody. Certainly not Mr and Mrs D, for whom I have the greatest respect. They only became involved because Bradley was their jockey. I rang Mrs D purely to mark her card, so to speak, to advise her to keep an eye on Bradley. It was a grave mistake, because it dragged into the maelstrom the last two people in the world that I'd ever want to upset. When I saw them at the Jockey Club inquiry, I felt dreadful. I was ashamed that they were involved. There was no way I wanted them there and they shouldn't have been.'

That inquiry, on Friday, 24 April 1987, was before Lord Vestey, the food services, farming and shipping heir, and chairman of Cheltenham racecourse; retired trainer and jump jockey Bruce Hobbs; and John Sumner, Typhoo Tea heir and racehorse owner. It lasted two hours, behind closed doors – as was normal then. The secret, 'star chamber' style of hearings of the Jockey Club, the sport's regulatory body, which dealt with disciplinary matters until 2006 (when its powers were transferred to the Horseracing Regulatory Authority, now the British Horseracing Authority), had long been questioned – as had its membership, summed up in a *Racing Post* headline in 2001 as being 'mainly male, mainly old and mainly rich'. Members were elected for life.

Curley appeared without a legal adviser, being told there was no need. He took along videos of Bradley's riding, but claims the committee wasn't interested. 'Their only concern was my "accusations" against Bradley.'

He told the hearing that there was no truth in Bradley's statement, published in the *Sporting Life*, that Curley made several telephone calls in which he said that should pay him the money he had lost. He added that the recorded telephone conversation to which Bradley alluded contained no references to payments.

Curley agreed that he also spoke to 'Mrs D' and

officials of the Jockey Club, but in none of these conversations did he make any reference to Bradley paying him money. 'Against all that evidence,' says Curley, the disciplinary committee made their decision in five minutes that he was to be banned for two years, starting a week later.

Curley, normally so self-assured, with virtue perched on his shoulder like Long John Silver's parrot, was shaken, utterly bewildered. His limited response could have been a line from an American 'B' movie. 'I don't remember much, except telling Lord Vestey, "You are making a big mistake."' As he agrees, 'Not exactly the most original retort – though I was proved right.

'As I walked out, I was in a state of shock. I told reporters: "I feel shattered. The decision is an absolute disgrace. I shall be consulting my solicitor now. This is only the beginning and I'm prepared to fight this all the way to the High Court."

'I added that I had had no warning that such allegations had been made against me and I had not been advised that I should be legally represented. I told reporters that I had been "conned" into attending without a solicitor.

'The verdict so depressed me that I said at the time that I was not sure whether I wanted to continue living in England. I regarded the Jockey Club as a great pillar of society. It was supposed to mete out natural justice. In this case, it had manifestly failed. My legal people considered it a perverse decision.'

Later in the week, at Sandown, he declared: 'I am backing down for no man or any organisation, including the Jockey Club.' That was some statement. He was questioning the Jockey Club's omnipotence.

In a Channel 4 interview, Curley explained how the Jockey Club's draconian punishment could affect his livelihood. 'I said, "My business is backing horses. I started off with nothing. We now own sixty horses. The money to finance that has all come from betting."'

The Jockey Club merely issued a bland statement, without going into any details. It raised again their policy of secret justice. 'Nobody could understand why I had been warned off merely for making an accusation against a jockey,' says Curley.

He continued to run his horses. Three days after he received his sentence, Saryan won a selling hurdle at Southwell – he had to go to 5,100 guineas to buy him in.

It wasn't until 70 hours later that the Jockey Club clarified that it was Curley's phone calls to Monica Dickinson and Bradley, and not his original complaint, that had formed the basis of the inquiry. In their statement, they explained that Curley's disqualification followed 'threats of a serious nature made . . . involving not only Graham Bradley but also another licensed trainer [Mrs Dickinson]'.

Curley was determined to fight what he saw as a clear injustice – that the Jockey Club had acted as both prosecution and jury – and told his solicitor Alan Walls to 'get me the best'. He did, in the formidable figure of top criminal barrister Richard Du Cann. 'Some might say it was unnecessary, but my belief was, although he was expensive, it was like getting Lester Piggott to ride for you in the Derby. He's a very busy man and hard to get. It gave you an edge, and it also did no harm to let the other side know that you were taking the matter deadly seriously.

'At the time, I was quoted as saying: "Not a question was asked by the committee. I felt they were under instructions to have no words with Curley. I got to feel they were dealing with a mad Irishman who had done his money at Ascot and was now doing his nut. Well, they will find out differently. The City had a Guinness scandal and this will be the equivalent in racing. I am not taking this lying down."'

Strong words, but Curley was aware that the Jockey Club was a self-electing oligarchy, and in many respects an anachronism by the late eighties, and its rules had rarely been tested in the civil courts.

Probably the most celebrated previous case in which it had been involved was in 1966, when 72-year-old Florence Nagle brought an action because the Jockey Club refused to grant training licences to women. It was considered that training racehorses was an unsuitable job for a woman, and the licence of her training operation had to be held in the name of her head lad. The Jockey Club backed down before that case could be heard and a significant battle was won, even if, today, it appears unthinkable that it ever needed to be fought.

CURLEY'S PREDICAMENT, HOWEVER, was an altogether different matter.

The Jockey Club didn't allow appeals, but an injunction was served by Curley's legal team on Nigel Macfarlane, secretary to the Club's disciplinary committee. On the day before the ban was due to start, Mr Justice Phillips granted an *ex parte* injunction against the Jockey Club, which meant the sentence could not be implemented until they were ready to appear in the High Court and present their case.

'My argument was that the committee's proceedings had offended the principles of natural justice' says Curley. 'Before that could happen, the Jockey Club climbed down and granted a rehearing of my case, saying that it had done so in order that I could be legally represented this time.'

There was a six-and-a-half-hour hearing, with a new committee chaired by Christopher Lloyd, along with General Sir Cecil Blacker and Michael Wrigley. On 3 August 1987, some 101 days after his original punishment had been meted out, Curley won his case.

Though the committee found that his phone calls did 'cause distress' and his conduct had been 'reprehensible', he was judged not to have infringed the rule relating to causing damage to the interests of horse racing. His licence was returned on 1 October. It was a landmark success. In the past, sentences had been reduced, but never completely quashed. Curley had beaten the establishment.

CHAPTER 18

Now it was Graham Bradley who could barely contain his ire and disbelief. He later described Barney Curley's accusation as 'one of the most malicious and unjustified attacks on my integrity'.

Yet there was a poetic justice of sorts for the Irishman. By the time Curley 'walked', having been reprieved by the Jockey Club, Bradley had just been banned, effectively for three months, after a Jockey Club inquiry found he did not make sufficient effort on a horse named Deadly Going at Market Rasen on 20 April.

Intriguingly, the jockey felt that, following the initial inquiry prompted by Curley's complaint, at which he had been exonerated, he was tailed by a Jockey Club security man – an ex-CID type – 'keen to see who I was talking to . . .' According to his autobiography, he maintained: 'I'm certain the Jockey Club were out to get me.'

Was it paranoia on Bradley's part? Or maybe Curley's message had, despite his doubts, got through to the powers-that-be.

Curley opines: 'It just went to show how utterly daft Bradley was at the time. I can only hope that one legacy was that it made the stewards of the Jockey Club realise that there were these things going on and maybe scrutinise them more. It may have made them think a bit harder, instead of dismissing everybody. Interestingly, since then, they've appeared to be far more stringent about non-triers.'

As for his resort to litigation, he says: 'I certainly don't think it did the Jockey Club any harm. It was a jolt to their complacency about the way they conducted their hearings.' He adds: 'I believe I was right to do what I did, but looking back, I shouldn't have put myself up as judge and jury on Bradley's behaviour. I'm not God and I shouldn't have taken it out like that on a fellow human being. It was a mistake. But the Jockey Club was also at fault in not taking me seriously in the first place.

'It was said I looked shattered as I walked out of that hearing, that I'd had a real mauling, but it was just the cumulative effect of hours with lawyers and travelling and worry about my future. The last six months had completely destroyed my life.'

The remainder of Bradley's 12-year career as a jockey was punctuated by accusations and run-ins with the authorities. He was arrested and charged in 1999 as part of a long-running investigation into alleged race fixing. The charges were later dropped. His career finished with something of a flourish when trainer Charlie Brooks appointed him as stable jockey. One of his biggest successes came under Brooks, when he won the 1996 Champion Hurdle on Collier Bay. Another notable win came in 1997 when he rode Suny Bay to victory in the Hennessy Cognac Gold Cup.

Curley actually booked Bradley to ride for him subsequently, on a horse called My Man In Dundalk at Lingfield in 1998. It was 12 years after the Robin Goodfellow affair, 'But that was merely because the opportunity had never presented itself before [in the intervening period]. I had nothing against him as a man, and certainly not as a jockey.' He adds: 'I know I wouldn't be first on Bradley's Christmas card list, but if he ever sat down and thought about it, I wouldn't be the worst person he's ever met, either. It was a bizarre carry-on and he was just caught up in the middle. Bradley, the Jockey Club and myself all learned a lot from it. Maybe once the stench had cleared, it allowed the winds of change to start to blow through the sport.'

On retiring from the saddle, Bradley became a blood-stock agent, but in 2002 he received a five-year ban from the sport, imposed by the Jockey Club, for passing on information for reward to Brian Wright, a man subsequently jailed for 30 years after being exposed as one of Britain's biggest cocaine dealers.

For Curley, it wasn't just his pride that had been bruised. Yes, he had successfully challenged the Jockey Club's power, although it had required fortitude and money. But by then he'd parted with his best horses, thinking that even if he eventually got his licence back, it could take months. The principle may have been won, but in pragmatic terms, it was a devastating few months.

'I sold a lot of my good National Hunt "store" horses' Curley says. 'They were ones that would eventually do well at the top tracks like Ascot and Newbury. I heard some won bumpers in Ireland and no doubt progressed into decent hurdlers and 'chasers.'

At least he'd kept his stable staff, and Declan Murphy had stayed despite interest elsewhere. Murphy was like a second son to Curley. When his boss was banned over Robin Goodfellow, there were tears streaming down his cheeks. Curley's faith in Murphy's class would be later thoroughly vindicated when he moved to become stable jockey with Josh Gifford, who could offer him far better horses. He won the 1993 Queen Mother Champion Chase at the Cheltenham Festival on Deep Sensation.

But the year after that triumph his career was effectively terminated, and almost his life, too. Murphy suffered seven skull fractures and a broken jaw, and also had a blood clot on the brain when Arcot fell at Haydock and he was trampled on by another horse. He was in a coma for five days and, it was said, he was four minutes from death. Curley, understandably if wrongly, shouldered some of the blame himself, for bringing Murphy over.

It seemed improbable that the jockey would ever walk again, let alone ride. He did both. He was passed fit and rode in the annual jump jockeys v. Flat counterparts race at Chepstow – and won. Two weeks later, he retired from the saddle.

The Robin Goodfellow episode had stymied any prospect Curley had of training high-quality horses. As he put it: 'I never played in the Premier League again. I just quietly had my team competing at the bottom of the third division.' He adds: 'I decided not to take any action to seek damages from the Jockey Club, although several people, including my lawyer, maintained I would have a reasonable chance of success. He also suggested I sue the Jockey Club for libel. My only response was to ask: "Have I got a licence to train?"

'He said, "You have."

'I said, "That's all I want."

'To be candid, I was fed up with courts and inquiries.'

One other significant event occurred in the wake of that episode. Finally, Curley was granted a licence to train under both codes after three years restricted to jumps.

'I applied for a licence to train on the Flat. I received it within two weeks, although it usually takes a lot longer. It had been expedited by Dick Saunders, who, as an amateur, aged 48, had been the oldest jockey to win the Grand National on Grittar in 1982. A wonderful man, great horseman,' says Curley. 'If I was a cynical man, I'd say that was an act of contrition on the part of the Jockey Club.'

As Curley contemplated his future, Tommy Stack called up. The jump jockey turned top-class trainer had remained close to Curley ever since the two men first met at the Brogans' place near Bellewstown, where he would stay at weekends to learn to ride. Today, Curley admits rather ruefully that he was never convinced Stack would make it as a rider or trainer, and definitely not that he would be twice champion jockey and become the only man other than Bruce Hobbs to ride a Grand National winner and train two Classic winners – which just goes to show that Curley's judgement is not infallible.

One of Curley's most emotional memories at the racecourse was the day he accompanied his pal to Aintree in 1977 and watched him partner Red Rum to his third Grand National triumph. He describes it as one of the happiest days of his life.

He and Stack are polar opposites, he says. 'Tommy would relish socialising with owners at the Curragh. I would abhor it.' He adds: 'There can't be a less egotistical man in Ireland. Maureen says he's the only man I'll listen to. He has the key to my moods and mannerisms.'

But now Stack's message was succinct and brutally direct. 'Now, Barney, please do us all a favour. Pack in training racehorses now and concentrate on what you're good at. Your game is backing winners.'

180

Far from tempering him, however, it acted as a trigger. Curley put the phone down and said to himself: 'The cheeky little bastard. I'll let him know who can train horses and who can't.' He is a man who has always responded to a challenge. One of his closest friends had provided him with one.

He rang round bookmakers and asked them to lay a special bet: that he could send out ten winners by the end of the year. It was September 1987. That gave him three months, with the possibility of winter weather causing abandonments. 'The bookies bit my hand off,' he recalls, and adds with a quiet chuckle: 'They were prob-ably surprised they weren't arrested for theft.' They laid him £126,000 to win £275,000.

The dispersal of his best horses when he thought he would lose his licence left him with only 15, and those were 'mostly broken down bit and pieces – it was more of a junk yard than a racing yard'. Even with decent horses, he'd only had nine winners in the previous jumps season.

As WILL BECOME apparent later, winning to order is a highly complicated task. Curley rarely planned too far ahead. A scheme would evolve as he watched the horses work on the gallops. 'I'd wander about the yard and people would think I was taking no part, but I was watching and waiting.'

He had one win early on, and then all went quiet. With five weeks remaining, he had only amassed three winners. Five winners in 18 days changed the complexion of the gamble, a ninth followed on 21 December, and the following day at Folkestone, in the 1.45 Sellindge Handicap Hurdle, worth £750 to the winner, Experimenting became number 10. He was one of Curley's invalids, who had broken down twice. Declan Murphy gave him a typically restrained ride, held him together and got him home with the gentle touch.

The reaction was remarkable. The crowd – and even the on-course bookies – began cheering as the horse hit the front. As people thronged around the winners' enclosure, someone shouted: 'Well done, Barney – that's shown 'em.'

He was to reflect later, 'I never realised such generosity of spirit existed. That day the racegoers saw me as one of them.' Yet not for the first time in his professional life, he says that he felt 'no real joy or exhilaration other than the satisfaction of overcoming a challenge'.

There was £401,000 in the pot. When he mooted a follow-up bet to bookmakers, suggesting he would train ten winners in the first three months of 1988, the phone was silent.

The money was soon gone. Curley organised a raffle to raise funds for Great Ormond Street Children's Hospital's Wishing Well appeal. The idea was that ten winners would all have one of his horses running in their name for a year. Tickets did not sell well, but Curley had guaranteed £100,000 to the hospital regardless. In all, it set him back considerably more.

CURLEY'S OBSERVATIONS about Graham Bradley's riding would not be the last time he reported his suspicions regarding the sport's integrity to the Jockey Club. In the late eighties, he believed doping of horses was rife.

Keep Hope Alive, another former Curley store horse, ran in his first bumper at Newbury in 1989. Curley told his putters-on: 'Take all prices. Back him until they will no longer lay him.' The five-year-old opened at 3–1 and was backed down to 6–4. He justified those odds easily. He followed up at Ascot, where, despite a penalty, he was backed into 9–4 on and again justified the faith in him, and at Wolverhampton. Curley had great hopes for him in high-grade contests and ran the gelding against a horse of Jenny Pitman's, Egypt Mill, in a hurdle at Ascot. Keep Hope Alive started 5–4 favourite and Curley had £50,000 on, but he finished only third, and 'distressed', according to his trainer. 'He was out on his feet. He could hardly put a hoof in front of the other.'

Curley claims the horse had been doped. He believes that, despite his instructions that 'under no circumstances is this horse to be left alone', it was still somehow got at. Keep Hope Alive never won again.

He told the Jockey Club that doping was going on wholesale, and presented a list of horses that he suspected had also been targets. He accepts the Jockey Club took his accusations seriously, but nobody was ever caught at that time, though in the late nineties three jockeys were arrested after horses were found to have been doped.

CHAPTER 19

The former *Racing Post* columnist Paul Haigh once asked rhetorically in an article: 'Who is Barney Curley . . . and why does he make such a bloody nuisance of himself?'

The Irishman himself maintains he never set out to make headlines or become a thorn in anyone's side. He actually decamped to Newmarket because he was relatively unknown in Britain.

Given his profession, one might expect him to prefer anonymity and operate in the shadows. Yet it has been his constant mission to put the racing world (and occasionally that beyond) to rights. Throughout his career he has warred with officialdom – stewards, bookmakers, horse-racing handicappers and even TV pundits.

Once his displeasure is incurred, he can be like an angry wasp returning to an open jam jar. If there's a perceived wrong to be exposed and corrected, Curley is your man. He will not flunk confrontation. Compromise is an unknown word in his lexicon. He has his principles and adheres to them vigorously. Some may contend that those principles don't always stand scrutiny, but he is unmoved.

Don Quixote would have readily had him as an ally.

Curley's attitude is: 'If I see a wrong, I'll fight it, no matter who it might hurt or what I might lose financially.' He has established a reputation, like a street fighter, for removing his jacket and taking on all comers.

He has even taken on racecourses. He accused officials connected with Fontwell of bidding horses up after they had won sellers – races designed to give the poorest animals a chance. (The racecourse receives a percentage of the difference between the opening or 'selling' price and what the horse actually fetches at auction. The amounts concerned can often be several thousands.)

When Above All Hope became his first winner after the Robin Goodfellow affair, he had to go to 7,300 guineas to buy him in. Claiming that the course had instituted the bidding and he had been set up, he described it as 'bloody daylight robbery'. It resulted in him being accused of slandering the owners of the Sussex track. He spent many thousands on lawyers' fees and prepared a defence, but the writ never arrived.

He also took handicappers to task. Now, it should be said that he is not alone in questioning their assessments. Unlike football referees, they will explain their rationale – and even alter ratings. After a five-year lay-off, handicapper Phillip Judge raised his horse Mullingar Con – named, it will be recalled, after that attempted scam many years before – 23lbs. After 'some discussion', according to Curley, the handicapper revised the horse's weight down. 'Phil, don't ever do that to me again,' he told him. 'Handicap the horse, not me. I'll forgive you once, but never twice . . .'

He was true to his word as well. Just before the start of a race at Lingfield, Curley withdrew My Man In

Dundalk, and instructed jockey Leighton Aspell to return to the weighing room, in protest at the horse's handicap rating. He claimed the horse had been handicapped not on his form, but on who trained him. The stewards fined him £1,400. Curley vowed to have Judge sacked over the matter and took it up with the British Horseracing Board, then responsible for handicapping. Despite Curley paying out a small fortune on legal fees, Judge stood by his decision and the BHB stood by their man.

But his most militant action was directed at the bookmakers over what he believed was their failure over many years to appropriately support the sport from which much of their profits are derived. He had long questioned the poor level of prize money, and had also voiced his concerns about the major firms' manipulation of starting prices. Curley's joint target was the leadership of the BHA, that had allowed this to happen.

Perhaps emboldened by his triumph over the racing establishment in the wake of Robin Godfellow, he opted for a campaign of disruptive tactics and 'disobedience', withdrawing horses just before the start. In March 1990, to protest about manipulation of starting prices, he instructed Declan Murphy to canter the stable's Ardbrin down to the start before an Ascot hurdle race, then return him immediately to the saddling enclosure. Curley was fined £1,000 for 'a wilful disregard of the interests of racegoers'. He believed the complete opposite was the case.

The following year, on a Wednesday evening in July, he made a late switch, substituting the Classic-winning jockey John Reid for Tony D'Arcy, a 7lb claimer who had never ridden a winner, for his horse Threshfield, due to contest a handicap at Sandown. The early price was around 9–1. After the jockey switch, he was backed down to 3–1 favourite. The horse won comfortably enough. Curley, who landed around £100,000 in winning bets, said: 'Kenneth Baker [then Home Secretary] says we've got to help ourselves. Well, I have.'

When an unrepentant Curley, together with owner Ken Higson, withdrew horses just before the off at Fontwell in 1992, for which he was fined, it led to a row – as we have seen, not for the only time – with the Channel 4 betting pundit John McCririck. Ostentatiously clad in daft hats and jewellery, and employing terms like 'the rag' (outsider) and 'double carpet' (33–1), McCririck had endeared himself to a proportion of the racing public. Curley, however, had never been impressed.

McCririck contended in a *Racing Post* column that the Jockey Club should withdraw Curley's licence at his next rule-flouting protest. An enraged Curley sought out the pundit in the press room at a Newmarket meeting and threatened to 'defrock' him – meaning, he says, that he would rip his microphone off him, rendering him as in-effective as a priest stripped of his ecclesiastical status – if he mentioned him on TV again.

A commotion ensued. Security was summoned, together with the police. The Irishman later observed: 'He went round like a hysterical child, complaining that "Curley was going to manhandle me."'

Nevertheless, sensing that there was 'an irresistible force for change' within the industry, Curley attempted to be a Pied Piper, leading the punters and galvanising the trainers into action to improve racing. On 6 March 1991, he launched the Independent Racing Organisation at a Greek restaurant in London. He put in £30,000 of his own money, and asked for a £25 membership fee. The organisation had offices, and offered discounts to racecourses and greyhound meetings, and a betting advisory service.

It attracted some diverse and high-profile support, including trainers Luca Cumani, Michael Stoute and Henry Cecil, jockey Lester Piggott, and former England footballer Francis Lee, who at the time was chairman of Manchester City, but who had also had a spell as a race-horse trainer.

Curley stressed that the IRO was 'no group of rabble-rousers out to revolutionise the sport. We still supported the Jockey Club as the best body to head the racing industry.' He launched a punters' charter to challenge a system under which, he believed, too small a fraction of the £4bn annual turnover (the figure today is around three times that) generated by punters was returned to racing. Other issues he wanted to confront included the strength of the on-course market, so-called 'early' prices, and facilities at racecourses.

He also called for the establishment of a regulatory body, similar to the Gaming Board, to oversee book-making. He believed there was a 'bewildering incongruity that while trainers and jockeys had their conduct scruti-nised minutely, with offenders often receiving severe punishments, bookmakers indulged in a free-for-all, over which there was no control whatsoever'.

He also wanted so-called 'ring-masters' who would categorise on-course bookmakers according to the level of bets they laid, up to a given amount, similar to the Australian system. Pitches should be allocated on perfor-mance, not on the basis of 'dead men's shoes', as was currently the custom. He hoped to persuade the govern-ment to order an inquiry. However, the seeds of change he scattered failed to germinate.

A tent was erected at Newmarket during Guineas week to promote his campaign. The *Sporting Life* described Curley as 'a lonely figure sitting in a Bedouin tent behind the grandstand', and questioned his suitability to be the punters' guardian, likening it to 'putting a fox in charge of the chickens'.

Only 290 members signed up. Curley blamed a 'wall of indifference' from trainers, owners, racegoers and punters. 'But you can't help those who won't help themselves.' He came to the conclusion that those who trained, owned and bet on racehorses were too single-minded to get involved in what was effectively a 'trade union' for the common good. The consequence, according to Curley, was that the big bookmakers would continue to rob the punters.

Meanwhile, he took his eye off his own training regime. Declan Murphy would complain: 'Barney, please concentrate . . .' He refused to let the issue rest, however, and appealed directly to the trainers.

At the beginning of 1992, he organised an informal get-together in the billiards room of his home at Stetchworth. He wanted to thrash out a plan for action. It was a distinguished gathering. Around 15 attended, including Christopher Haines, then chief executive of the Jockey Club, and trainers Michael Stoute, Henry Cecil, Luca Cumani, Alex Stewart and Bill O'Gorman. But most had wealthy patrons, and there was no real incentive for them to act.

Finally, in desperation, he organised a meeting at the Jockey Club's HQ in London's Portman Square. Curley described it as D-Day, time for all concerned to put their heads above the parapet, and advocated a strike of trainers.

Now, not for a moment does he stand comparison with

Peter Sellers' magnificently pompous shop steward Fred
Kite in the 1959 film *I'm All Right Jack*, but the message
was uncannily similar: 'There's only one way – all out!'
He said at the time: 'The only way is for the BHA to say
"no racing" until it's sorted.'

Again there was an impressive turnout: John Dunlop,
Guy Harwood, Michael Stoute, Harry Thomson, 'Tom'
Jones, Luca Cumani, John Gosden and Paul Cole. Curley
sensed empathy with his sentiments, but all were paying
lip service. Nobody really wanted to destabilise the
industry.

When the meeting broke up for lunch, Curley walked
out and didn't return. 'After four years, racing politics
had consumed me, frustrated me and virtually destroyed
me financially. In hindsight, I should have recognised
well before then that they weren't prepared to suffer to
improve the state of racing. They wouldn't stand up for
what they knew was right.' He would later name a horse
All Talk No Action.

After the millennium, Curley threatened to quit racing
on more than one occasion. The betting landscape has
changed considerably since then, with the proliferation
of online betting, but his attitude towards the bookmakers
has not altered an iota. 'Their contribution is derisory,
they're rigging the market, and people like me can't get
a bet on.'

In late December 2008, a *Racing Post* story suggested
that he was putting his yard on the market and preparing
to sell his string of around 20 horses. An advert he had
placed in that edition emphasised: 'In the present
climate we no longer feel it's justified to provide at a
very substantial cost, with no hope of a return, however
small, free entertainment for the big bookmakers and

the racecourses which seem to have a stranglehold on racing in England.'

In the event, he didn't carry through with the threat.

Yet well over 20 years on from first articulating his grievances, his beliefs have never wavered. He still advocates an owners' strike to highlight concerns over poor prize money and the bookmakers' overriding power. 'Direct action is the only thing that gets people moving,' he says. 'I learnt that lesson when I was young and the Troubles began. Nobody stood up for what they believed in; everybody left it to the politicians and the madmen.'

In his book *High Rollers of the Turf*, author Raymond Smith reflected on Curley: 'I have no doubt the crusader in him will go with him to the grave.'

CHAPTER 20

Many years ago, when I was 17 or 18, there
was a programme on Channel 4 at about
midnight called *After Dark*, a discussion show
for people who couldn't sleep! I came in from
a night out and there was McCririck and a
couple of others sitting there on the TV talking
a load of rubbish. But there was this guy, sitting
there quietly, who would chip in every now and
again and say something which was quite
outstanding. That was Barney Curley and I was
drawn to him like a magnet.

– Frankie Dettori in a *Racing Post* interview

In August 1997, that fine miler Cape Cross was disqualified and placed last of four after being first past the
post in the Celebration Mile at Goodwood. Barney Curley
had no direct interest in the horse – John Dunlop had
been its trainer – yet he stepped in unhesitatingly.

On most occasions, his skirmishes with authority arose
as a result of his strict principles. Here there was also a
personal interest.

The jockey was Frankie Dettori. The Italian had been
found guilty of irresponsible riding, his horse having been

adjudged to have interfered with Peartree House, ridden by Dane O'Neill.

Curley was incensed by the stewards' verdict. He claimed that it had actually been the other jockey's fault – O'Neill had admitted that his horse 'just rolled away from the rails, created a gap for Mr Dettori and just rolled back on him again' – and he offered to appear at the appeal at the Jockey Club's Portman Square office as a witness. More than that, he went so far as to engage his wife Maureen, who by now was a qualified lawyer, to act on Dettori's behalf.

The appeal failed. Afterwards Curley claimed that the disciplinary committee – which proceeded to uphold the stewards' decision – had their minds made up before they went in. Maureen, he said, had been 'horrified that justice could be dispensed with such obvious lack of consideration of the facts'.

The intervention would not have surprised Dettori. Curley had taken a paternalistic interest in the irrepressible Italian rider from early in his career. The pair had met at the Tattersalls autumn sales at Newmarket in 1989 when Dettori was 19 and an apprentice based with Luca Cumani. Curley, never a jockey himself, but a perceptive judge of the breed, was of the opinion that he had the potential to become the heir to Lester Piggott.

Dettori had bounced into racing's consciousness and beyond, his smiling features and natural charm entrancing racegoers; his talent in the saddle captivating trainers. He soon became a celebrity figure; and that worried Curley, who by the early nineties was concerned that he had begun to lose concentration.

In the 1990 season, Dettori rode 149 winners to become the first teenager since Piggott to hit a century. The following year, he was on the slide, with only 14 by Derby week in early June.

The Irishman took his protégé to task after he had given Ian Balding's Mt Templeman an undistinguished ride in May 1993 at Goodwood. As Dettori himself admitted, his riding had been 'sloppy'. Indecision had cost him the race. Curley was furious with him, and not simply because his £6,000 bet on the horse to win £15,000 had gone down.

On the way home in a cab together after their plane from the Sussex course was diverted to Cambridge, Dettori disclosed that the *News of the World* was preparing to publish a story that he had been warned by the police over possession of drugs in London. He had also fallen out with his guv'nor, Luca Cumani, over plans to ride for trainer Gary Ng in Hong Kong, having, he admitted, been 'seduced by the night life'. He was in limbo where his career was concerned. As Curley put it rather more starkly, he sensed that the young Italian 'was at the last station on the line to oblivion'. 'He had achieved too much, too soon,' he said. 'At that moment, he wasn't a popular, confident, wealthy jockey, but a drifter.'

That evening, Curley invited Dettori around to play snooker at his house in Stetchworth. It would be, appropriately, the cue for some home truths.

In his own autobiography, Dettori recalls: 'He [Curley] asked me if I was serious about being a jockey or just playing at it. It immediately set me on edge.' However, he adds: 'It was a meeting that altered the course of my life. I listened in shock as Curley laid bare the shortcomings of my lifestyle over the past two years.'

Curley emphasised that he was convinced that Dettori was riding badly because he wasn't concentrating, as though his heart wasn't in it. He was playing around like a Jack the lad.

'Frankly, it was a relief to have a wise old bird like Barney to share my burden,' says Frankie. 'My prospects looked bleak until Barney intervened.'

Curley says: 'I told him, "You have a God-given talent. Very few people have that. You're one of the best I've ever seen. You can be as good as Lester. But you're ruining it."' According to Curley, Dettori accepted the criticism without bluster, and pleaded guilty without demur.

The following day they drove to John Gosden's yard at Stanley House in Newmarket. Gosden had been installed there as Sheikh Mohammed's trainer in 1988. He had an impressive CV, having been assistant to Vincent O'Brien and Sir Noel Murless, and had spent five years training in California, close to Charlie Whittingham's barn, where Curley had first encountered him.

At the time, Dettori's lifestyle was coming under scrutiny. There were stories about him turning up late for work, or not at all, because of his night-time excesses. In a place like Newmarket, the carrier pigeons of bad reports are swift on the wing.

It was against this background that Curley asked Gosden to employ Dettori as first jockey, to succeed Michael Roberts. It was a job coveted by every other rider in the land. Curley says: 'When I arrived with Frankie to stake his claim for the job riding for Sheikh Mohammed, it was a bit like Jesse James taking his brother Frank down for a job in the bank as a clerk. A lot of people would have seen him as a toerag of a jockey; this little arsehole from Italy making a mess of his life with this Curley fella, a punter, going down to secure the biggest racing job in the world. *In the world.*'

Gosden would be taking an enormous risk. Sheikh Mohammed had some of the world's best horses. The job required an impeccable attitude. Dettori couldn't afford to put a foot wrong. Curley, however, was confident that Gosden would extract the best from Dettori, support him and give him time to develop. Gosden laid down the law about what he expected. He demanded 100 per cent dedication to the job, and a thoroughly disciplined approach.

As they departed, Curley had a simple message for the Italian: 'Get stuck in, talk to no one and work.' Follow that advice, he told Dettori, and he would become champion jockey. As an incentive, Curley offered to sell him his house if he achieved that ambition. Dettori had always admired his home at Stetchworth.

Both target and reward came to pass. That same season, 1993, Dettori amassed 149 winners and finished second in the championship. However, the following year and 1995 he partnered over 200 winners to become champion. He also claimed a third title in 2004 during a career in which he won all five English Classics.

In 1996, Curley and Dettori 'swapped' houses, Dettori and wife Catherine moving in to White House Stables; the Curleys setting up home at Dettori's Newmarket residence. Curley admits that he felt a personal accountability for Dettori's every ride. He suffered more nerves than if he had had £50,000 on a horse.

When the Italian was due to ride 1995 Derby winner Lammtarra in the King George VI and Queen Elizabeth Diamond Stakes, the Irishman couldn't face being there. An hour before the race he just drove for miles and ended up watching it at a betting shop. Dettori got the colt up by a neck inside the final furlong. Curley compared the moment to Tommy Stack winning on Red Rum. He didn't have a pound on the horse. His initial faith in the young Italian had been completely vindicated. Dettori called him to say 'thanks for everything'.

Maybe Dettori would have overcome that 'too much, too soon syndrome' and successfully fought the symptoms alone, but you suspect that Curley played a significant role in his rehabilitation.

More than two decades on, in 2012, Dettori would be bedevilled again by the scourge that blighted his career early on. He failed a drug test after racing at Longchamp in September, and was banned from riding for six months.

It should not be ignored, however, that for two decades his character had transcended racing. With his flying dismounts from big-race winners, he retained his seemingly boyish enthusiasm even as the years passed, helping the sport to reach out to an audience beyond its traditional supporters, just as Lester Piggott had done. For that, Curley must take much credit.

CHAPTER 21

Phil Bull, founder of Timeform, once described racing as 'the great triviality'. It is a view to which Barney Curley subscribes. 'If I'm honest, I feel I've wasted my life,' says the man who has never felt comfortable having his life defined by his betting exploits.

If that sounds incongruous for one of the country's most notorious backers, he has long protested that it is not his intention to arrive at Heaven's gates clutching a list of winning bets as evidence of his achievements on earth. He has no desire that his tombstone should be inscribed with 'Legendary Punter'.

It took the death of his son Charlie in a car accident in December 1995, at the age of just 18, to change his direction and priorities. Charlie Curley – known as Chuck – harboured ambitions to follow his father into the racing game, though he was determined to do the job in the conventional manner, and not back horses to ensure survival. His father arranged for him to spend time with Newmarket trainer Bill O'Gorman and with Michael Dickinson, who was by then based in the US. But he issued a warning. 'I used to tell him, "I've lived all my life at this, and it's not a game to be in." I urged him to think about doing something else, but the horses were addictive.'

He was a deliberately tough taskmaster. He had considered eventually moving back to Ireland and leaving the horses in Chuck's hands. But he was determined that nothing was going to come too easily to his son. When Charlie was late for work a couple of times, he told him he was sacked. At one time, Curley junior had some rides as an amateur. 'He promised: "I'll stop riding if I have a winner." He never did, though he was runner-up a couple of times.'

Chuck Curley was driving to work when his car skidded on ice and plunged into a ditch. 'His death destroyed a dream I had for him,' says Curley, who was left distraught by the loss. He took to his bed for two days.

SINCE THEN, his life has changed radically. His thinking has been dominated by the charity he founded in 1996, DAFA (Direct Aid For Africa), to help the desperately poor and sick in Zambia. His target was £1m, and that has been achieved several times over. 'But for the tragedy there'd be no DAFA; so I suppose a bit of good came out of it,' he reflects.

It should be stressed that the charity has never been simply about raising money in order to feel good about himself, and ego plays no part in it. In a *Racing Post* article, he once made this request to the writer Brough Scott: 'Don't paint me as a saint or anything silly like that. This is just me taking out a bit of fire insurance in case things get tricky at the Pearly Gates. I've always believed whatever you give, you get back a thousand times.' He claims it all goes back to his father's old adage: 'Wise men don't forget to give a little back.'

DAFA is not involved with relief. It is about making tangible improvements in Africa. Its primary purpose is to provide the opportunity for the poor to help themselves. There is virtually no waste. Curley demands that all projects, predominantly concentrating on two areas – Lusaka and the copper-mining area around Ndola – are costed and approved by the committee he has formed.

His representatives out in Africa are mainly Catholic priests, men he's known since his schooldays in Ireland and who were his original inspiration. Some have been in Africa since the sixties. He is inspired by 'their disdain for material things, their wisdom and above all by their contentment'.

Those priests take responsibility day to day, but Curley scrutinises projects personally and, indeed, gives those who request funds a tough time. The money must be fully justified, with an end result. In that sense, he approaches charity with the same attitude with which he conducts his betting: he seeks excellent value before committing himself.

He first went out to Zambia in 1995 with Father James O'Kane, a friend from his college days who became a missionary, and brother-in-law Dolan McBride. Out there, he was reunited with Father Eugene O'Reilly, his friend from college.

'No one persuaded me,' he says. 'I was out there in 1995 and just saw the poverty with my own eyes, and was impressed by the people working there. If I hadn't done that, I would have considered my life a waste. Having done it, it's still a big waste, but at least I've contributed something. People don't realise what you can achieve out there – to have 1,500 kids at two schools and supporting them.'

He adds: 'No, I wasn't confident. I remember some members of the committee saying, "Let's run this for three years, see what we can do, do as much as you can, and then close it up. It'll lose its momentum, vitality." It's coming up for twenty years later, and it's still flourishing.'

'You can give money to charity, but that just wouldn't have satisfied me. You have to walk the walk, go out there and live with the people. That's where I would get the satisfaction from. Anybody can give money if they have it.'

Areas of running a charity required talents beyond Curley, and when he established DAFA, he brought in Ben Lewis who volunteered to organise the charity's website and administer its affairs. Everyone involved pays their own way. There are no rake-offs for well-paid executives, or extortionate expenses; no jollies.

Anyone accompanying Curley out to Africa, as three big-name jockeys – Johnny Murtagh, Jamie Spencer and Tom Queally – have done, at their own expense, will attest to the fact that he demands value for every pound spent.

In 2011, he invited me out there. This is an excerpt from a *Racing Post* article that appeared as a result.

> We head into the bush down a pitted track, past the BP oil depot, near Ndola in Zambia's copper belt. Regional Superior Margaret Musonda, a Dominican nun, is the somewhat unlikely figure at the wheel who handles her powerful truck with the expertise of a rally driver.

Barney Curley, seated beside her, can barely quell his anticipation as Sr Margaret eventually pulls into Yengwe Basic School in rural Fatima. It is an institution that exemplifies some of the best work of DAFA (Direct Aid for Africa), the charity the trainer formed 15 years ago.

Four thousand feet above sea level, the sun bears down pitilessly. It is not ideal for a man of 71 years with a countless-a-day habit and circulation problems, the legacy of serious illness in 2009 – these days a slowly negotiated furlong is about his limit at one stretch – but you rarely find the Irishman more at ease with himself.

'When we first came out here, this was just a very small school,' he says. 'Now there are 1,500 kids getting an education. That's very satisfying and a great privilege to have seen it all grow. And who knows – there might be a Nelson Mandela or Mother Teresa among them. They are talented. All they need is a chance.'

That phrase encapsulates what the renowned gambler is doing here, why he first came out to the former British colony in 1996 and why he has returned many times since.

A group of children perform a play, with some splendid harmonious singing, in homage to DAFA's contributions, before Curley makes an impromptu speech in front of the entire school, enforcing the importance of education. It can be the passport out of poverty in a nation where less than 10 per cent of the 13 million population are in 'formal' employment.

The pupils are clearly intrigued by this mysterious white man. Forget coups and controversy. Out here, a world away from the Victoria Falls and luxurious safari lodges, all they know about him is that the work of his organisation has contributed towards their school buildings, a water bore-hole and their 'lunch'.

When he first visited, Curley discovered that the school run meant literally that. Some pupils' daily journey was 15km to school and back. The average was 10km. And on empty stomachs. By midday many were asleep, shattered by the rigours of just getting there. Now the day starts with all the children queuing to fill their plastic bottles with a soya-based drink prepared for them each morning.

Among 11 projects that we survey in a week, Yengwe Basic School and the nearby Kavu clinic (where Curley submits somewhat tentatively to a dental check-up) in Sr Margaret's diocese fully confirm the evidence of money well targeted.

He had set out from Heathrow on a high – or as exultant as a winner in the last at Yarmouth the previous night could leave a man, with Shouda, backed down to evens favourite, just getting home under Queally. But for Curley, this experience represents something that transcends any achievement on the turf.

Though the priests, with whom we stay, enjoy the craic his company provokes and relish hearing about his gambling exploits, Curley is acutely aware of the incongruity of discussing such enormous sums in the company of men whose life's work is among those existing in abject poverty.

'I believe that, some day, I have to meet my maker and will be judged,' he insists. 'I don't want it said of me: "He was a great gambler." I'd rather it was: "He tried to help people."'

Not that he compares himself for a moment with our hosts. He adds: 'I'd like to go up [he gestures towards the heavens] on one of these fellas' CVs.'

Out here his aura of inscrutability and irascibility dissipates in their company. Beneath the bonhomie, however, he demands value for DAFA's financial commitments. This is no indulgent game-show host, liberally bestowing largesse to the deserving poor of the developing world. 'There's no free hand-outs,' he explains. 'Because people don't appreciate it if they get something for nothing. If we give money for a building, the locals all have to muck in.'

On a tour of 11 projects, including schools, an orphanage, medical facilities, a hospice (we even find ourselves at one stage within Kamfinsa State Prison, Zambia's largest such institution, with 2,000 inmates existing 30–40 to a cell, where it is agreed that DAFA will consider funding books and computers), Curley expresses his faith in more than 30 priests, Dominican nuns and volunteers involved in DAFA projects.

Fr PJ (Patrick James) Gormley epitomises these men and women. As we approach his parish off the main Ndola–Kitwe road, there is a banner advertising the services of 'Doctor Top Miracle Chibwanga' – a character best described as a witch doctor. It suggests that the area we are to visit would be some way from providing state-of-the-art health and educational facilities.

This is Mulenga, a dusty compound where cheap Chibuku beer known as 'shake shake' and HIV are a toxic combination. 'When I first arrived here, I asked the local leaders about the reputation of the place,' says PJ, in whose parish we stand. '"The cheapest beer and the cheapest women," I was told.' Both were magnets to miners from the local copper mine on payday.

Such issues were what the redoubtable priest encountered when he first arrived to a hostile reception two years ago. 'Initially I was abused and insulted, but now I'm accepted,' he says. Testimony to his energy and resourcefulness is the pre-school building, under construction with the help of a £31,000 contribution from DAFA, which PJ is overseeing. It is designed for three- to six-year-olds, who will be taught the basics of language and maths. Legally, children only receive education from seven onwards.

Hopefully, it will help reduce the numbers who end up as street children in the centre of the city (Kitwe), engaged in begging and prostitution.

The treatment of HIV has improved vastly since Curley's first involvement. Antiretroviral drug treatment is not a cure but it does prolong life. However, myths still abound. When we visit St Agnes Clinic outside Lusaka, we are told that one such belief among some men is that having sex with a virgin is a cure for HIV, with attendant horror stories of incest.

The clinic asks for €12,000 for equipment and accommodation for nurses. Curley nods his approval. 'You've an 80–20 chance.' He elaborates. 'That's 1–4 in a two-horse race.'

Our visit is injected with sadness. We are here only days after the sudden death of Fr Eugene O'Reilly, who Curley had first encountered when both were schoolboys at Macartan's College in Monaghan Town and whose work here first inspired Curley to form DAFA in 1996. 'It'll be up to the Zambians now to carry the torch,' Curley says as we visit Fr Eugene's grave. 'But I don't worry about that. There's some great men among them.'

They include Fr Gustav Mukosha Chisenga, who proudly shows us around the centre he has developed in his parish of Mufulira, with £15,000 invested by DAFA. He is now seeking a similar sum to fund agricultural courses for 50 local women with families.

'People will do more for them [local Zambian priests],' says Curley. 'We gave them £20,000 but there's far more than £20,000-worth of buildings here. That's the way I hope the thing will progress. The aim is to leave things in good hands. It's what gives me peace of mind – and that means far more than a big touch ever can.

There was one slightly worrying episode out there, for me. While staying at a priest's home in Zambia I was bitten by a security dog (don't ask . . . it's a long story). With rabies not unknown in this country, a doctor was summoned. Curley laughingly reassured me, readily offering 1,000–1 against me surviving. I said that not only was that decidedly poor value, but when precisely would he pay out? When I started foaming at the mouth? Or when I was in the mortuary?

'Oh, your widow will thank me,' he said thoughtfully, before generously raising the odds to 10,000–1.

Top jockeys Johnny Murtagh, Jamie Spencer, Tom Queally are among those who have been out here before with Curley. You can appreciate why they were so moved by the experience.

'They heard me talking about it and how satisfying it was, the greatest experience of my life, and volunteered,' the Irishman explains. 'They had plenty of experience in racing, but this tops it all.' He adds: 'One of the reasons I've liked them to go out there is that it gave them an understanding of life. That it's not all about fast cars and helicopters. They could appreciate what they've got. It's a great experience being out there. It's a privilege.'

The first volunteer was Johnny Murtagh, the Classic-winning Flat jockey and now also trainer, in 2001. 'He just said, "I'll go." It didn't surprise me. I always loved and admired Johnny, for his ability. He's a great jockey, and I have a huge regard for him. But he's also great fun. We laughed our way round Zambia.'

In December 2008, Tom Queally told Curley, his long-time mentor, that he was going to be riding as stable jockey for the acclaimed trainer Henry Cecil. Curley suggested that the young rider accompany him on one of his trips to Africa.

'This year is a big year for you,' he told Queally. 'It'll do you good to come to Zambia. Some day when you're stuck in traffic, on the way home from Sandown after getting beaten on two favourites, or maybe you'll be doing light [weight] the following day and you'll be feeling a bit sorry for yourself, you need to be able to appreciate how good things are for you, you need to be able to put things in perspective.'

Queally spent 10 days in Zambia. He observed later: 'I think I dealt with it fairly well – apart from the orphanages. The orphanages got to me. It wasn't so much the little kids, you can humour them, you can make them laugh, but go further down the corridor and you get to the handicapped children. There's nothing you can do. They don't know who you are; they don't know who they are themselves. Nobody wants them.

'One thing I noticed out there, though. You ask anyone how they are, and they say, "Great." Everyone is great, everyone is smiling. Some of the kids walk 10 miles to school, there are 1,500 kids going to the school that

Barney set up. There's hope there. It was good to go there, makes you think about things.'

Jamie Spencer, who visited Zambia in August 2006, was another rider in whose burgeoning early career Curley had taken a keen interest.

Spencer had started out as a jump jockey. He rode a hurdle winner for Curley as a conditional rider on Magic Combination at Ascot in February 1999. Four months later, the same partnership was part of Curley's assault on the Galway Festival. It was something of a retrieval mission. In the early eighties, he had lost £100,000 on I'm A Driver and other horses.

His son Charlie used to ask him: 'Did you really lose that? How much would that be worth today?' Curley retorted: 'Never you mind. Some day we'll go over and get it back.' Until he did so, 'It was like walking around with a stone in my shoe.' Curley did as he'd promised in 1999 – alone. By then, his son had died.

Magic Combination barely knew he had been in a race as Spencer steered him home in a Flat handicap, disdainfully looking around for dangers. Mystic Ridge, owned by Patsy Byrne, also won under Spencer, and Curley came away with well over £200,000 in total. It should have been more. The trainer-gambler complained bitterly that, with the horse available at 9–4, his bet of IR£20,000 to win IR£45,000 was refused by Graham's (the firm started by his old friend Sean). His representative was told he could have IR£1,000 at SP, and the price was immediately slashed to 7–4. Curley took umbrage and said he would not be back betting or running horses in Ireland until the situation changed.

Those performances in the saddle confirmed that he was right to advise Spencer to stick to the Flat. 'There was more money in it and it was less dangerous,' says Curley. 'I also told him he'd have a better chance in England. He had natural talent and I gave him all the help I could. In the late nineties, I said that he was a champion jockey in the making. It worked out well for him. He climbed the ladder very quickly.'

Curley said that Spencer was probably the best jockey he'd seen since Frankie Dettori started. Already Irish champion jockey, he became the British equivalent in 2005 and 2007, when he shared the honour with Seb Sanders. Other protégés, and those who have benefited from Curley's advice, abound. They include flat jockey Shane Kelly and jump counterparts Paul Moloney and Denis O'Regan.

Since the day Barney Curley sat down and founded DAFA, it has altered his psyche; certainly his relationship with racing has become tenuous at times. In the winter of 2007, declaring that he wanted to commit even more of his time to his charity, he even relinquished his training licence and handed over the training operation to his long-time assistant, Andrew Stringer. For over a year the yard's horses ran in Stringer's name.

That was because DAFA had received a major boost. Sheikh Mohammed had decided that following the sale by Trinity Mirror of the *Racing Post*, whose licence he owned, four charities should receive £10m between them. One of these was Curley's. He felt a heavy obligation to utilise the donation wisely: 'I'd had to organise a lot concerning the charity. It's quite tricky. We have a committee and have to make difficult decisions. Everyone's starving out there, and you have to be very careful who you give the money to.'

In February 2009, Curley took charge at the yard again. 'There had been snide remarks about Andrew Stringer and me and how I was still calling the shots,' he recalls. 'It was disrespectful to him, though he's well capable of running the show. So I came back again.'

Meanwhile, the winners had continued to flow. While the rest of the world was more intent on following the Grand National in 2007 – won by Silver Birch – Curley landed a gamble on his Le Soleil at Newcastle and won more than £100,000. Overall that horse won him over £250,000. Enormous winnings to most of us, but those figures have to be placed in context.

'I worked on turning a profit over a year,' he explains. 'I just had in my head how much it would cost to run and buy horses – say, two, three or four – and I knew I had to get that back. I had a very simple way of looking at it. Let's say my costs at the start of the year would have been £400,000 in total. I had to get that back. At least. I always had that in my mind.

'I was pretty bright at having a bet. I knew what horses to bet, and I made money every year. I had to, because I had no other means of income – unless I sold a horse to offset some of that, I would have gone skint. Nobody's owed a penny by me, and I've been here around 30 years. Not that I got a fortune. I just made sure I could live, and get a few extra pounds. I was never that much interested in hoarding of money.'

In later years he cut back significantly on numbers. He could handle 10, 12 horses and their expenses. But if you were in to 25, expenses were big and it was harder to make it pay. At one time he'd had 40 to 50 horses, and the overheads were enormous.

It all explains why his stakes had to be eyewateringly large. 'Getting £50,000 on was easy; to get £100,000 on you were struggling. But if you had £50,000 on a 4–1 and it turned up, that was £200,000 – you had covered half your outlay for the year. That was how I operated.'

Nevertheless, towards the end of the decade, Curley's world had gone quiet. The suspicion was that he had finally been drained of his initiative and drive, and desire for a challenge. Maybe, approaching 70, he was accepting the limitations of his years, concentrating on his charity work and just stabling a few horses and punting on occasions.

In fact, the decelerator had been of necessity applied to his foot-down approach to life. Serious illness had intervened. It was not the first time he had come perilously close to a greeting handshake from his Maker. He had already used up one life when he survived TB as a young man. And, in 1992, he had used up another.

He had been to a York afternoon meeting with Michael Roberts – chasing the jockeys' championship at the time – and Jimmy Quinn, and was travelling back by light plane via Chester, where both had evening rides at the Roodeye. Curley was a reluctant passenger. He didn't really want to go to Chester.

The pilot, Neil Foreman, attempted to take off from a farmer's field. The aircraft struck a bump, and though it climbed into the air, it did not have sufficient power. They just about cleared two large trees before the pilot was forced to put the plane down. He cut the power and the aircraft careered through a hedge and finally came to rest in a stretch of deep, dirty water.

Fearing that the plane could explode, they all baled out.

Quinn shouted that he couldn't swim and 'I'm going to drown!' He clambered on Curley's back, and they made their way to safety. 'I'm no hero,' said Curley, who added: 'All that passed through my mind was "How unlucky can you be?" I didn't even want to be here, and I'd lost £20,000 on the day – what a way to go out.'

The quartet were taken to hospital, but got away with bruises and cuts. They were to be detained for observation overnight, but Curley wouldn't have it. Around midnight, he called a cab and offered the driver £150 to take the group home to Newmarket. They crept out of a side entrance and climbed aboard.

As the taxi negotiated the side streets of Chester, they spied a still-open kebab shop. It was well past Curley's dining hour, and he was starving. The other customers looked on open-mouthed as these four unlikely characters – the two diminutive jockeys, Quinn and Roberts, towered over by Curley and the pilot Neil Foreman, and all clad in white operating-style hospital gowns – entered the shop. 'They obviously thought we'd broken out of the local asylum,' said Curley. 'But at least it got us to the front of the queue quickly!'

There was an amusing postscript. Curley owed one bookmaker, Pat Whelan, £13,000 from that night. Whelan sent him a note addressed to 'Barney Curley (nearly Barney Rubble)': 'The next time you owe me, will you please travel by car!'

His latest brush, though, was a rather more protracted matter. He had been suffering from sweats and fatigue for months, and had been particularly poorly on a visit to

Zambia with Tom Queally in September 2008.

He turned out to be suffering from a rare and near-fatal virus; according to Michael Gaunt, consultant vascular surgeon at Addenbrooke's Hospital, it was almost certainly the first case in the world. Gaunt's colleague, Professor Andrew Lever, a specialist in infectious diseases, discovered that Curley had contracted the human version of *Streptococcus equi*, which causes a disease called strangles in horses. It sounds nasty, and it is.

The infection was congregating around a lower abdominal stent, which had been inserted to repair an aneurysm several years ago. Removing these stents has a high mortality rate, but he came through it.

Though Curley has often said he has no fears about meeting the Boss, it's rather different when you have an appointment pencilled in. 'I thought it was curtains and I'd never be coming back,' he admits. 'Going to the operating theatre, I thought, "If the Man Above's thinking properly, I don't think he'll let me go this time. I have these kids in Zambia and I have quite a bit to do there yet."

'If I didn't make it, I had instructed Maureen to sell all the horses – nobody could run this business except me. It takes a lot of money to run this yard and make it pay.'

Through faith and medical expertise, he pulled through.

'When I got the cure, it was like God had won the pools. After the op, I did look bad, but I had been on the table for ten hours. I have those surgeons to thank. They did a wonderful job.'

It was just as well. He would require a strong constitution for what he had in mind. It was 2009, and he was planning the most ambitious scheme of them all.

CHAPTER 22

Thirty years on from his Yellow Sam coup, which caused Ireland's bookmakers to flutter like startled hens in the path of a farmyard tractor, Barney Curley and trainer Liam Brennan were invited back to Bellewstown by the racecourse committee to commemorate an intriguing part of racing history.

It was a moment purely for nostalgia and reminiscence. No one imagined that such a scheme could be repeated in today's technologically more sophisticated environment. Certainly not JP McManus, who was an on-course bookmaker at Limerick's greyhound track, the Market's Field, before becoming a racehorse owner and punter. He is also a long-time associate of Curley's, who tells the story, against himself, of the evening after a race meeting at Killarney when he went back to the Gresham Hotel in Dublin with JP and a heavyweight gang of poker players. They included bookmakers Terry Rogers and Teddy Rice; Flavio Forte, who owned cafés in Dublin; and Curley's solicitor in the Republic, Tim O'Toole.

They played poker all night, through till six. Curley lost £100,000. He conceded: 'I should have stayed clear. It was not my game.' Afterwards he went to a nearby church, where one of several promises he made to the priest was that he would never play poker again . . .

McManus was one of several who declared when Betfair spearheaded the coming of online betting exchanges at the turn of the millennium – arguably the most significant gambling development since the advent of legal betting shops in 1961 – that the new form of gambling wasn't for Curley. He was correct, in a sense. The technology revolution had roared past and seemingly left Curley's gambling aspirations for dead.

And there was another consideration. Noel Furlong – 'Big Noel', one of the major players in the Irish betting ring, who had been involved in dog racing in Dublin until horses seized his imagination and he won £1m on his horse, The Illiad, in the 1991 Ladbroke Handicap Hurdle at Leopardstown – offered a sharp piece of advice: 'You may only get one chance of catching the bookies for the kind of gamble from which they will not easily recover.'

Furlong spoke from experience.

HE CLAIMS TO have collected £2m when his Destriero got home by four lengths from the future Champion Hurdler Granville Again in the Supreme Novices' Hurdle at the same year's Cheltenham Festival.

Furlong had doubled Destriero with The Illiad, his runner in the Champion Hurdle, and was 'going for the jugular and the kill'. The Illiad made a bad mistake and never recovered, finishing 21st of 24 runners. Furlong would have won at least £4m.

The belief amongst many of Curley's peers was that his sole kill had come in 1975. He had other ideas. Even then, on that visit to Bellewstown in 2005, he was contemplating a bold sequel.

He was certain that, despite all the advances, the book-makers' armour had a weakness. He had long believed that, with the right strategy, he could penetrate their defences – though it would require a significant feat of training on his part and a meticulously planned betting operation.

Since Yellow Sam had saved his financial skin in 1975, gambling had witnessed the advent of the internet. Betting firms had become increasingly automated. Their odds now were based on statistics, and caution was embedded in their framework. As the *Racing Post*'s Steve Palmer once put it: 'Daredevil layers are pretty much a thing of the past and contemporary bookmaking is just about spreadsheets, accountants, fixed profit-targets and ultra-conservative risk-management. Stake restrictions and account closures are commonplace for even relatively modest winners and many punters are now getting turned away if they show the slightest hint of a threat to a company's prosperity.'

There are exceptions, as Gary Wiltshire will attest. He was the bookmaker that day at Ascot in September 1996 when Frankie Dettori secured his seven deadly wins – at least where Wiltshire was concerned. His judgement was that Fujiyama Crest, the Italian's seventh mount of the afternoon – with the first six having won – had no chance and he fearlessly laid other bookmakers, who were desperately attempting to lessen their own liabilities. He was left owing £1m, but went on a retrieval mission and recovered it all.

But in general, the battle no longer involved the flashing blades of duelling swords. It had become an increasingly one-sided contest of punter against automation and the massed ranks of technologically agile betting traders.

Paddy Power, the human face of Ireland's eponymous bookmaking chain – a company started by his great-grandfather Richard in the 1890s – placed the changes in perspective in the *Sunday Times* magazine when he said: 'Gone are the days of the bookie with a pencil behind his ear. We employ mostly IT and maths graduates, so lots of very young whizz kids looking at computers all day. In one department, we've got the "quants", the quantitative analysis team. They do things like study tens of thousands of football matches to predict future results.'

A Paddy Power recruitment ad for a horse-racing risk manager demonstrates the type of recruits bookmakers seek today: 'preferably a graduate with third-level qualification in mathematics/statistics or business'. The successful candidate will be expected to 'manage customer stake factors and identify unprofitable business and customers for the warm punters' portfolio', 'refer any accounts to senior managers thought to warrant closer attention' and 'hedge excess liabilities in accordance with limits set by the group's Board Risk Committee – singles and running on multiple bets'. Caution is the overriding feature.

It was the security of such Fort Knox-like institutions that any serious backer now had to penetrate. This leads to the inevitable question: just what, over three decades on from Yellow Sam, possessed Curley to focus his mind against the algorithms and mathematical and trading geniuses of today's gambling businesses worth over £10bn between them?

The overwhelming, almost obsessive desire for a new challenge had never receded. Curley has a nose for them. He seeks them out like a pig hunts for truffles. Though his life had altered significantly since that move to Newmarket a quarter of a century before, his fertile brain and imagination were rarely in a state of hibernation, and the concept of a coup designed for the twenty-first century niggled away at him. He needed the 'buzz', as he calls it. Challenges are uranium in his mental reactor, and not just those associated with bloodstock. Indeed he seemingly takes a delight in entering an alien arena.

There aren't too many individuals who would consider running a nightclub, and having to deal with the associated drug issues, which he did after that attempt to organise a trainers' strike was aborted in 1992. It was one of a number of alternative business ventures he contemplated around that time. 'Irish gambler eyes Mecca's casinos' was a *Sunday Times* headline in 1992. Mecca wanted to sell four London casinos: Maxim's, the Connoisseur, the Victoria and the Gloucestershire. They hoped for £90m, though it was thought that a figure of around £60m was likely to succeed.

Curley had raised the money through two financial institutions, one British and one American. His backers insisted he had to be seen around the casinos as a gambling 'face', though he had never considered himself a man to press flesh. Eventually, however, the casinos were sold to another bidder.

The Mirage nightclub in Windsor was in receivership – the third time in 18 months – and Curley paid £1.2m for it. It was originally called Blazers, and in its heyday had been a major nightclub, featuring such stars as Shirley Bassey. But the acts, he claimed, had got greedy. Agents for leading comedians were allegedly demanding more than £12,000 a night. It all took Curley back to his days in Ireland managing showbands. He put an end to the cabarets and instead turned the club into a disco.

By then having attained middle age, it wasn't exactly his scene. Neither were certain elements of his clientele 'the nice young people' he had thought the club would attract. He swiftly realised that the place was a magnet for drug-taking and selling, mostly of Ecstasy. Curley was from an era where the curse was predominantly alcohol, and he knew as much about drugs as he did about contemporary popular music – nothing. To educate himself, he attended meetings of Narcotics Anonymous in London.

The dealers were brazen. Curley was even offered a bribe of £2,000 cash a week to turn a blind eye. He made it clear that he was totally opposed to drugs and was determined to eradicate the problem. When he and his manager ejected culprits, there were threats aplenty.

His concern was justified when, within five months of each other, two youngsters collapsed in the club. One died in hospital; the other was dead before they got him there. 'Both were very upsetting and frightening episodes.'

Curley visited the parents of the first boy. They did not blame him. It was established at the inquests that both youngsters had died of drugs taken before they came to the club. Nevertheless, the local MP called for the place to be closed down – a stance that infuriated Curley, given the efforts he had made to forestall the drug dealers.

He introduced thorough searches, CCTV, and a

photo-membership policy. In addition, two paramedics were on duty all night. He worked closely with the drugs squad and even paid undercover observers to detect dealers. There were no second chances for anyone caught. They were handed straight over to the police.

A couple of years earlier, Curley had put £250,000 into starting his own betting business, Curley Credit. Maureen was the licensee. He proudly posed outside his home with his Mercedes, complete with personalised number plate: 1 BET. Just as had occurred when he owned betting shops in Northern Ireland, however, he discovered that he was not destined to be a bookie. The venture was not a success and he returned to punting, primarily backing his own horses. At times, it was a dire necessity. In the early nineties he fell into a financial hole because of non-racing liabilities, and had to work diligently for days and evenings on end to extract himself from the deep red.

Everything he owed, he paid back from his winnings. 'I didn't have that many horses, but the ones I had I used well. I had to with that magnitude of debt.' He once admitted ruefully: 'I've had to keep punting, you see, because I have never been involved in a business venture in which I didn't lose me tonsils.'

That could well have been the case, too, had he been successful in heading a syndicate bidding to take over Sunderland Football Club in 2006. He has always maintained an interest in football, ever since those days in Manchester watching United's magnificent team. He believed that Sunderland's supporters deserved better than what was on offer. But negotiations broke down and he walked away. Followers of the Black Cats will have their own views on whether he would have done better than the current custodian . . .

Opportunities come along, and he lets them pass, or grasps them with total conviction, regardless of advice proffered by friends and associates.

The scheme that would be enacted in May 2010 was in part a response to those who warned, 'It's not for you, Barney' – just as he had responded to Tommy Stack's declaration after the Robin Goodfellow affair and sent out those ten winners. It was a typically uncompromising retort to his friends in racing who had suggested that his gambling prowess was on the wane. 'The word on the street is that you've lost your touch,' Frankie Dettori had mischievously mocked him.

Curley had eyed him with a stern look and replied mysteriously: 'I'm going to earn more in one day than you earn in a year.'

'Dream on,' retorted the former champion jockey.

In truth, Dettori had long been aware that Curley was a pragmatist, not a dreamer. He had spent a lifetime defying logic and spurning perceived wisdom. Chiding from friends and prodigies didn't rile him, but it did provoke him into action. In this case, he was primarily spurred on by the prospect of launching one last major advance on the bookmakers and becoming a part of racing history.

'People were telling me that our day had gone,' he recalls. 'Punters I knew over the years said, "It's finished. It's over." I never thought like that. Bookmakers are always trying something new, to rob punters, to get them to bite. But that's what beats them in the end: the greed.'

The layers would assert, of course that no one is forced to bet on horses, greyhounds or football, or feed cash into a one-armed bandit. If they were guilty of anything, it

was possibly complacency. It was more that weakness that
Curley was determined to exploit. 'I wanted to prove that
it could be done,' he explained. 'People said a Yellow
Sam would never happen again, but I was convinced that
an updated version could succeed. It had always been on
my mind, and when we entered the new millennium, I
said to myself, "I'm going to do something as big as
anything anyone will attempt this century."'

While 'Yellow Sam' had been orchestrated out of sheer
necessity, this time Curley was driven purely by the desire
to outmanoeuvre the old foe. Profit was a supplementary
aim. There was no desperate requirement for funds. He
has long argued that you can't take antiques and oil
paintings into the afterlife. He has no desire to accumulate wealth for its own sake, or acquire powerful cars or
yachts. He claims to have never had £1m or more in the
bank.

Yes, he has lived in some decent gaffs – Middleton
Park and Terry Ramsden's property at Stetchworth, White
House Stables, bought at 'a reasonable price' before it
went to auction, were scarcely two-up, two-downs. Yet
you'd no more associate an ostentatious lifestyle with
Curley than suggest that the Eurovision Song Contest is
a celebration of highbrow music.

Pull into the driveway of his Newmarket home, and
you'll park adjacent to an ageing VW that he uses to
drive his St Bernard, Arnie, around in. 'I've got a T-reg
Merc, which I never use, which I'm sending out to Africa,
and I used to have a V-reg horse box,' he says.

Back in 1975, Curley had engineered the Yellow Sam
scheme alone from his Wicklow base, delegating to a
team of putters-on and ultimately involving many troops
on the ground. But the era of online betting accounts

and mobile phones had altered the whole landscape. He required an accomplice; someone with the skills to organise a twenty-first century project; a man who had a comprehensive knowledge of betting.

It occurred to him that there was an obvious contender.

CHAPTER 23

At the back of a lecture hall at Royal Holloway College, University of London, an economics undergraduate sat and scribbled notes. The new millennium had just been beckoned in, offering so much promise for many of Martin Parsons' fellow students. He, however, had rather more radical ideas.

The lecturer would not have been at all enamoured had he been aware of the subject of Parsons' jottings. Some complex calculations were involved, but not closely related to the subject being taught. They involved horses, odds and potential gambles.

Parsons recalls, 'The earliest notes I remember making on the kind of scheme we organised were at the back of my university lectures in 2000. I hardly did any work. I made more notes on horses than I did on economics. I was daydreaming. A few of the lecturers would have liked to kick me off for poor attendance. But I scraped through, and got my degree.'

Parsons, who tends to opt for the casual look, put his first student loan cheque to good use. 'As soon as it cleared, I went and spent most of it on a tailored suit from Bond Street – and started following the horses properly,' he recalls.

While some of his peers might possibly have been more preoccupied with drink, drugs and sexual liaisons, odds were this student's principal vice. 'I was signing in, then jumping out of the window and running down to the William Hill shop every day.' He pauses and concedes: 'If it'd been my son and I'd known about it, I'd have kicked his arse.'

Yet the time he spent in the company of fellow clients at betting shops in Egham, Surrey, where Royal Holloway is based, and in Staines and central London during his three years as a student was essentially a research project. 'Most of the time I just watched the racing. I very rarely placed a bet. Some of the regulars in the shops used to have a laugh about that. Every now and again I might write out a betting slip asking for a tea with one sugar as a bit of a joke.'

It was to prove a valuable grounding. 'I learnt a lot about how different trainers campaigned their horses as their charges' careers unfolded; the type of bloodstock they filled their yards with and what they did well with, like precocious two-year-olds or slower-to-develop staying types. I soon cottoned on that far too many punters base their form study on purely visual aspects of racing, with little regard to race times and how races are run to suit certain types of hold-up or pace-setting horses and their jockeys.

'A fast finisher who just fails to get up on the line is invariably classed as "unlucky", and yet very few would dare to suggest that maybe getting beaten by a short head is as good a result as that runner might ever achieve in that race, in those circumstances, no matter how the race is run.

'I studied jockeys' riding styles and levels of ability. I

learnt what a well-handicapped runner looks like when winning his first race before then running up a sequence of good form. I think I quickly got a good eye for reading races and gained great faith in my own judgement; others' opinions were irrelevant to me.'

Elements of racing can be abstruse for the uninitiated, but Parsons explains: 'The reason why racing is rapidly losing betting turnover compared to other sports like football, especially from younger people, is the very reason it fully engaged me at that time. I loved the endless amounts of information to study – it filled my time at a point where I had made the choice to have plenty free.'

He adds: 'There wasn't enough work to do in a day to keep me interested at university. I was never going to get motivated. I am an "all or nothing" man and I've always believed you do something properly and the best you possibly can or you shouldn't do it at all. Incompetence frustrates me. I think there is a lot to be said for finding what you are good at, what you enjoy, and specialising in it. I thought about dropping out or transferring but decided to see it out. I found I was able to do the bare minimum *and* give racing a hundred per cent at the same time.'

He secured a 2:1. On graduation day, instead of celebrating with fellow students, he went racing at Newmarket.

While some of his fellow students might have headed for the City, for employment within the Square Mile, Parsons had one ambition in mind: to work for the country's best-known gambler. He had not even been born when the Bellewstown coup was orchestrated, but he had studied Curley's autobiography, *Giving a Little Back*, as intently as a textbook and gleaned information about his methods from afar. Indeed, if there had been a degree

228

course in 'The Life, Times and Wisdom of Barney Curley', he would have graduated with honours under one of the most learned of tutors.

Parsons had learnt how Curley had amassed a vast knowledge of gambling from diverse sources. He had read about Curley's early experiences, and how he had witnessed how his father's gambling on greyhounds had culminated with the family landing in serious debt. He was aware of his training to become a Jesuit priest, his smuggling enterprises and the showbands he managed before owning betting shops in Enniskillen. And he knew the full details of Yellow Sam. He had read how all those experiences had provided the Irishman with a valuable education as a man of God, in the world of commerce, and on both sides of the betting business.

He explains: 'I had started following his runners religiously in the late nineties. I was in awe of him. For me, there was no greater sight than a jockey in the Curley colours looking round for dangers at the furlong pole. The war against the bookmakers will always be lost by the punters but it makes the occasional battle won all the more sweet.

'I remember writing to Barney after reading his book, and a couple of times after that as well. I can't remember what I said but I'm sure it was something along the lines of if he could think of anything I might be able to help him with to let me know.'

It wouldn't be the first such missive received by the Irishman; any applications to be his apprentice would probably have gone out with the recycling – not out of malice; simply because Curley had always been a lone operator.

Yet in time, the pair of kindred spirits were attracted

like magnetic forces: the older man who, though in his late sixties, still possessed an agile brain and the remarkable energy and imagination required to overcome the might of the major betting companies; and the younger one, earnest student of professional betting who had applied himself diligently to his subject.

Their conjunction was not a swift process. It can take years to earn Curley's trust and respect. Eventually, however, he realised that this young man was blessed not just with knowledge of gambling and racehorses but, crucially, also expertise in the technology of modern-day bookmaking.

Just as the experiences of Curley's father should have acted as a deterrent against the world of gambling, so Parsons, raised in a strict Christian household in which gambling was denounced as unacceptable, should have been deflected from that particular sin. Instead, it became an obsession, sparked initially by the father of a primary school friend who had greyhounds in his own kennels a few miles from the Parsons home.

'I remember being impressed by the fact that Frank invariably had a grand in his pocket, was always well dressed and drove a top-of-the-range BMW. He had always been in greyhounds and was a notorious gambler. Purely by coincidence, he had backed horses for Barney Curley in the eighties and nineties and had also backed horses for Michael Tabor [the former bookmaker, gambler and businessman, best known for being part of the Coolmore operation].

'My friend had no real interest in his father's dogs but I had always wanted my own pet dog from a very early age and was never allowed to have one. My friend was completely spoilt by his parents, so spending time with them was an indulgence.'

Parsons was only ten when he started attending the local greyhound track with his friend's family. 'My parents were never comfortable with this, but it was tolerated as long as I followed strict instructions not to participate in any gambling.'

The greyhounds weren't just destined for the track. Most were home-bred for coursing. Parsons attended his first coursing meeting in his early teens, and admits: 'I was hooked for life.' He adds: 'The annual pilgrimage to Southport in February for the Waterloo Cup soon became the highlight of the year. These were my first real experiences with punting. It was all about knowing something the bookmakers didn't and trying to exploit that advantage.'

He enjoyed observing the punters around him – spotting their strengths, but mostly their mistakes. 'People who don't understand gambling think there's people out there who never lose.' He learnt very quickly the folly of that perception. 'I realised that anyone taking on the bookmakers and playing them on a level playing field in terms of information couldn't hope to make a profit over the long term. Any wins would just provide temporary respite from the general trend. Overall the profit would be similar to the 78 per cent payout of the fruit machines. The books always had the margin working for them.'

He recognised that patience and self-control was everything, keeping the baseball adage to the forefront of his mind: 'Wait for the good pitches. It's not how you swing but what you don't swing at that matters.'

Greyhounds provided an excellent grounding, but he knew that horses offered more opportunities. 'I started to watch racing knowing absolutely nothing about it other than what I knew about bookmaking,' he says. 'I realised that while I had an edge over the bookmakers with my four or five bets a year on the dogs, the horses were going to be a different matter altogether.

'I have always believed that if you can't price a race up yourself, as a bookmaker does, you shouldn't be having a bet on that race under any circumstances. A punter has a bet because they think a price is too big, but ask them what price the selection should be, in their opinion, and what price this makes the alternative selections, and you very rarely get an intelligent answer.'

There are definite echoes of advice proffered to Curley in his younger years, as Parsons recalls: 'I remember my school friend's parents being concerned that I was starting to take an interest in the horses. They sat me down and told me categorically that it was not possible for me to win backing them; that it could only go one way. But I hate being told I can't do something.'

He adds: 'Barney was first described to me as someone who owned and trained horses purely so he could back them. I remember thinking, "Why else would you own and train horses?"

'Frank called Barney at some point after I graduated to ask if we could visit him so that he could meet me. We went to the yard. I told Barney I thought I'd be a good racing manager for someone. He said he would "have a think".'

At that time, Parsons was working for an IT company at home, installing and managing tailored network systems. 'I started with the intention of doing six months' work, but this turned into a few years.' In that period, he had been turned down for a job with a racing publication as a form analyst.

Then, in 2005, he fell asleep driving his car not two miles from his home in East Anglia. 'I leaned on the accelerator and flipped the car over a dyke into a field,' he recalls. 'The car was unrecognisable and the ambulancemen were certain I was dead when they saw it. I was helped out of the window with just a sore shoulder where the seat belt had held me in. The seat had gone flat back with the roof caved in on top of me.'

He adds: 'I sat in the ambulance on the way to hospital thinking how my life wasn't really heading where I had hoped and that it could have just ended so easily. I kept thinking of the line from the film *The Shawshank Redemption*, "Get busy living or get busy dying." I decided to make a list, which could have been titled: "If you could do anything . . ." I wanted to pursue each entry on the list until it was exhausted before moving on to the next.'

Number one was B. J. Curley.

'I never got to number two, and I'm not sure what it would have been. I remember the late Eugene O'Reilly, Barney's great friend from school who went on to spend his life in Zambia, describing the car crash as a Damascene experience for me.'

The following week, when his shoulder permitted, Parsons wrote to Curley again. He concedes it wasn't the most enticing proposition or CV. 'I tried to put myself in Barney's position,' he recalls self-deprecatingly. 'Here was a young guy with a background of gambling who kept pestering him. I could talk, and write, for ever, but it was only by being given chances that I could prove I was capable and could be trusted. After a letter that I remember contained just about everything I had left to say, I called him and then met him at his house.

'He kept asking what I thought I could do for him. In

233

truth, I didn't know enough about what he did on a daily basis to answer that question. I just wanted to be useful. I would have mucked out and done yard work on the ground if he had wanted me to.

'I had the greatest respect for how Barney operated and felt I would be achieving something if I could assist him in any way. I still would do anything he asked of me without question.'

As has been stressed before, Curley has never required an aide, other than a trainer to organise his horses. Initially he attempted to find Parsons employment else-where, including as a jockey's agent and also on the Darley Flying Start programme (a two-year full-time management training programme for the thoroughbred industry), but without success.

Curley has many contacts in Newmarket and has often been approached by would-be young jockeys and work riders. Such is his reputation for taking emerging riders under his wing that he has often received knocks on the door from young wannabes, many from Ireland, and their fathers. 'It's like the Irish embassy here at times,' he once told me.

But this was a little out of the ordinary. Curley remem-bers: 'He wrote to me three or four times. He said he'd do anything. I usually throw those letters in the bin because I don't have any jobs. I was a one-man show, didn't want assistants. Eventually I thought, "I have to see this fellow." I thought he must have something.'

Finally, in 2006, he took him on. In his inimical way, Curley describes Parsons as 'the stone the builders rejected [who] became the cornerstone of the temple'.

Parsons recalls: 'He told me if I played ball he would treat me like a brother and that was the truth. I will always be grateful he did give me a chance.'

Not that Maureen Curley was enamoured by this development. Parsons says: 'Maureen likes to know who's in the house. She's got a genuine interest in young people. When you call in, she invariably likes to have a chat with you. She asked me at the beginning: "So, what are you really interested in, Martin?" Then Barney cut in and said abruptly: "Maureen, he's interested in horses and greyhounds . . ."

'She just said, "Oh, dear . . ." The words hung in the air but betrayed her disappointment. And that was the end of that conversation. She just thought it was a wasted life.'

Not so Curley. He recognised a man who could be trusted. He was also acquiring an assistant whose primary interests in life were racehorse form and betting systems – a background that would be invaluable in the coming years as a major scheme was devised.

CHAPTER 24

There was no eureka moment. It was a concept that slowly evolved; one that smouldered in Curley's brain like a damp Roman candle touchpaper before bursting into life.

It probably wouldn't have come about without the chemistry between Curley and his first lieutenant Parsons, and the latter's exhaustive research. 'The idea was a natural progression – from my ideas and Barney's experience,' says Parsons. 'We would talk about it frequently.'

The gambler-trainer's new colleague hailed from a very different background, but rather like Curley, he possessed an air of quiet confidence and contentment. Now in his early thirties, Parsons could still readily pass for a student who'd just got up in time to watch *Countdown*. He is somewhat introverted, but wields a quiet authority. When he speaks, people listen. He has a dry humour and smiles knowingly at life's little idiosyncrasies.

But crucially, where this project was concerned, he was obsessed with prices. You can imagine that if life had taken a different turn, he would have been a dynamic trader in a betting firm (Parsons disagrees vehemently, incidentally, saying it would be like sleeping with the enemy).

Now he would be in direct opposition with the bookies.

In the three years leading up to 10 May 2010, Martin Parsons became a man possessed. He would get up and sit at his desk, with just coffee for company, waiting for 9 a.m. when he could scrutinise the betting markets. He was like a gamer mesmerised by the latest edition of Grand Theft Auto, except this was no violent fantasy.

His groundwork only confirmed what he had suspected about the volatility of single bets – and in particular how cautious the layers were about Curley's runners. The off-course bookmakers had long ago refused to do business with him directly; serious winners are not desirable customers.

Of course, there are the one-off spectaculars – generally the consequence of pure good fortune and something that can be converted into advantageous PR. Steve Whiteley, a north Devon heating engineer, won £1.45m on the Tote jackpot after placing an original bet of just £2 at Exeter racecourse. Mr Whiteley was 'not a horse-racing man' and only went once or twice a year. He selected the final horse of his six-race rollover jackpot bet – Lupita, who won at odds of 12–1 – because the surname of the winning rider, Jessica Lodge, appealed to him.

Curley presented a persistent, more serious threat to profits. When the letters arrived, they were polite and formal – and in a sense, a backhanded compliment. William Hill acted on 7 July 1988, after Curley had taken £200,000 off them in two years. Their letter stated that credit clients' accounts were reviewed regularly, 'to ascertain whether it is economic for the Company to maintain them . . . I am obliged to tell you that your account comes into a category by virtue of which we are unable to continue to offer you credit betting facilities . . .

Therefore your account will be closed.' They described it as 'a commercial decision'. The following day, a *Daily Mirror* headline read: 'Banned! Punter who beat the bookies.'

Even then, a quarter of a century ago, the betting environment was in a state of transformation. The late journalist and broadcaster Graham Rock responded in *The Times*: 'The commercial attitude of major book-makers is now governed by chartered accountants of public companies, interested only in earning the approval of shareholders; the nip and tuck of the duel which inspired the leviathans of the ring before the 1960s is regarded as obsolete, an unseemly impediment to profit-ability.'

Curley overcame this attempt to close down access to his betting in two ways. At one time, he bet 'underground', in a private network of gamblers. What else could he do, he asked rhetorically, with on-course bookmakers refusing to accept his size of bets, and off-course bookies not at all? 'Ladbrokes love the fiver, tenner or twenty from cannon fodder, but they don't like anything else. All they want to do is recycle hard-earned money and take their rake-off,' he once said.

The advent of Betfair, founded in 2000, improved matters by forcing the bookies to sharpen up their act. Such betting exchanges are not bookmakers that offer odds based on judgement and the weight of the market (although today you can take an SP with them if you prefer). Instead they match layers – those who 'want to be the bookmaker', as Betfair's original blurb stated – and backers. For the first time, the punter had the chance to legally 'lay' bets; in other words, to bet *against* something happening.

Curley still preferred to take on the bookies, and managed to continue to place bets with the major firms, utilising his team of putters-on to back horses for him. It was the only way to bypass a system designed to render gamblers like him impotent. Yellow Sam had taught him the value of having a close network of trustworthy friends and associates to bet on his behalf.

He had performed that task himself for one of the great Irish gamblers of the seventies, Crawford Scott – the father of the trainer Homer Scott. Scott was straight, but trusted no one; not his trainers, jockeys or anyone associated with him. He handed that approach down to Curley, who recalls, 'Crawford would go into the parade ring and talk to his trainer and jockey before deciding if his horse was "off" that day.

'If it was, he wanted the best prices before everyone else involved with the horse dived in and drove the price down. He'd have a prearranged signal. He'd say: "Young fella, watch me in the ring. If I bend down to tie up my shoelaces, have the money on," and I'd rush to place it for him. If there was no signal, I'd hang fire. It was never huge amounts; maybe £3,000 to £4,000.'

Curley's own putters-on have all been anonymous, for obvious reasons, save for a fellow named Peter Begley, whom Curley referred to as 'my man in Dundalk' (naming a horse after him). He placed bets for Curley for close on 30 years. 'It wasn't the money. He loved the mystique of it, the excitement of being involved in something covert and conspiratorial,' explains Curley. It was an attitude that would also be evident among the team who were involved as his latest plan came to fruition.

Curley had always needed to deal in five-, if possible six-figure sums to make his betting worthwhile. But even with his putters-on spreading the money around, the bookies had long been highly wary of single bets on the yard's horses. Understandably, they restricted stakes.

Then there was the volatility of prices. Parsons had experimented enough to appreciate the unstable nature of the price of a single bet on a Curley runner, and the generous prices available early. His theories about morning markets were tested with an experiment in February 2008, when Curley's The Bonus Ball, an unraced four-year-old made his racecourse debut at Southwell in a two-mile bumper.

The race was late afternoon, but several hours before the off, sufficient money had been staked at prices ranging from 16–1 to 10–1. Not surprisingly, the momentum this support created meant the price collapsed and the opening show of prices in the betting offices came in at 100–30. The Bonus Ball went off at 2–1 and accounted for the favourite, the Alan King-trained Awesome George.

The Bonus Ball was as good as his name on the day, and victory yielded a healthy return, but it was clear that singles, even with prices taken early, simply did not provide enough scope.

Parsons had been pondering an alternative strategy. 'I knew there were possibilities with multiples three or four years before I met Barney – having, say, three winners on the same day. I thought, "Can we exploit the bookmakers who put up these early prices? Can we put them in a corner so that they cannot easily lay off with each other or through the exchanges? Can we make them swallow the best part of a hit themselves?" I threw a fair bit of money away with some firms, having real multiple bets to test certain aspects – a sprat to catch a mackerel, if you like.'

He recalls that Curley was initially sceptical. The Irishman's doubts centred around the conundrum of organising sufficient winners at beneficial prices on the same day. Experimentation intensified. 'We looked at the differences in the markets of different types of race: handicaps, maidens, claimers and sellers.'

Meanwhile Curley began entering and running two and three horses on the same day in order to see precisely how bookmakers treated runners when coupled or placed in trebles, with relatively low stakes. The results gave the pair the confidence to continue.

'It's about spotting that loophole and going for it,' says Parsons. 'The value available for such minimal investment struck a chord with the way Barney operates. The way I saw it, he was not going to go on for ever and this was a great chance to have one last big swipe at the bookmakers and become a part of racing history.' A Yellow Sam Part II.

It should be emphasised that there was nothing novel about an attempted coup involving multiples. But crucially, this scheme would not be illegal or contrary to the rules of racing, unlike the Gay Future affair, which, though imaginative and audacious – inspiring documentaries and a film called *Murphy's Stroke*, starring Pierce Brosnan and Niall Tobin – was a scam and would end in court for the conspirators.

Gay Future, a chestnut blessed with some ability, was owned by millionaire Irish businessman Tony Murphy, who'd made his money from construction and drove a gold Rolls-Royce with wheelbarrows, cement bags and shovels poking from its permanently open boot. His associates were known as the Cork Mafia. The horse was secreted away in Tipperary, where he was trained by the leading trainer Edward O'Grady, who over a long career has enjoyed many Cheltenham Festival successes.

A remarkably similar-looking horse, though actually a distinctly inferior individual, named Arctic Chevalier but registered duplicitously as Gay Future, was placed with stockbroker and part-time trainer Tony Collins, based in Ayrshire. As far as punters and bookmakers were aware, this was the Gay Future that arrived to contest a hurdle race at Cartmel, a scenic Cumbrian course, on August Bank Holiday 1974. Any hope he had was further diminished because he was apparently due to be ridden by an unknown amateur jockey.

In reality, the team had quietly brought the real Gay Future across the water, and the jockey listed as 'Mr T. A. Jones' was in fact Tim Jones, the top amateur rider in Ireland.

Hundreds of small bets were placed on Gay Future with bookies in Cork and London, totalling more than £30,000. A crucial element of the plot was that the betting involved Gay Future being doubled with one of his two stablemates – Opera Cloak and Ankerwyke – who were due to run at other courses the same day. That presented no fears for the bookmakers, who readily accepted such bets, believing it was fools' money. Opera Cloak and Ankerwyke were subsequently pulled out of their races, so the doubles were transferred to single bets. All the money was now on Gay Future, who eventually started at 10–1.

In a situation that would have echoes the following year when Curley struck at Bellewstown, bookmakers at the remote track could only communicate with their head offices by the one public phone, and that was deliberately kept occupied by the plotters.

The deception was completed by soap flakes being rubbed into the horse's legs before the off, to give the impression he was sweating – usually a negative sign just before the start.

Gay Future prevailed by 15 lengths. Estimates of the 'win' vary from £100,000 to £300,000, but there was never a payout. Unusual betting patterns betrayed the plotters, and bookmakers refused to pay, pending an inquiry. It was also discovered that the two withdrawn horses, which were said to have been in horse boxes that broke down on their way to the courses, had never actually left the yard. The matter was considered so grave that Scotland Yard's Serious Crimes Squad was called in.

Collins and Murphy were convicted at Preston Crown Court of conspiracy to defraud the bookmakers and fined the minimum amount, £500. Justice Caulfield, it was said, was a racing enthusiast who suggested that any possible crime had been 'very minor'. He even praised Murphy as 'a true sportsman who must be admired for coming over to this country and facing the jury'. O'Grady was also arrested during the investigation but charges against him were dropped.

Murphy, who died suddenly eight years later, aged 52, declared: 'Our real crime was that the Paddies, as they like to call us, fooled them by proving too clever for their big bookmakers.'

At the time, there was a grudging admiration for Murphy and his cohorts, because of the vibrant, charismatic characters involved and the sheer temerity of the scheme. Indeed, there was an assertion in some quarters that the jury only found them guilty because of anti-Irish feeling provoked by the Troubles. Yet running a ringer was not only illegal, but also in serious breach of the rules of racing. Both men were banned from racecourses for ten years.

Curley knew Murphy well, though he stresses he had no involvement in the scam. Neither did he borrow anything from it when planning Yellow Sam. 'It was a good idea, but I don't think they thought deeply enough about it,' he declares.

The use of doubles had been an important aspect in deceiving the bookmakers back in 1974. Now Curley planned to use multiple bets, but legally. This, he believed, was the one way to undermine the bookmakers' defences.

Parsons' research had demonstrated that while trading departments carefully monitor win and each-way singles in order to manage liabilities and alter their prices accordingly, selections included in doubles, trebles and larger exotic multiples are scrutinised much less rigorously.

There is a simple reason for this. For all the dreams of multimillionaire status, exotic multiples are about as futile as purchasing a National Lottery ticket, reaping a dividend on exceptionally rare occasions but mainly destined only to swell the bookmakers' profits.

In general, if a horse is being seriously supported, and particularly at a long price, mostly it will be backed on its own and not as part of a double or treble with other runners. Why would anyone take the risk? In general, coupling that prospect with one or more other runners would be considered utter folly – unless, of course, the punter was supremely confident of all the runners winning – normally an unlikely scenario.

According to Parsons, stake restrictions placed on Curley's runners for win singles mostly evaporated when they became part of multiple selections. He discovered that 'the stakes permitted when runners were included in doubles, trebles, Trixies (a three-selection wager, consisting of three doubles and a treble) and Yankees (involves 11 bets on four selections: six doubles, four trebles and a four-horse accumulator) were a real eye-opener'.

He adds: 'Where firms were cautious in accepting singles, the advantage they assumed from the multiple overrounds left them potentially exposed.'

The overround is what gives a bookmaker that satisfied smile (normally). Put simply, he adjusts the odds on offer so that he makes a profit regardless of the outcome – assuming he is able to lay all the runners in the event.

In a simple example the true price of a coin toss is even money, heads or tails; a fifty-fifty chance; a 100% book. A coin toss would be priced by a bookmaker at perhaps, 4–5 both heads and tails representing a book of 111%. The overround is the difference between his 111% and the fair book of 100% – a theoretical profit margin to the bookmaker of 11%.

That figure is magnified to the detriment of the punter by doubling, trebling or quadrupling selections. A winning fair coin toss £1 double at evens on each toss would provide a return to the punter of £4, but the same winning double at 4–5 each toss would provide a return of just £3.24. The more bets involved, the worse it gets. If you were lucky enough to correctly guess 4 consecutive coin tosses, a fair book would give you back £16, a 4–5 book would give you back just £10.50.

However, such were the possible rewards available through the removal of stake restrictions, the multiple overround drawback could be overlooked.

This difference in strategy would require a radical change in approach for Curley, a man who, like most serious professional backers, had always regarded multiples

as a no-go territory. Though he was persuaded, the problems remained: could sufficient bets be placed, at generous
odds? Could he organise his horses to do the business on
that one day? His talents would be extended as never
before.

No one should be under any illusion that organising
two winners, let alone three, on the same day – and at
the kind of price to make it all worthwhile – was going
to be straightforward. It was hard enough to send out one
winner with a degree of certainty. Ask any trainer.

True, Curley had one significant advantage. Finding a
race in the calendar where conditions were ideal and
coordinating this with bringing a horse to its peak was
something he had long mastered. To try and do it with
more than one horse, though, was a different proposition
entirely. Yet, as has been stressed previously, he thrived
on such tests of his ingenuity and sagacity. The planning,
testing and tweaking of the operation appealed to him as
much as, if not more than, the potential yield.

The plan initially was to start off with four or five
horses in mind and take it a week at a time. One or two
of them were bound to fall by the wayside, as Curley had
seen so many times before during the many years of
preparing horses to land gambles.

He had not only to find suitable races on the same day
for his horses and dispatch them to the racecourse in peak
condition to win, but also do so with the veil of secrecy
he normally operated under intact. Few, if any, other yards
could have prepared such an operation without it being
exposed before the money was down on the day itself.

When Curley contended that he was the only man in
racing who could pull this off, it was not purely arrogance.
It was the truth.

CHAPTER 25

Barney Curley and his young aide believed they'd only ever get one shot at this opportunity because it would expose the 'back door' the bookmakers had obligingly left open.

'We would have left money behind with them but more importantly also taught them how to tighten up their operations,' says Parsons. As word spread as to what was attempted, everyone would have been on the lookout for multiple entries on the same day again. It would have been game over from every angle.'

Strangely, that was not quite how it panned out.

A live test was organised before the full nuclear option; a trial run to sound out the possibilities of multiple bets. Curley identified a date: 13 April 2009, a Bank Holiday Monday when there were seven race meetings in the UK, both Flat and over jumps, which increased the options. In the event, the pair came agonisingly close to a multimillion payout with that five-horse assault – ultimately failing by the length of a horse's thrusting neck. They also learned just how problematic such an exercise could be.

As has been emphasised, Parsons' unstinting exploration of the territory had long established that single bets would yield only a limited dividend. 'We started off looking at a double,' he says. 'Then we realised we'd need at least three winners to make the jackpot worthwhile. But to do that we'd probably need four, maybe five runners, to give us a good chance of getting the three up.'

Eventually Curley decided to run five horses on the same day, with a series of trebles placed in different combinations. Three of five runners were required to win. A daunting quest, by any estimation. A whole host of multiples were placed across the board, with one treble in particular – involving horses named Agapanthus, Northern Dune and Elusive Hawk – weighted more heavily.

The Curley quintet did not go unnoticed, at least by one onlooker. Many major stables have several runners on what is traditionally a busy racing day, but Curley's declaration of a quintet was such an unusual occurrence that one alert journalist was sufficiently intrigued to bring it to the attention of his readers.

Twenty-five minutes before the first horse, Northern Dune, ran at Redcar, Chris Cook, deputy racing editor of the *Guardian*, posted the following on his blog, under the heading: 'We need to talk about Barney':

> Barney Curley, the gambler-turned-trainer who claims to have taken £300,000 off the bookies in 1975 with the Yellow Sam coup at Bellewstown, has five runners around the country today – more than he had in the whole of March.
>
> Is something up?
>
> As far as I can make out, Curley hasn't had

more than one winner on the same day in the
last 10 years, but today could be the day and
I wonder if we'll see any money for any of
these.

It was the last thing the plotters wanted.

On a Bank Holiday, the course at the north-eastern
seaside resort of Redcar was overflowing with visitors. It
is a family-orientated track, where the quality and the
prize money, with the exception of the season's principal
events, the Two Year Old Trophy and the Zetland Gold
Cup, tend to be modest.

Micky Fenton was booked to ride Northern Dune. The
Limerick-born freelance was highly regarded by Curley;
his triumphs had included riding Speciosa, trained by
Pam Sly, to victory in the 2006 1,000 Guineas. In 2009,
he had enjoyed a successful association with Steff
Liddiard's Group winner Mac Love.

This contest bore little relation to those elite events.
Northern Dune was entered for the 2.35, a low-grade
but seemingly open two-mile handicap, worth £1,942.80
to the winner. The horse had won his previous race,
at Great Leighs (one of the few winners at the all-
weather course in Essex, which opened in April 2008
but closed less than a year later). He was available at
14–1 on the morning of the Redcar race. His starting
price was 7–1.

Northern Dune trailed the field until entering the
straight. It appeared hopeless turning for home, and
even making progress in the final furlong it still
appeared a lost cause, yet despite having to come wide
of the entire field of 15, Fenton somehow galvanised
a remarkable burst of finishing speed out of the five-

year-old to win by a head in a photo finish. 'Something had kicked him down at the start, then he got interfered with on the first bend, and he was 50–1 in running [on the betting exchanges], but he got up on the lollipop [the finish post],' says Curley. 'It shows you how organising anything like this is so difficult to do.' The next two races confirmed it.

Just over half an hour later, Curley's Andorn, four times a winner when starting his career in Germany before arriving at Newmarket the previous year, finished eighteenth of 20 in the 3.10 at Redcar, a seven-furlong selling race, having started at 5–2. Fenton, again the jockey, could only comment that the gelding was 'never travelling'.

Within a few minutes, some 150 miles south, at Fakenham, Faith and Reason, a 5–1 chance partnered by jump jockey Paul Moloney, was tailed off last in the 3.15, a novices' handicap hurdle.

It was looking like an increasingly futile afternoon, and that was confirmed after the fourth of the quintet, Elusive Hawk, the 5–2 favourite, had run in the fourth, the 4.00 at Yarmouth – in thick fog. The frustration was all the more intense because the Curley runner, under Joe Fanning, was a fast-finishing close second, beaten by just a neck. The winner's jockey Jamie Spencer, ironically one of Curley's protégés as a young rider, could not have given the Andrew Haynes-trained Seneschal a more vigorous ride to get his mount home. Elusive Hawk failed to get a clear run until too late.

So much for the Irishman knowing precisely when an ace would be dealt in his favour, as his critics would put it. Whatever a trainer's estimation of his own horse – and even that is frequently far from certain – he or she cannot anticipate with any conviction the running of any of his rivals. This was a perfect case in point. Seneschal, though eight years of age, approaching the veteran stage for a Flat horse, and with plenty of miles on the clock from his six-year racing career, was evidently striking his seasonal peak at that time; he went on to win two of his next three races.

The fog had lifted slightly when, just under two hours later, Curley's fifth horse of his quintet, Agapanthus, got home by half a length, under Fanning's driving ride, in the last at Yarmouth – a warm ten-furlong handicap. The winner returned 4–1, having been as big as 20–1 that morning. It was a pyrrhic victory; an irrelevance in terms of the day's betting plan.

The treble had gone down. Two winners was not enough. 'That was a sort of chancer operation,' says Curley. 'There weren't loads of people involved, and there was no great organisation. Three would have won a fair amount.'

True enough. It's worth illuminating the fact that if Elusive Hawk had beaten Seneschal in that earlier race, bookmakers would have been paying out £3.8m on the winning treble.

Bought at the sales, unraced, out of Sheikh Mohammed's Godolphin operation for a mere 12,000 guineas, Elusive Hawk more than paid his way over the years. Overall Curley made over £300,000 backing him.

But what of Andorn and Faith and Reason, the two horses whose running had appeared too bad to be true? There was no ulterior motive. Parsons is adamant that the aim was three winners from the five. Nothing less.

'Andorn had looked well at home and showed good

speed working with Elusive Hawk but couldn't translate this to the racecourse and ended up needing much further. He was disappointing,' he says. 'Faith and Reason was rushed to get ready and was a bit of an afterthought. There was no surprise he ran badly.'

However, the day has to be put into context. It could only be regarded as a failure by Curley's standards. It still ended well in profit. The whole outlay of the enterprise was covered, and more won besides, as soon as Northern Dune had crossed the line in front at Redcar. Agapanthus too had been backed to win as a single over £100,000 alone.

Curley and his accomplice withdrew and reassessed their options. The gamble of 13 April 2009 may have come close to realisation, but it also confirmed just how problematic it was to get three winners up, even from five runners. But at least the exercise removed any lingering doubts for Curley that his strategy could reap rewards.

Parsons says: 'I think it took that to fully convince Barney. What we learned in defeat made us sharpen up. The fact we had come so close, if anything made Barney more determined not to fail next time. A lot had been learned on the day itself from actually carrying out the operation. If it was possible to try again, this time we were coming back stronger and even better prepared.'

But would it prove possible? The one overriding concern was that their cover had now been blown. The bookmakers could, and should, be on high alert. The major concern for Curley and Parsons was that the industry's security would be set at an amber warning.

Certainly one man had kept a close eye on things. At 6.50 p.m. Chris Cook updated his blog:

> How about that Barney Curley? It's two wins from five runners for the trainer today, after his Agapanthus won the last at Yarmouth, having been hammered down to 4–1.
>
> Curley also won with Northern Dune (7–1) at Redcar, so even an SP double would have paid 39–1. I wonder if he was on?

Parsons says: 'Such coverage shows what you are up against trying to remain under the radar. Had we, as feared, blown our one shot at the prize? It was some time before we dipped our toe in the water again to see if the bookmaking industry as a whole had put up the shutters.

'When we did, there had been a mixed response. A small number of operators had made changes to company policy regarding all horse-racing multiples. Others had moved the restrictions they placed on Curley runners in the win market to now cover stakes where these were added to multiples. Remarkably, though, the vast majority of firms were carrying on as they were, regardless. It was as if they were unaware of the near miss.' The value of the exercise was that it demonstrated that once you got into multiple bets, bookmakers left themselves vulnerable.

By late 2009, the two men had formulated a new plan. Ostensibly it had even less chance of fulfilment than that potential Bank Holiday bonanza. In many ways, it evoked Yellow Sam, only revised to take on a betting environment that had changed dramatically in 35 years. Its potency lay in its simplicity, but it would hinge upon the delivery of a sophisticated betting operation. What Curley was planning to attempt with his team could be likened to a film director adapting a twentieth-century classic for the new millennium. 'It was much the same system operating and, like Yellow Sam, would require a lot of people,' he says.

Distilled to its essential details, it came down to this:

One day – four horses. Curley had to identify a quartet to run at sufficiently rewarding odds on the same day. The horses should be linked in many hundreds of accumulator bets, principally Yankees and trebles, but at such low stakes – we are talking here £5 or less – that bookmaker alarms would not be triggered, or at least not until it was too late.

At least two, hopefully three, and ideally all four horses had to win. They had to be fit and trained to a peak within the window of a few hours, but not such obvious contenders that their prices would be prohibitively short. 'It would have been no good picking four even-money chances,' says Curley. The advantage of running such horses was that the bookmakers would be unprepared. The plan was dependent on odds, certainly well before the races, and before the bookies caught on, being relatively generous.

All these elements were necessary if Curley and his team were to win the kind of money he had in mind.

If four winners did the business, the rewards could be many millions, depending on their prices. Three would still ensure a substantial profit. Two would probably only constitute a consolation prize. One would represent a washout.

Curley was confident he could organise the horses, but how to place sufficient money to secure a significant win? To exploit the full potential of the plan there had to be a major raid on the shops – legally, of course – just as Curley had done 35 years previously. This was the part he reprised from Yellow Sam: placing hundreds of bets surreptitiously.

Stakes would be low enough not to set off the book-makers' security klaxons and hooters, but the aggregate result, if the whole plan came together satisfactorily, was a substantial payout.

The bets were to be strategically varied depending on the firm, but Parsons' subsequent on-road checks suggested that £4 Yankees would be likely to be accepted without hesitation by betting shop staff – whatever the runners, and prices. His research had told him that if the bet was £5 or more, staff had to refer it to head office. The team would also place £16 straight trebles; again he was confident these would not be referred upwards.

Crucially, enough bets had to be placed at maximum odds in a short period of time before bookmakers reacted and slashed the prices on the horses involved.

But how to ensure that beneficial odds could be obtained?

With Yellow Sam, the coup had been based on a 20–1 SP, a figure that remained artificially high because of the intervention of Benny, the phone-box man. There was no equivalent of Benny this time. Instead, the plan hinged on the maxim: strike early – while prices were high – strike often, and strike as far as possible in unison.

It would require a large team on the ground: a disci-plined, well-briefed group who, most important of all, were utterly trustworthy and would not jeopardise the mission by attempting to fly solo.

Such was the scale of the project, Curley decided to enlist another key individual.

CHAPTER 26

J ack Lynch offered entirely different skills from Martin Parsons, and a contrasting background. The Irishman hailed from a family who followed horse-racing avidly, and who enjoyed a regular flutter. As a child, he often accompanied them to the races where they'd place bets for him. In consequence, Lynch had been besotted by the sport. He bought his first pair of binoculars as a young boy after a win on the Tote placepot at the races.

Lynch had first met Curley when he had done work for him as a currency broker. They had kept in touch. At one time he'd had ideas about being a big-money backer of horses. 'Y'know, I really fancied myself as some kind of player in my youth,' he explains. 'I always liked punting, but I moved from opinion betting when I was 18, 19 to more mathematical-based schemes around pool betting and arbitrage.'

Racing was regarded with caution. 'I concluded pretty quickly that you had to be incredibly smart to survive in that game, let alone prosper.'

He adds: 'I still follow racing as a sport: all the group races and big National Hunt events. But I'm no longer an anorak of racing, and unlikely to return. I don't like half doing things. I need to throw myself entirely into projects.'

Lynch had been summoned to Newmarket by a phone call out of the blue from Curley in August 2009. When Curley broached the scheme he had in mind, the words immediately fired Lynch's imagination. He admits: 'As someone brought up with racing in his blood in Ireland, it was like every boy's dream to get that call. I was humbled. Just to play a small part was enough for me. Barney was about to go in to hospital for his operation, but we got together in early October.'

Lynch had crucial assets. While Parsons knew his way like a veteran around odds and technology, it was Lynch's organisational qualities, bulging contacts book and networking skills that Curley demanded from this third man, and he asked him to be involved in the planning of the operation. It was a timely meeting. Lynch had just embarked on what was intended to be a sabbatical from his career as a City trader. It was to prove a defining moment in his life. He would never return to his job with a major banking institution.

Sharp-tongued and sharp-suited, intense, in his forties, Lynch is loquacious and resourceful. Predominantly he is an ideas man, not money-orientated; he is also blessed with integrity, which in part is why Curley held him in such regard. 'Barney wouldn't trust too many people,' says Parsons. 'He wouldn't take too many chances. With him, you're a hundred per cent – or not on the list.'

Once Curley was content with the chemistry between Lynch and Parsons, he had the confidence to send them on their way to organise the betting operation in tandem.

'I put in my dollar's worth, but generally left the betting side to them. I just said: "This is on your head. No mistakes. You work it out. I'll get the horses."'

Lynch's recruitment, though necessary, was a further departure from Curley's normal strategy of maintaining absolute control. For decades he had been solely dependent on his assistant trainer Andrew Stringer and his small team of stable staff, and in more recent years on Parsons. The more people were involved, the more it multiplied the risk of the stratagem being exposed, not necessarily deliberately, but with an idle word. It went against all Curley's instincts to subcontract in this way, but he knew this time that needs must.

Lynch, who was now reporting to Parsons, swung into action. According to Parsons, the new recruit's work ethic and professionalism honed the operation to another level. The new man was responsible for the scheme that became known as Operation Chainsaw, simply because the aim was to cut down the Big Three – Hill's, Ladbrokes and Coral – as well as many others. Not financially, of course; just a symbolic psychological blow to their prestige with a significant hit. The idea was to show that their defences could be breached like a computer hacker penetrating a nation's weapons system.

With the exception of drafting in two of his own relatives, Curley left the task of recruitment entirely up to Parsons and Lynch.

There were countless possible recruits, going back to his university days, but Lynch recognised from the start that he would have to be highly objective in his approach. Candidates had to be judged on a strictly professional basis. This was no time for jobs for the boys.

'I've always been scheming, conjuring up ideas in my own little way, without carrying it through,' he says. 'I'd always had names in my head if ever a plan like this presented itself.' Just as Curley himself had done 35 years before, Lynch prepared a comprehensive long-list and agonised over his selections.

He demanded trust, reliability and intelligence. Betting and knowledge of horse racing were not required. Indeed, they were not even desirable qualities amongst the contenders. Only one individual, Dara O'Malley, who would join the team late on, was an experienced punter. Another, who had worked briefly in a betting office was also recruited. But the remainder weren't gamblers; not in a serious sense. That was deliberate policy. Parsons and Lynch needed a disciplined team who would readily accept instructions without question; not a group of individuals who might be tempted to cash in on the knowledge they would glean from their involvement.

Lynch admits it was a difficult process. Some of his closest friends were excluded. 'I had to be absolutely ruthless. Anyone with a connection to racing in any way was eliminated from my thinking. I couldn't take chances with anyone if there was the tiniest doubt.' He explains his quandary. 'It's a dichotomy. If you've someone who knows where they're at, they have an understanding of betting and there's no risk they'll screw it up. But the risk is that it means something to them, it's significant, so there's the danger of leaks.'

Extracts from Lynch's notes read:

SF: shared house/flat with him . . . loves being involved. He bet 200K on GAA last year. We trust each other.

PMc: shared house/flat. Became my right-hand man. Was key.

MG: a great friend who I really trust to be discreet.

HMc: can keep a secret. High roller.

DO'M: likes a punt so he might find it hard not to whisper. Also, he's more a leader than follower. After deliberation was brought on to the London pitch – late.

Others – possibly ideal – were excluded or unavailable:

WW: is a driver, bookmakers are his customers.

XX: best friends with, but a real punter type. Too risky.

YY: can keep mouth shut, but I might prefer him not to know.

ZZ: accountant, was nervous about committing, and with brother said no. Still a top man.

'The common theme amongst those picked was that I had done something with them in the past; either a business venture or raising money for charity,' says Lynch.

A sense of mischief encouraged him to email out basic details to his final selections with the subject name 'Omerta'. It became the code word for the scheme and was the password on all documents. Its origin could be traced back to a passage Lynch had read in Curley's autobiography, relating to the period when Curley took Frankie Dettori under his wing early in the Italian's career.

The trainer-gambler had always placed honour and thoughtfulness from his protégés as high priorities. Back in 1993, he put Dettori to the test, inviting him to his house at Stetchworth and telling him that he might have a winner for him the following week. The horse was named Case for the Crown and was due to run at Folkestone in a ten-furlong handicap.

On his way out of the door, Curley looked the jockey in the eye and said: 'Omerta', the word denoting honour and silence and always associated with the Mafia. It told Dettori that he had to keep to himself the knowledge that Curley had high expectations for Case For The Crown. He did so, and, in a supremely confident ride, the Italian steered the mare to victory at Folkestone.

Coincidentally, Curley had a horse named Omerta at one time, bred by Jim Barry, but sold him early on in his career. Omerta went on to win the Irish Grand National and the Kim Muir at Cheltenham for Martin Pipe in 1991.

The expression appealed to Lynch, who had long been enthralled by the history of the Sicilian Mafia. 'Those boys were fundamentally immoral, but the way they operate is unbelievable. They would die for each other.' Failure here would have somewhat less drastic consequences.

For weeks, men were enlisted through an exhaustive selection process. Surreptitiously. No fuss. Discretion was absolutely crucial. Lynch took everyone to dinner individually and explained the fundamentals of the plan. 'I made sure to meet each individual eye to eye and told them what was expected. The great thing is that money was never mentioned by any of them.'

All those approached were identified as trustworthy.

All were sworn to silence. But as Lynch concedes: 'The way I looked at it, we were probably combining 33–1 on shots, and the more you combine, the greater the risk of leakage – simple as that.' As melodramatic as it might appear, a whiff of the plot being sniffed by the bookmakers would have blown the whole operation. His recruits also needed to possess an aptitude for acting out a role unfamiliar to the majority: betting office punter.

By April, Lynch's long-list of 200 original 'possibles' had been distilled down to 30 'definites'; 15 located in Ireland and 15 to be based in London. They ended up being called into action at various stages – some not until the day itself.

What prompted them to agree to being involved? What was in it for them? They certainly didn't need to be press-ganged. Most, it appears, were doing it solely for that frisson of excitement that came with being associated with such a plot.

These were not mercenaries. There was no huge reward. 'They were just asked to give up their time to help us and told that all their expenses would be covered. That was it,' says Parsons. 'They came just knowing they were doing a friend, or, in the case of a couple of them, a relative, a great favour.'

All these diverse individuals had day jobs. Some were highly successful in their fields. A number of them were aware of Curley's reputation, as both a gambler and a charity founder, and had great respect for both aspects of his life.

The job spec was limited at that early stage. All they were told was that it would involve some travel around London in casual clothes – with the exception of one

263

recruit for whom there was a special operation planned – for a couple of days. It was to remain a secret before, during and after.

Lynch's other responsibility was to organise a base for the operation. Location was key; it had to be central to many of the clusters of betting shops, with all Tube lines easily accessible.

The concentration of betting offices in particular areas, often the most socially deprived localities, is a phenomenon that is anathema to many politicians, including Labour deputy leader Harriet Harman, who has been vocal on the subject. Now, however, close proximity of shops throughout London was an important benefit to Lynch and Parsons and their team.

Lynch established his headquarters in London: two serviced furnished apartments off Carter Lane, in the shadow of St Paul's Cathedral, costing around £250 a night each. They were considered more discreet and private than a hotel. The apartments were described in the promotional bumf as 'majestically erected in the heart of the City of London, a prestigious development ensconced in a tranquil and secluded courtyard just behind St Paul's Cathedral'. Not that these particular guests would have too much time to enjoy the facilities.

The apartments were rented for a week. 'And we needed every hour,' says Parsons. 'We got new mobile phones for all the foot soldiers and set up group texting software from laptops in our temporary office so that messages could be relayed to them more effectively.'

He adds: 'Most of the guys would use the Tube network or walk their routes. But we also hired fold-up bikes and a conventional bicycle, and there was also a moped available. We printed out paperwork so that they could write down the bets as they placed them; these could then be recorded and potential returns calculated when they returned to HQ.'

Back in Newmarket, Curley didn't have to give any thought to that side of the scheme – which was fortunate, because for several weeks now he had had enough headaches of his own.

CHAPTER 27

Barney Curley was like a champion pugilist, intending on retaining his title. He had done all his roadwork and sparred relentlessly. He had set the operation in progress, staged that so-nearly-successful rehearsal with his quintet on Bank Holiday Monday 2009, and dispatched Martin Parsons and Jack Lynch to prepare a well-drilled betting ground force.

He was finally eyeball to eyeball with his opponent ahead of a championship bout. He wasn't about to blink now. But could he muster a suitably powerful uppercut?

Just ask any of his peers, at whatever level of competence and experience, and even the most confident individual would tell you that this was a major test of his talent. He had to identify four horses, probably lacking recent form in order to guarantee the kind of odds required, and who looked to be approaching their peak.

Even given his reputation for thinking outside conventional parameters, it appeared an impossible mission. Most of racing's training masterminds would have said 'pass'. It would have been a tough ask even for a trainer with 50-plus charges.

Certain powerful stables in Newmarket and beyond –

Mark Johnston, for instance, with his 200-plus stables in Middleham, Yorkshire – could conceivably prepare four top-quality individuals on the same day to win their races – though not with the certainty required – but their prices would have been prohibitively short. There are few secrets within the major yards.

The time was long past when Curley had trained anything of that quality. His charges bore little comparison with the equine bluebloods, some possessing classic potential, of Sheikh Mohammed's Godolphin operation, who would have been searing the gallops near Curley's stables.

No one but Curley would have attempted such an undertaking with such a dearth of numbers and quality. Even he had been sceptical at first. 'It's a serious operation to try and get four horses right on the day. Most people are satisfied with a winner. Their bonus ball is maybe two, but to go for four?' He ponders the question, before adding quietly: 'That takes a lot of thought . . .'

Over the years, he had owned, and in some cases trained, some high-calibre performers. But his choice now appeared absurdly limited.

CURLEY HAD ACQUIRED his horses from numerous sources. Some had come from Ireland, but in the last decade several of his contingent had arrived as rejects from the German banker and breeder Baron Georg von Ullmann's Gestüt Schlenderhan stud.

Though Curley's yard has always necessarily been a closeted affair, he has close contacts with many diverse characters in racing. They include a number of British and Irish trainers and jockeys, who seek his counsel on many issues. Once when I was with him, a prominent trainer even called him up for advice on a matrimonial issue – possibly not amongst Curley's specialist subjects, though it did not deter him from offering his expertise.

He first met von Ullmann, one of Europe's leading racehorse breeders and the chairman of the supervisory board of one of Europe's biggest privately owned banks, in November 2002. They are not the most obvious bed-fellows. The German had read Curley's autobiography. 'He told me I should be in prison,' recalls Curley ruefully.

A member of the Oppenheim family through his late mother Karin, Baroness von Ullmann, the Baron owns and runs Germany's oldest and most successful private stud, in Bergheim, close to Cologne. He owned Shirocco, the home-bred 2005 Breeders' Cup Turf victor and Coronation Cup winner the following year, and also the top-class Manduro and Getaway. All three were sons of von Ullmann's exceptional stallion Monsun. Curley has maintained close links with the German, who sends him a number of his mares in foal to Darley stallions. Curley oversees them at his Newmarket stud.

While never claiming to be a horse whisperer, he has also helped out with von Ullmann's problem horses, including Manduro, the world's top-rated runner in 2007. He came here for three or four months and we got him sound,' he recalls.

Curley once asked von Ullmann if he could train a horse for him. '"I've never asked anyone else," I told him.'

'"You certainly cannot," he replied. "You're a gambler; I'm a banker – but I'll give you a horse for nothing."' True to his word, he sent him El Tiger, who had won a Listed race in Germany, and been placed sixth behind Shirocco in the German Derby. He yielded a 14–1 victory at Lingfield for his new owner.

A by-product of their relationship has been that Curley

purchased several of von Ullmann's horses, many of which had been winners in Germany but had failed to progress to the high standard the owner-breeder demands. Curley could give them the time they required. Most cost no more than £60,000, but at one time he speculated considerably more on animals that appeared to have a future over jumps, purchasing two of von Ullmann's best-known horses, Tareno and Subiaco, for a total of £300,000.

'I just thought at the time, "Let's get a decent horse." When I lost my licence [during the Robin Goodfellow affair], I had to sell a lot of good ones, and never replaced them. The reason had been that I wouldn't give the prices for National Hunt horses: £150,000, £200,000 for unbroken three-year-olds. The thing had become crazy.'

Tareno, the most expensive yearling sold in Germany, had previously won two Group races in 2002 and finished fifth in the Group 1 Premio Roma in Italy. He only raced once for Curley, in his friend Patsy Byrne's colours. Starting 9–4 favourite for a hurdle race at Huntingdon in November 2003, Tareno collapsed and fell after the third when leading, and died.

Subiaco had been second in the German Derby and winner of four Group races. He ran three times for Curley, once in a Group 3 at Newbury, when unplaced, and twice over jumps. He fell on the final occasion, at Sandown, and never raced again.

Sereth was another potentially useful import. He had won five races in Germany, including a Listed event, before joining Curley, who had the 2009 Cesarewitch handicap in mind for him. Sereth finished third in the major end-of-season long-distance betting showpiece at Newmarket, behind the favourite Darley Sun.

'He would have won if Darley Sun hadn't been in it,' says Curley. 'He was third, beaten a head for second. I told Johnny Murtagh, his jockey: "I'm on big each-way [he had backed him at 50–1] . . . so as long as you're in the first four, don't be hard on him. I have a plan for him.' The plan was a hurdling career. Sereth won first time out over timber at Huntingdon, but then got a knock at Ascot and never recovered.

What Curley had to choose from as he planned his May operation, however, were horses of rather lesser talent. For months, he sat in his cluttered little office, with his dozen horses stabled a few yards away, assembling his forces against the might of a multibillion-pound industry. As he attempted to identify suitable races for the right horses on the same day, working through his racing calendars, it was like an astronomer waiting for Jupiter and Mars to come into conjunction. Even then, to borrow a line from 'Aquarius', it would take more than love to steer home his stars.

Curley invokes the image of a draughts board to describe how problematic his task was. 'You'd change the pieces hundreds of times,' he says. 'Put horse A there, and have horse B in here. But this one's not going well, that one's lame. And we're operating with very few horses, you know. Take horse B out. A week later, back in again. It's not easy. Horses are so unpredictable.'

He adds, with a dry laugh: 'You'd have wanted to see my office, littered for day after day with racing calendars as I pencilled in dates. I had everything I'd planned laid out on the floor and the next morning they were in the bin as horses didn't stay sound. I must have changed my plans twenty times. It was something else. It's like a general finding that there's no powder for the guns or his troops aren't fit enough. Horses have to be trained to a peak, and that doesn't happen at short notice. I guarantee the best trainer on earth would find that a daunting proposition. It's not an exact science.'

He had scrutinised his horses at home. But he had to be certain, and organised a private trial gallop at Lingfield racecourse. In early April, an enormous horsebox negotiated its way out of his stables. Aboard were four horses.

Sommersturm, a six-year-old bred and previously owned by von Ullmann, had arrived from Germany in 2008, having won his first two races at Frankfurt and Krefeld. He was a son of Tiger Hill, the stallion who had been a multiple winner in Germany, including that country's 2,000 Guineas, and progressed to finish third in the 1998 Prix de l'Arc de Triomphe.

Sommersturm had been considered good enough to contest Group races and had finished ninth of 15, behind Alderflug, who hailed from the same stable and owner-ship, in the 2007 German Derby at Hamburg. He had run promisingly on his English debut, finishing sixth of nine at Kempton off a handicap rating of 85,* but had shown nothing since and had subsequently been dropped 30lb in the weights by the handicapper. He had also contested jumps races.

*   As a rough guide to Flat handicap ratings, the best horses are 110+, good quality 90+, better standard 70–90, moderate 50–70, the poorest 50-. A team of 11 BHA handicappers interpret and study form and publish ratings, expressed in pounds, every week. These ratings, or marks, determine the weights carried by horses in handicap races and are produced partly on the basis of math-ematical fact and partly on interpretation.

Savaronola, a five-year-old by the American stallion Pulpit, had been placed in Ireland before joining Curley, also in the autumn of 2008. 'A right nasty piece of goods when he arrived,' according to Curley. 'One day at Southwell he kicked the place down. But after a while we had him as quiet as a lamb. The horses here had the best time of any stable in the world.'

Though mystique surrounded Curley's training and running of his horses, his success was founded on extraordinary patience and an astute eye for a horse approaching peak fitness in his home work. If he thought a horse displayed potential, he gave it all the time it required to perform before reluctantly conceding defeat.

Despite running what he calls 'a tight ship', his 18 inmates at the time included five or six 'pets' – 'horses that had done you a turn and you didn't like to give them away'. It belies his pragmatic, hard-nosed reputation. 'I had no plan for those. They shouldn't really have been in a racing stables. But you can get to like them.' He pauses, before adding quietly: 'Most of the likeable horses are no good.'

During one visit, he confided to me: 'I watched four horses work this morning. I came back and rang a fella, asked him if he wanted a horse, just to go riding. The horse was no good. I'd had him four months, and he'd showed nothing. He was gone an hour later, to a girl for riding.'

Savaronola had not been rushed. Placed as a three-year-old at Navan and Dundalk, he had been lightly raced under Curley. He had been unplaced three times on the all-weather on the Flat at Southwell, dropping 20lb in the process, and had been well beaten on his last two starts, both over hurdles at Huntingdon, on the latter occasion starting at 80–1.

The party was completed by Me Fein, a six-year-old who had won four moderate races on the all-weather tracks at Southwell and Wolverhampton, and Sure Fire, a lightly raced five-year-old, also bred by von Ullmann. He had not won in Britain.

There was not much between the quartet on official handicap ratings, and Curley approached the exercise with an open mind.

Four highly experienced jockeys had been lined up – Tom Queally, Jamie Spencer, Micky Fenton and Paul Mulrennan – to participate in the gallop at the Surrey course, once regarded as one of the country's most attractive. 'Britain's most beautiful', its own posters used to describe a track which was the scenic backdrop for the racing scenes in the raunchy 1979 Joan Collins movie *The Bitch*, but that aesthetic appeal has been rather diminished by the addition of an all-weather course.

On this morning, it was a soulless arena – none of the baying of bookmakers' prices, clink of glasses in the bars or exhortation for the runners of a race day; just the echo of hooves and a sense of intrigue as Curley allocated jockeys to horses and issued instructions about how they were to be ridden in (what should perhaps be named) the 'Barney Curley Trial Stakes', over a mile and a half.

The jockeys were paired with the horses as follows:

Sommersturm: Tom Queally
Savaronola: Jamie Spencer
Me Fein: Paul Mulrennan
Sure Fire: Micky Fenton

Queally, who rode for Curley when available, and Spencer, who had done so in the past, were obvious participants, but the trainer explains: 'I went out of my way to get Micky Fenton to ride the lead horse because he's a great judge of pace. It was crucial we had that.' He also has a high regard for the northern-based freelance Paul Mulrennan.

Trainers often prepare their horses with racecourse gallops, particularly if, say, a classic contender has been unable to get in a suitable 'prep' race, or maybe to tune up a big handicap hopeful. Normally gallops involve pairs, with the horse in question given a lead by a lesser stablemate.

This was different. It is doubtful whether one had been organised for such a purpose before. 'It was a proper mile-and-a-half gallop, with the best jockeys,' recalls Curley, who insists it was a 'blind' test. 'They almost certainly weren't aware of the identity of their horses.'

The jockeys all rode at their natural weights, which are within 2lb of each other, and were issued with precise instructions. Micky Fenton was told to set a decent gallop in front on Sure Fire. Mulrennan and Spencer were to track him on Me Fein and Savaronola respectively. Queally had to hold up Sommersturm in behind. Spencer and Queally were told to go on at the two-furlong pole.

A couple of groundsmen, finishing some paintwork, surveyed the scene when Sommersturm swept around the outside and took it up in the home straight, finishing two lengths clear of Savaronola, who in turn was six clear of Me Fein, with Sure Fire a further length behind. It appeared obvious from that piece of work that Sommersturm was the superior horse.

Things didn't go quite to plan, however – such is the competitive nature of jockeys. 'I told them to go at a nice gallop, and to let them run on in the last furlong,' recalls

Curley. 'So off they go, Jamie Spencer sitting with his arse in the sky on the third horse, Savaronola; Tom Queally sitting and watching him on Sommersturm. But jockeys . . . they're little rascals, really. I knew Tom Queally would have been looking at Spencer and thinking, "I'll do him." So, he came earlier than he should have. But that's par for the course. As long as you know.'

That said, they had, seemingly, all run on their merits, and largely as Curley had anticipated. 'Sommersturm worked a bomb that day – though Tom took a bit of a liberty – but he was still the best horse on the day.

'I sent four because I wanted to have a proper gallop,' he explains. 'I told Micky Fenton, "It's got to be a proper mile-and-a-half gallop" – and he made sure it was. If they didn't go a proper even pace, you learn nothing.

'Afterwards, as always after any work, you listen to the jockeys. But the buck stops with you. I was very pleased with what I'd seen. It confirmed that my initial feelings had been correct.' He pauses. 'As I thought . . .'

CHAPTER 28

Curley decided he could dwell on his decision no longer. He recalled the words of John Magnier, the Irish business magnate who established Coolmore Stud. 'John said many years ago: "Nothing in life is ever perfect." I said to myself, "Right, we're going." I thought, "If we're going to wait until things are perfect, we're all going to be dead . . ."'

He adds: 'Don't forget this is about the fifteenth time we were going for this, constantly changing things because horses weren't right.'

After months of selecting horses and then discounting them, and employing the evidence provided by that outing at Lingfield, Curley decided on three of his runners; though a glance at the form of the names he eventually circled in red would not have inspired confidence amongst anyone looking on.

Of the three definites on his team sheet – a late decision would be made about a fourth – only one had won a race in this country. Unless the name of the trainer was taken into account, they would have had potential backers in retreat.

Opportunities were severely limited. But Curley's eyes were drawn to Monday, 10 May, when there was Flat

276

racing on the turf at Brighton, Redcar and Windsor, and a meeting on the all-weather at Wolverhampton. There was also an evening jumps meeting at Towcester. All offered opportunities for his charges. If that day's races had been postponed for any reason, as others had been, it might be months before another suitable opportunity arose.

He placed his faith in three of his own horses, who would run on the Flat. Two were formerly with Baron von Ullmann. Faith was maybe a misnomer. These were moderate, inconsistent individuals whose level of performance could never be guaranteed.

In the wake of that Lingfield gallop, Savaronola and Sommersturm were declared for an amateur riders' handicap on the all-weather surface at Wolverhampton. Fortuitously, the race was split into two divisions due to the number of runners. One would be run at 5.00, the other at 5.30. The conditions were ideal for both of them – although as a precaution, Sommersturm had been entered in the 1m 6f handicap on the same card as well.

'In recent years, I'd become very familiar with those kind of races,' Curley explains. 'They were usually poor quality . . . though you could run into an Arkle, with some fella lining him up. Not often. But you could.

'I had to go for that level of contest because I refused to give big money for horses. It would have been a waste of time spending £150,000 on a horse. It could get a leg [an injury, often involving a tendon], and be worth nothing. It wasn't viable.

'There had been a time when I loved sending decent horses to the big meetings, the festivals like Cheltenham or Goodwood. That was the only time you could get

277

serious money on. But things had changed a lot since then. Now, you could get the same money on a selling plater as a horse costing millions.'

Curley's representatives for 10 May had barely cost six figures. Savaronola was 'not a huge amount', while Sommersturm was 'maybe £40,000'. His third selection, Agapanthus, who had been one of the brace of winners amongst the quintet sent out in that failed Bank Holiday coup the previous year, had cost no more than £50,000. Curley had not bothered to include the five-year-old in his Lingfield gallop. It would just have complicated things. As will become evident, he believed that he had the measure of the horse and knew what could be expected of him in a race.

Named after the herbaceous perennial originating in South Africa – for those not green-fingered amongst you – the gelding was another son of Tiger Hill. He had won his debut race at Bremen, but after finishing sixteenth and last in the German Derby, he had arrived in Newmarket in the autumn of 2008.

The early signs had not been propitious. Before his win at Yarmouth, he had been last or second last in all his runs since arriving from von Ullmann's operation. After that victory, he had run five times on the Flat and had been beaten by an aggregate 112 lengths. In his previous two Flat races he had gone down by 62 and 60 lengths. However, coincidentally, he had also slid down the handicap like Franz Klammer on an Alpine downhill.

Curley's trio of horses had all been rated considerably higher when they arrived. Savaronola first contested a race in the UK off a rating of 75; Sommersturm had been allotted 85. The indifferent form of both meant they had slipped to 55.

Agapanthus was given a mark of 89 when Curley first brought him to Newmarket – the consequence of his debut win in Germany, followed by a close fourth in the German Derby trial. He would be the first of the Curley quartet to run on 10 May, having been lined up for the 4.10 at Brighton. By now he was rated 63 – 26lb less than his debut in the UK and 2lb lower than when he had won at Yarmouth the previous year.

His most recent outing had been over jumps, in a maiden hurdle at Fakenham four months earlier. On that occasion, he had started at 40–1 and been a tailed-off thirteenth of 14. Not everyone's idea of the ideal tune-up. Curley was convinced, however, that it had been a valuable exercise.

The booking of the jockeys was a lot more straight-forward and was confined to one family. Tom Queally, otherwise employed as number 1 rider to Henry Cecil, was designated to partner Agapanthus at Brighton. His Ireland-based brother Declan would take the Wolverhampton mounts in the two divisions of the amateur rider handicap. They were both men in whom Curley had utmost faith.

Tom Queally knew his intended mount well. Or perhaps it would be better to say he knew his idiosyncrasies well. 'He could be a law unto himself,' the gelding's trainer admits. Queally had ridden Agapanthus nine times already, without a victory, and had also partnered him in his work at home for Curley.

The young Irishman was the latest in a sequence of riders, going back to Declan Murphy, whose careers Curley had helped nurture in their early years. The former Southern Area pony racing champion and Irish champion apprentice made the move to Britain at the age of 19. 'I'd been at Aidan O'Brien's, and things were happening very slowly. I wanted to give myself every chance of making it as a jockey, and England was the place to do it,' he explains. 'Barney was a massive help to me. 'My father [Declan Queally Snr, who trains a few horses at Cappagh, County Waterford] was a little bit concerned for me, and said, "Why don't you give him [Barney] a call? He'll look out for you."

'I did. Barney helped me along quietly, without being too much of a big noise. He always told me to let my riding do the talking. He said, "If you ride well, work away and keep your nose clean, the rest will happen."'

Curley recalls in his forthright manner: 'At first he was going nowhere. So we made a plan for him to become champion apprentice.' He achieved that in 2004. The following year, the trainer suggested that Queally should visit his ally of old, Michael Dickinson, at his 200-acre state-of-the-art training facility, Tapeta Farm, on the eastern shore of Maryland. From what was described as 'the Chantilly of Chesapeake', the Yorkshireman's finest feat had been to train Da Hoss to win the 1996 and 1998 Breeders' Cup Mile.

'I got a lot of help on the clock there,' says Queally. In American racing, where courses are more uniform in size, much more emphasis is placed on times than is the case here. 'That paid dividends when Midday won at Santa Anita,' he says, reflecting on Henry Cecil's prolific mare, which Queally partnered to Breeders' Cup triumph in 2009.

Queally had first linked up with Cecil in 2008. When he informed Curley of that proposed move, the latter's immediate reaction had been to invite the 24-year-old out to Zambia to witness his charity's work first hand. It would be the prelude to a rich association between Cecil and Queally and, for the latter, that trip to Africa placed subsequent events in perspective.

The following year, Queally became first jockey to Cecil, honoured to be the latest in a line of succession that had included such illustrious names as Steve Cauthen and Lester Piggott. He could not have imagined the bonus it would entail – in the shape of the invincible Frankel.

When Khaled Abdullah's colt was retired to stud after the 2012 season, his victory standard hadn't been lowered in 14 races – all under Queally. He had been victorious in 10 Group I events, between 7f and 10f. He is regarded by many Turf judges (those prepared to accept that different generations can be compared and overlook the fact that Frankel never raced the Derby distance) as the finest racehorse ever. At the finish of his career, when he was retired to stud, Frankel was rated 140.

Yet even as Queally became the envy of all other riders, he remained Curley's unofficial stable jockey. 'I rode for him for a long time,' he says. 'He understood me and I understood him. It was a little like working for Henry in a way. Barney would never tell me what to do on a horse. I'd ride the horse work. I'd give my opinion and he'd tell me what he thought. He'd leave the rest to me. It rarely went wrong.

'It was a unique stable in Newmarket, wasn't it? Nobody really knew what's going on. When you went in there, and there's just letters on the stable doors [instead of names], it told its own story. But he knew I was trust-worthy.' He adds: 'When I first landed off the boat I might have been tested [by Curley]. I wasn't told too much, or I might have been told a few lies to see how far the lies would get. Pretty soon, he realised he could trust me a hundred per cent anyway.'

There was one embarrassing episode over the years of their association, albeit one with a beneficial outcome, when Queally was handed down a 21-day suspension after stewards found him not to have ridden Curley's Zabeel Palace to achieve the best possible placing at Nottingham in May 2007. Curley was fined £3,000 and the horse was banned for 40 days. Zabeel Palace, purchased at the horses in training sales for 28,000 guineas, had started at 16–1. He had been held up by Queally, then hung badly, but had stayed on well to finish a three-length fifth of seven. Curley described his charge as a 'thoroughly bitter individual, determined to do the exact opposite of anything that was asked of him. He also had terrible legs and resented the ground that day.'

He was adamant an appeal would clear Queally, but made the mistake of attending the hearing of the Horseracing Regulatory Authority's disciplinary panel (which had taken over those responsibilities from the Jockey Club), in London's Shaftesbury Avenue, only a few days after leaving hospital following his heart operation. 'I land up at this inquiry to defend Tom, but can't sit right because of the op. They'd put a tube up through my groin, and I'm not feeling myself at all. I was in desperate pain and I was full of drugs. I was sweating like a pig. I wasn't up to scratch. I'm sure they're wondering what the hell I'm on. I wasn't really compos mentis.'

He adds: 'The horse had come from Godolphin, Sheikh Mohammed's organisation. All I had to do was get their vet to explain to the panel the problems they'd had with the horse which meant he was hanging right, left and all sorts.'

The appeal was dismissed, and Queally received a further week's suspension because a previous incident from 2005 was taken into account. On top of that, he had another 20-day ban at that time, following a 'non-trier' offence two days after the Nottingham race. That had been on one of Henry Cecil's horses. 'What a laugh. Henry didn't stop horses,' says Curley.

Curley, vehemently annoyed with the outcome at the time, says now: 'I don't blame the panel because it must have been a surreal situation. I'm sure I didn't make a very good case. All I wanted to do was get out of there.'

It left Queally with a lengthy 'holiday' to contemplate. 'I told him, "Clear off – as far as you can go . . . and think about the job,"' recalls Curley. '"Think about life." Tom was floating at the time. Taking things easy. Getting a few rides, but not bothering a terrible lot. He went to Australia, and came back a new man, so it did him a turn. I believe it was the making of his career; a great gee-up for him.'

A sequel to that incident occurred the following year, when Curley entered Zabeel Palace in the John Smith's People's Race at Aintree on Grand National day. It is a charity event, on the Flat over 1m 1f, not run under the rules of racing. His assistant, Andrew Stringer had persevered with the horse, massaging and treating his legs for months. 'He had begun to remain sound for much longer periods than we had managed with him before, but more importantly, he was no longer at war with the world.'

Curley put up a Newmarket accountant, Clare

Twemlow, who had been riding out for trainer Neil King, and had offered to ride in the race for DAFA. 'Zabeel Palace was difficult to get sound, but I had him on fire,' recalls Curley. He was not wrong. The partnership won comfortably, and the prize pot of £55,000 for Curley's charity.

'I watched the race with my friend Tommy Stack,' says Curley. 'He can't hear well [the legacy of meningitis in 1998], and doesn't know how loud he is talking. He declares at the two furlong-marker in front of everybody in the stand, "What a bandit you are. This has absolutely sluiced up." I fancied it all right. I may have had a couple of hundred quid on, but nothing more.'

In the ensuing months, though, he made hay as fortune shone on Zabeel Palace. His suspect legs held out as he proceeded to land five hurdle races from six races, including contests at Ascot and Sandown. 'I never really got too involved in backing him as I always knew he could break down,' remembers Curley. 'But I won over £150,000 during this period, none the less.'

Returning to Tom Queally, Curley's early instinct that this was a gemstone from which a fine emerald could be polished was correct. The trainer-gambler's judgement of riding talent has never been founded purely on horsemanship, but on attitude as well. 'He'd be thoughtful. Tom could have worked all morning at Henry Cecil's, then ride two pieces of work for me. No problem. They don't have to be mean or "the great I am". That turns me off.'

Queally's association with Frankel was a daunting responsibility, but one that never fazed him. If Curley had set out to create a template for success as a jockey, Queally would have been a model for it. As the jockey reflected in late 2012: 'I'm just a normal guy who likes to do his job, go home and chill out with as little fuss as possible.'

You suspect it's in the genes. Tom's brother Declan is a talented horseman on the point-to-point circuit in Ireland, where he also rides under rules, mostly but not always in races confined to amateur riders. He has a degree in economics and, unlike his elder brother, has no plans to ride professionally. He rides often for the jockey-turned-trainer Adrian Maguire, and had been runner-up on Kilty Storm in both the Foxhunter Chase – known as the amateur riders' Gold Cup – at Cheltenham, and at Punchestown Festival in the two months before Curley booked him to ride on 10 May.

But steering two horses around the tight all-weather surface of Wolverhampton? That was a different matter entirely. Curley, however, had no reservations about nominating him to ride, even for this vital task. Brother Tom had no doubts either. 'Declan's as cool as I am, and as good as anyone, given the opportunity.'

Significantly, Declan Queally had ridden his first winner under rules on Curley's Cristoforo, in a gentlemen amateur riders' event at Windsor in August 2004. He was barely a gentleman; he was then a 16-year-old schoolboy, who had been staying with brother Tom in Newmarket that summer and working in Curley's yard.

Like many before him, Declan Queally's allegiance to his compatriot is absolute. He says of being asked to ride on 10 May: 'I was not really surprised to get the call. I'd do any favour for him. I helped him when I was 16, and bits and pieces along the way. He trusts me and I trust him.'

So Curley had three winners, or so he believed, primed for 10 May, and jockeys booked for them. He was determined to proceed with that trio. The plan could not be aborted now. Too much time and preparation had been invested by all concerned. But the matter of a fourth runner remained unsettled.

CHAPTER 29

It was an acute dilemma. The previous year, Curley had eased his foot off his opponent's throat with at least one of his choices. This time he would not countenance completing his raiding party with an optimistic selection.

He was determined not to let the opportunity pass, so convinced was the trainer-gambler that his trio were at the apex of fitness. 'I had a few other possibilities mapped out; at that time, I would have watched racing twenty-four-seven and it was my nature to identify betting propositions elsewhere. There were two or three with other trainers, but no connection with me, that I thought would win.'

However, to complete his quartet, Curley looked to the north-east and the yard of the former top jump jockey Chris Grant. The horse he had finally elected to include was decidedly out of left field. Jeu De Roseau was one of his own cast-offs, a horse that had shown so little when under his charge that more than two years previously he had sent him to the sales, where he fetched a mere 1,000 guineas. Since arriving from Ireland, the gelding had exhibited promise but precious little else, and Curley had readily let him go. His departure had been the equivalent of sending a rarely worn jacket to

Oxfam. Possibly someone else would get more use out of him.

If that fact meant he lacked authenticity as a contender, there was another negative to consider: the distinct possibility that rust had set into his mechanism. Jeu De Roseau hadn't run for over two years, not since 28 April 2008, when he was eleventh of 12, beaten 54 lengths, at Towcester – where coincidentally it was intended he should become the final part of Curley's plan.

It was sheer serendipity that Curley's assistant Andrew Stringer had been visiting Grant's Teesside yard around the time that the Irishman was searching for a fourth contender. Grant and Stringer had forged a friendship when Grant was stable jockey at Denys Smith's yard many years before. Stringer was then a young conditional jockey.

Stringer happened to be present when Jeu De Roseau completed an impressive piece of work on the gallops. To the experienced eye of a man who knew the horse well – he had officially been in Stringer's charge as trainer when he last ran – the gelding worked with rare promise.

By another welcome coincidence, Grant planned to run the horse in one of two hurdle events at Towcester at the evening meeting of 10 May. Jeu De Roseau became the fourth of Curley's quartet; the only one to contest jumps.

Ostensibly, it appeared to be folly. Could this Curley reject seriously be considered a suitable component in a potential multimillion-pound coup?

Well, yes and no. Curley had a huge respect for Grant, regarding him as an excellent judge of horses. A number of the Irishman's former charges who had failed to flourish under him had benefited from moving to Grant's yard in County Durham.

Before turning to a training career, Grant had been a tenacious National Hunt jockey of distinction and was as tough as they came; his nickname in the weighing room, 'Rambo', dates from his time as stable jockey to Denys Smith and then Arthur Stephenson.

He had achieved an unwanted reputation as the 'nearly man' of Aintree, three times finishing runner-up in the Grand National – on Young Driver and Durham Edition twice – and was also placed twice in the Cheltenham Gold Cup. But that could never detract from his prowess in the saddle. He partnered 790 winners between 1977 and 1994. For many years he was the leading jockey in the north. His highest total was 94 wins in 1989–90.

Grant, assisted by wife Sue, began training both Flat and jump horses in late 1996 and has excelled at it. He is based at the idyllic location of Low Burntoft Farm, near the village of Wolviston. He recalls: 'We'd bought horses off Barney in the past and had a bit of fun with them, a bit of success, to be honest. I remember My Man In Dundalk was the first we had from him, and we've had a few since then. My wife Sue hunted him and he loved it. It was just something different for him. He was in his element. That did him the world of good. He won his first two races for us but collapsed and died in the third. Since then, we've had the odd one that hasn't achieved anything, but the majority have won races.'

Jeu De Roseau was a son of Montjeu, who sired horses of exceptional quality. The dam, Roseau, was a daughter of Nashwan, winner of the 2,000 Guineas, the Derby, the Eclipse Stakes and the King George and Queen Elizabeth II Diamond Stakes in 1989. Jeu De Roseau had originally gone through the sales ring as a yearling for €70,000.

The bay gelding had been placed in Ireland on the Flat and over hurdles before Curley had bought him. But he had never managed to get Jeu De Roseau right, and hoisted the white flag. He was sent to the Tattersalls sales at Newmarket in 2008.

'I said to Chris: "You should buy this one – there could be a turn in him. He's been sick, given us nothing but trouble. But he did show a bit of form back in Ireland. A thousand quid . . . you can't go wrong",' Curley recalls. There may have been a touch of the used-car salesman about his words, but there was mutual respect between the pair and the advice was genuine.

Curley says: 'I've sold him numerous horses over the years. If there are five gentlemen in racing, Chris Grant is one of them – he's a decent, honest, hard-working fella. Chris would always help you out with no plus for himself.'

One of Grant's owners, Bill Raw, a farmer, who had a permit to train his own horses several years ago, was up at the stables, saw Jeu De Roseau and said he'd be interested in him.

Like humans, some horses become stale but flourish in a different environment. Jeu De Roseau had certainly taken his time about it. More than two years on from his last run for the Curley stable – albeit officially in Stringer's charge – he had yet to race for his new trainer. It hardly seemed conceivable that the horse could be depended upon to do the business now.

'It was about ten days before the race,' says Grant. 'Andrew had been up at our place a fortnight before he ran, saw him work and thought he'd never worked so well, and he was coming back to himself. We were going to run him at Towcester because there was a low-grade handicap – though we didn't think he'd get in the race because he was too low in the weights. I declared him, not being certain whether he'd get in, but he did. That's how it came about. It was exactly the same day they were running theirs and they put mine in with them.'

If Grant's judgement of Jeu De Roseau's renaissance was correct, this was a heaven-sent opportunity. Yet despite being told that the horse had begun to thrive, Curley was understandably sceptical. It was a leap of faith. Including a horse from another stable in his plans still perturbed him. What quality of horse would Grant have to work him with? However, the County Durham trainer was insistent.

'I told Chris Grant, "We're looking for something at a price",' explains Curley. 'The horse had a very bad virus when he was here, and looked terrible. But Chris was saying he was looking well now, that he'd turned a corner. I still always thought Jeu De Roseau would be the weak link, if any. But Chris had assured me, "He's going well, he's turned the corner, though I think he won't be a hundred per cent fit." But I knew he'd been a good horse previously and I thought, well, if he was even eighty-five per cent fit he would win a very poor race at Towcester.'

And there weren't too many alternatives – unless he took a chance completing his quartet by selecting a runner from another stable that he expected to win.

Curley recalls a horse of fellow Newmarket trainer Jeremy Noseda's in whom he harboured confidence. That was Noseda's Brannagh, who would, indeed, comfortably win a maiden earlier on the same card Agapanthus was due to contest at Brighton. But he was 5–4 favourite. Even opening at more generous odds, 13–8, that kind of price would have been too short for Curley's purposes.

He adds: 'I thought about going out and buying a horse

to run in a seller at Towcester, but it never worked out. But whatever I did, I was determined to go now, otherwise my own horses would have gone over the top. They would no longer be at their peak. That's the problem you'd have. The way I looked at it was: there was Jeremy Noseda's horse, a good thing, but he'd be around evens; I thought Jeu De Roseau would be around 20–1. It was no contest.'

Curley's accomplice Parsons admits that initially he hadn't been completely persuaded either. 'Barney had never been able to get his coat right while he was in Newmarket but Grant reported he now had a real shine to him and was thriving in his work like never before. However, I was very apprehensive about including a runner from another yard. When Barney fancied one strongly they were rarely beaten. He has fine-tuned his set-up over the years to know exactly what the jockey has underneath him when he sends one into battle.

'We had been saying since April 2009, if we were able to try again, the next time they all had to be five-star naps, no small ifs or buts which were present in April 2009. This was the last chance. The greater magnitude of this attempt with the vast number of betting shops now being targeted was going to cause waves in the bookmaking industry win, lose or draw.

'But Chris Grant was adamant he was in rude health and he could surely be competitive off a lowly handicap mark over hurdles if he retained anything that resembled the ability he once had.'

There was another factor in its favour. Curley is a fervent admirer of the jockey Grant had in mind, Denis O'Regan. 'The lad came out of the womb seeing a stride,' it was once said of him. Curley concurs. 'He's as good as any jump jockey in the country. There's nobody better.

He has everything; great hands, and lovely balance on a horse.' He also knew there were few more voracious riders around. At that time, O'Regan was 'angry and hungry', and when he got the call from Grant, asking him to partner Jeu De Roseau, he knew he would be riding for a trainer whose own feats in the saddle were an inspiration to him.

O'Regan had turned freelance after departing the 180-horse powerhouse operation of trainer Howard Johnson in Crook, County Durham. His three-year retainer with Johnson's owner, the computer software tycoon Graham Wylie and wife Andrea, had not been renewed.

For the first two seasons, it had been a prosperous union. Indeed, O'Regan had declared that he had been 'privileged to be in such a wonderful position'. He had replaced Paddy Brennan as stable jockey for the start of the 2007–08 season, and went on to partner the World Hurdle victor Inglis Drever and the Arkle Trophy winner Tidal Bay at the 2008 Cheltenham Festival. In his last season for Johnson, O'Regan had ridden 66 winners and had just finished runner-up on Black Apalachi in that month's Grand National.

However, relations between O'Regan and Johnson had deteriorated in recent months. The trainer, who would retire the following year after being found guilty of welfare breaches at his stables, made his disappointment clear when O'Regan was found to have weighed in 3lb heavy after finishing a three-length runner-up aboard Arcalis in the previous month's County Hurdle at the Cheltenham Festival. (On the basis of one pound equalling a length, it could be said that the partnership would have dead-heated for first place at the correct weight.)

O'Regan's exit was not entirely unexpected. At that

293

time, Johnson had something of a reputation for a revolving-door policy. O'Regan had become the trainer's third jockey to leave in four years. But it was still a devastating setback for the man from County Cork

O'Regan had come under racing's spell when he had ridden out at his cousin John Crowley's yard, before spending a summer, aged 16, with Francis Flood. He had 13 winners as an amateur before turning professional. His first big winner was on Dermot Weld's Ansar in the 2005 Galway Plate.

'It was a very upsetting time, I must admit,' he says of his split from Johnson. 'I had gone from riding a lot of winners to no winners. My attitude changed a lot; I wouldn't say bitter, but edgy and angry.' He adds: 'I didn't actually do anything wrong. It was just that I didn't have the horses. I still rode 66 winners in my last season, and four in Ireland – 70 winners in one season is a lot for anyone.'

As a freelance, O'Regan was often called on to ride by Grant, so the booking had been expected. The pair had long been friendly. He had also ridden out for Curley in the past. The trainer-gambler's belief in the jockey never wavered and he gave him words of encouragement when he needed them. 'Words could not describe what I think of him,' says O'Regan. 'He's a very caring man. If you're on the team, you're on the team. That's the way it is with Barney. I just feel very lucky that he ever took an interest in me.' He adds: 'Barney made me believe that it wasn't my riding that was the problem. He made me realise that the trainer I was riding for was not an easy man.'

Curley was blessed by further good fortune. There were two opportunities for Jeu De Roseau at Towcester. His preferred target was the 7.30 race, a handicap hurdle, but would he get in?

All races have a maximum number of runners for reasons of safety. This differs from course to course. If too many are declared for a handicap event at the overnight stage, they are normally 'cut', just as in golf, from the bottom upwards, so that the horses of highest quality are left in.

There was so many runners declared at the four-day stage for the 7.30 at Towcester on that Monday night, the two-mile Niftylift Handicap Hurdle, that it needed 22 to come out at the overnight stage in order for Jeu De Roseau to get a run. That had appeared extremely unlikely. This was a race for moderate horses, rated 0–105.* Jeu De Roseau had dropped down the ratings and was now on a mark of 82. Yet somehow he snuck in as the bottom weight of the maximum field of 15 declared to line up for the handicap.

As a precaution, the horse had also been entered in the selling hurdle two races earlier on the same card to ensure he got a run. Sellers are usually considered the lowest-quality races. However, on this occasion, the consensus was that the subsequent winner of that race, the John Flint-trained Den Maschine – a future winner at a higher grade – would have been too good for Jeu De Roseau that day.

But the doubts persisted: would Grant's horse be good enough to win the handicap hurdle, even off a low weight, after such a substantial lay-off?

---

* Jump ratings differ from those on the Flat. A rough guide is that the best horses are 150+, quality ones 130+, better standard 110–130, moderate ones 90–110 and the poorest 90- .

Hopefully it would not prove too crucial. By the time Jeu De Roseau set off for that 7.30 at Towcester, Curley would have a good idea if the day had been a success – or one best forgotten.

CHAPTER 30

While Barney Curley perused his racing calendars, and scrutinised his charges as they pummelled the Newmarket gallops, his first lieutenant pounded the streets of London on an arduous reconnaissance mission.

From the end of 2009 into 2010, Martin Parsons had been assiduously preparing the groundwork for the betting operation, conducting an in-depth sweep of the target areas in London. He produced maps of possible routes for the team Lynch would assemble and, just as crucially, researched betting shop etiquette and how staff reacted when confronted with various bets.

Parsons also pondered the question of transport: how to organise the most efficient means for the punters to travel from cluster to cluster and shop to shop. Stations on the Tube lines would be a vital consideration.

Parsons recalls having a close relative who was a Christian minister working with the homeless for the London City Mission, much of whose time was spent on the Underground in Greater London evangelising and finding ways to help the homeless and vulnerable there. Keeping them out of betting shops would have been one. 'As a child, I was fascinated with the giant map he had on his wall. There was a story about each strange place name. He often used to take me out for the day just so we could visit different lines and stations on the map. He would not have approved of my own mission leading up to May but would have appreciated the use of the form of transport. Amongst the "evils" he encountered were drink and gambling. Occasionally I mused on what he would have thought of my work here . . .'

Curley could not have wished for a more diligent associate than Parsons. He printed off lists from the shopfinder sections of the bookmakers' websites and visited each potential target betting office armed with map, navigational device and stopwatch. His research was exhaustive – and exhausting. As he would later reflect: 'Bookmakers' own online shop locators would have never been used against them to such great effect.'

Some days he ended up with feet blistered and swollen from his efforts. If he had been sponsored per mile, he could have raised a fortune for charity. 'I spent a couple of weeks solid in London to break the back of that, and when I had a free day I would travel about to visit potential clusters nationwide,' he recalls. 'I visited each UK shop used, chatted to hundreds of staff, and placed countless bets purely to test staff reactions,' he says. 'I walked, biked, Tubed and taxied every relevant route to time the quickest ways to get around.'

Parsons added: 'The plan of the locations, routes, shops to use and bets to place was changed time and time again before ending up with the one carried out . . . in much the same way as Barney did with his plan for the horses. I would have been to the shops we eventually used at least three times.

'I remember one night in a Premier Inn in Victoria, in a hot bath with my feet swollen like balloons. It had rained most of the day. I worked out I had walked about twenty-five miles. Mapping out the routes, knowing what was to come, was the greatest buzz – despite the blisters.'

He could be thankful that the premises he inspected bore little comparison to their original incarnations. Back in 1961, when cash betting was made legal, such places were known as 'turf accountants' – what a wonderful euphemism that was – to give them a veneer of respectability. In those days gambling was perceived by many as an evil, and the welcome for would-be customers was deliberately intended to be grudging. It was decreed that premises should not be attractive and should be 'more like undertakers' premises'. There was to be no enticement to bet.

It shouldn't be forgotten that there was a more puritanical attitude then, born in part out of the fact that Britain was still in recovery after the war years. It was not that long since rationing had ended. What kind of man, or woman, would consider frittering away the family's income in such a place?

The early shops' interiors could not be viewed from the street. There was to be no encouragement for punters to loiter. Walking into these dingy, smoke-permeated shops – if you weren't a 20-plus-a-day man, you were seemingly an exception – was an act of shame only a notch better than patronising a Soho strip club.

There were no live TV broadcasts of races then; just the 'blower' commentary, provided by Extel, the Exchange Telegraph. The commentators were no Peter O'Sullevans, but men who seemingly contrived to make the finish of every race sound like a thriller. Boardsmen scribbled prices, as they came in from their representatives on course, with chalk or magic markers. On the walls, pages of the *Sporting Life* were pinned up with the runners, form and tipping pieces, but not a lot else.

Years ago, any unfamiliar faces would have been regarded with suspicion, and the operation Parsons was preparing would have been considerably more problematic. Then, bets were primarily on racing and greyhounds. Today, with the interest in betting on football and the arrival of one-armed bandits in shops, the 'footfall' – that word wasn't around in the sixties – is far more diverse.

From a just-about-tolerable evil when they were legalised, betting shops and their online spin-offs have become a key component of the leisure industry. The metamorphosis of those earliest shops into today's heavily advertised operators has been remarkable. Today they are emporiums of excess where punters can bet on 'virtual' as well as real racing. The message is: 'Gambling is cool.' The National Lottery – no more than a voluntary tax for the many; a windfall for a relative few – in part accounts for that.

Just about every high street has at least one bookie, sometimes many. The total number – 8,500 – has not altered drastically in recent years; just the betting opportunities, as those ostentatious frontages summon you inside. Once undesirable, they have rebranded themselves as the acceptable face of avarice. Beneath the gloss is a highly profitable industry. And there are all manner of different betting possibilities – many with bonuses attached. In general, those are accumulator bets.

Anyone seriously successful is the subject of the full trumpet of publicity. But that is a rare occurrence. Bookies love multiples precisely because they're so darn hard to get up. It was this fact that Curley and Parsons and his team were determined to exploit – together with another factor in the development of betting offices, the 'clustering' in areas of major cities.

Around a week before 10 May, the first of Lynch's recruits, Patrick McGovern, a primary school teacher, was summoned ahead of the main contingent. 'I didn't have time to do everything,' explains Lynch. 'I needed someone I could trust implicitly, and he came to mind. Patrick was then in further education, and he agreed to do things for me at an hourly rate.'

McGovern had one principal task: he was asked to obtain the postcode of every UK betting shop, and find mapping software that would plot these and identify clusters. This complemented the preparatory work that Parsons had carried out earlier. Most of the information was usefully provided by the Gambling Commission – the body that oversees the industry in this country. It publishes a directory, listing all addresses.

McGovern, an economist by background, was to make a vital contribution to the cause, yet he had no idea of the implications of what he was doing. Neither did he ask. Security dominated every bit of thinking, and that extended even to Lynch's close associates.

There couldn't have been anyone more innocent in the ways of gambling. McGovern was not a racing man; he had no great interest in betting. Odds were largely a mystery to him. He had emerged from everyday life into an atmosphere of mystery and subterfuge. He was intrigued, but also somewhat uneasy.

He had been recruited by Lynch. Their trust was mutual. Yet so clandestine was the operation, he had been told nothing of the precise role he was expected to perform, nor the nature of the enterprise. He was not even entirely certain how much those around him knew.

When he arrived at the modern, plush corporate apartments, McGovern rang Lynch. Instead it was Parsons who
appeared, clad in a rugby shirt. 'Jack had intimated that
Martin was a man to be respected and admired, but in
his civvies he could have been a painter just finishing up
for the day,' recalls McGovern.

The pair set off to meet Lynch in central London. 'We
took a cab through the early evening traffic to Leicester
Square. We discovered we had a mutual friend interested
in dog racing.

'I was cautious about giving too much information away
after Jack had sworn me to silence over my involvement
in the affair, so while I was anxious to make a good
impression, figuring I would be spending a few days in
Martin's company, I was conscious of keeping a certain
distance. At that stage I didn't know how much he knew
about me, whether Jack had trusted him with all the
details, and what his part in this plan was.

'Jack turned up on a bicycle in a few moments, with
folded sheets of paper in his hand and a biro sticking out
of the corner of his mouth. It was a fresh May evening
but he was wearing just a worn rugby shirt and tracksuit
bottoms that could have dated from his time at secondary
school. He seemed busy and preoccupied, mostly talking
to Martin, and he didn't make a big deal of my arrival.

'After a while chatting, Jack joking about my ignorance
of what was to come, we boarded the Tube to Edgware
Road, where I was asked to check out two betting shops.
It was a simple enough task; just to establish how busy
those offices were. I wondered if I was being skived off
already, given a menial job while the main guys were to
do the real business elsewhere.'

That first night, McGovern dined with Parsons and

Lynch in a French restaurant near the apartments. He felt awkward, an interloper in their environment. On a visit to the gents, he paused to consider just what kind of scheme he had walked into. 'I was still on the hook as to the object of our mission, which my dining companions would obliquely refer back to every now and again. I was here in a new city, for a job I didn't know anything about, with two men who seemed very focused and almost compulsively secretive,' he recalls. 'It didn't take a huge leap for me to speculate on the possible illegality of the enterprise . . .'

After dinner, though, he was reassured. 'As we strolled back to the apartment, perhaps I had used up my chit-chat, perhaps I was just quiet. Whatever the reason, Jack must have sensed something; he put his arm around my shoulders and promised all would be revealed shortly.'

Finally, the nature of the enterprise was laid out for him in easy-to-understand terms. The absence of information was regarded as a necessary state of affairs. Everyone was given instructions and information on a need-to-know basis.

McGovern adds: 'I was not an expert on betting, having confined my modest activity to a few small wagers on soccer and other non-racing sports. I knew little about horse racing. But the plan was simple: bet on four horses in combination, all over town, within a short period of time. The various systems the bookies used were explained to me, as were the technicalities of the bets.

'At this juncture, the enormity of it was only partially apparent, the realisation coming to me and then slipping away again. After two hours' tutoring in the complexities of the plan, of what could go wrong, what we had to do, I felt I had grasped it.'

According to Lynch, however, he hadn't entirely cottoned on: 'You know, he'd been briefed, tirelessly, on what we wanted. The day before, he was sent out for milk, and on the way, he popped his head round the door and said: "One last thing. It's going to be crucial the horses we pick." He thought we had used some kind of mathematical formula, we'd worked out the probability of winning, just picked them out of the paper.'

Lynch and Parsons had burst out laughing, but it was born of affection. Such an absence of guile was somehow reassuring. 'His very limited knowledge of gambling and horse racing proved a real bonus as he concentrated purely on the job in hand without becoming caught up and distracted by the unprecedented nature of the operation,' says Lynch. 'He is intelligent in an academic kind of way, but wouldn't have had a clue about what it was all about. He's massively trustworthy and not greedy or opportunistic in any way.'

And so damnably cautious. 'He's the kind of guy who, if he jumped in the back of a taxi with you, would immediately put his seat belt on even though we were stuck in a traffic queue! You'd have thought he was on a roller-coaster ride.'

Lynch adds: 'When it came to understanding horses and punting, he would have been ninety-nine per cent no use. In all other ways, he was a hundred per cent. He's a machine. He'll do what's in front of him superbly – within his limitations. It's not just trust, though. You've got to have someone who is intelligent enough to under-stand why they've got to not say anything – without explaining to them exactly what it is they're not supposed to be telling people.'

That was true of all the recruits. 'They all arrived only vaguely aware of what would be expected of them. If just one had turned up having told, say, his wife or girlfriend, and she had passed anything on to, say, her father, who had been an avid punter, then the game could have been over.'

Even Lynch refused to allow his instinctive curiosity to betray him. He deliberately remained detached from the equine operation being organised by Curley. 'I didn't want to know,' he says. 'I had no control over that part of the scheme, so it was irrelevant.'

Only Parsons, who liaised with Curley every day, was aware of that side of the scheme. Indeed, he had prepared analyses of each race the Curley horses would be contesting.

It said everything about McGovern's innate caution that he had arrived at Gatwick from Dublin on the Thursday night, but had also booked a trip on the ferry as well.

For some weeks it had become evident that the Icelandic volcano, and the consequent ash cloud over Europe, which had started in mid April and continued into May, could have had a damaging effect on their plans. Flights were being delayed and cancelled to and from European destinations. There was considerable anxiety about whether members of the team would be able to arrive in London by air on agreed dates. This was not just an irritant. It could threaten the whole enterprise.

Over the next few days, McGovern barely rested from his labours as he prepared for the incoming team of 'punters'. His work included checking routes, collecting bookmakers' slips, managing Lynch's cash flow, withdrawing cash to fund the day-to-day outgoings and sourcing mobile phones and Oyster cards.

Even as the day approached, he was still ignorant of the names of the horses being lined up by Curley. 'I knew I could easily check them, but to be honest, I had enough to worry about and it seemed like bad faith to go checking them when so much trust had been invested in me up to now. Martin even joked with Jack that if Barney had been told they'd get a guy to do all of this, set everything up and not know the names of the horses until the day before, he'd have been happy enough.'

CHAPTER 31

Sunday, 9 May

The majority of the London workforce began assembling at the apartments that morning. Most were animated. Some were more than a little anxious. It was as though they had been transported, like a *Star Trek* crew, and were entering an alien dimension, one that exuded mystery and intrigue. But to boldly go where . . .?

It would not be until that evening that they discovered the truth. For extra insurance, some of the team in Ireland would not even be called into action until the day itself.

One other man, though, had been told to report early. Henry MacCormack had a specific role detailed for him and had arrived from his home in County Meath, late the previous evening.

Back in January he had been summoned to dinner with Lynch. Even though he had been on the periphery of some of his betting schemes over the years, the obviously clandestine nature of this enterprise made him all the more curious. 'I confirmed that I could be relied upon whenever the call came. Some months passed with no further word. In late April I got the call to clear my diary for 10 May. Everything was in place. I was told to bring my best suit.'

On MacCormack's arrival at the apartments on the Saturday, Lynch had led him into one that had the appearance, he recalls, 'of a cross between a student flat on the day before a big exam and an undercover police operation in a movie – computers, wires, takeaway boxes and lots of *Racing Post* newspapers'.

He adds: 'Jack introduced me to Martin and Patrick. My initial perception of Martin was of a deeply suspicious, closed character. A man used to working in isolation. A man who viewed the world through odds. You could almost see him working out the odds of this clown who had just walked in undoing all of his planning and preparation.'

Patrick was the precise opposite. 'Whilst obviously hugely competent and in control, he used wit to defuse the tension that was building.'

Like virtually all the others, MacCormack was not a gambler. 'It meant I was very edgy, as I did not fully understand the task in hand. But in hindsight I would say ignorance is bliss.'

ON THE SUNDAY morning, MacCormack and Lynch took a cab to Park Lane and MacCormack checked into the Dorchester – where a room for the night would set you back at least £400 – before the pair attended Mass at the beautiful Farm Street church.

They then headed for Victor Chandler's Mayfair shop, just around the corner from the Dorchester in Deanery

Street. It is Chandler's only shop in Britain since he sold his other offices to Coral and concentrated on his online business.

MacCormack assumed the role of a high-flying passing businessman who clearly had some sort of gambling problem. Deliberately selected by Lynch because of his modish dress sense, he went about turning over plenty of money in Victor Chandler's and the surrounding shops of the affluent area.

'Jack left me to spend the afternoon there. I was given instructions to bet £1,000 over the course of the afternoon,' he says. 'I was to get to know the staff and let them know that I was in town on business for a couple of days and was staying "next door" in the Dorchester.'

The plan was for MacCormack to portray himself as some kind of poor man's James Bond: flirting with the ladies behind the counter; a bit of a player with too much money to burn. He also swiftly established himself as a sucker for a Trixie and a Yankee, in order that his bets the following day would not be out of character.

London-based much of the time as an upmarket commercial estate agent, MacCormack was used to significant money passing through his hands. 'During the Celtic Tiger years I regularly worked on investment acquisitions in London on behalf of high-net-worth clients,' he explains. 'I suppose Victor Chandler were used to rich boys with more money than sense staying in the top hotels in Mayfair and were therefore happy to take my cash.'

Having flashed his hotel key to highlight his temporary home around the corner at every occasion, he became well acquainted with the local staff. The idea was that they should be more concerned with what time their new friend was heading to the airport the following night, rather than the selections on his slips.

'It was very nerve-racking because I had to establish a relationship and betting pattern,' he says. 'The office was very quiet, so there was no hiding from the staff. We were chatting away openly, and again on the Monday. I am still not sure if my naivety was a positive or a negative.'

He adds: 'I actually won a few hundred on the Sunday, which gave me a good excuse to return the following day. After a few very pleasant hours in Victor Chandler's, I headed off to do a dry run of my other target betting shops for the next day's mission.'

Later, he returned to the St Paul's base where by now the rest of the team had reported in and had been instructed to go out on a dummy run and familiarise themselves with their individual routes.

'The excitement and nervous energy really started to bubble,' says MacCormack. 'A couple of us were very stressed about not making a serious mistake that would threaten everything.'

Even 24 hours before the quartet of horses would run, the finer details had not been divulged. Circumspection still dictated Martin Parsons' thinking. He was determined that the tap operating the flow of information should be opened only slowly. As the team leader, he was concerned less about a treacherous tongue than about a loose one, even at this late stage. He also required concentration, not distractions. To ensure that all remained fully focused on the logistics of their personal roles, it was not until Sunday night that the full details were revealed.

Most of the recruits had hectic lives back home. The background of the team members was varied, though most were young professionals. A few white lies had been uttered to explain their absence. Even their closest family had to remain in ignorance. 'We were off to London for a "behind the scenes look at Reading FC", as I communicated to anyone who asked . . .' recalls Mike Green, a sports scientist, while Dara O'Malley, a financial analyst, informed his family that he was heading to the city to do some consultancy work. Not for a moment could the folks back home have envisaged the true nature of his business.

That pair were the last to arrive. They were both hurlers and barely had time to towel themselves down in the changing rooms after tough, bruising games before flying into London and what O'Malley refers to rather grandiosely as the command centre.

'Opening conversations were based on sport and the weather. Typical Irish conversations. There was a slight edginess as we got to know each other, but this was quickly overcome as we focused on the real business in hand.' The fact that O'Malley was there at all was only because Lynch had disregarded his own criterion: no punters on the team.

It had been a month earlier when Lynch had invited his old friend to a hotel in Athlone on the pretext that he wanted him to do some consulting work for him in London. O'Malley had attended without question.

The pair had known each other since college, and were kindred spirits. 'We were always involved in different initiatives together, sporting fund-raisers and betting coups – somewhat smaller coups than Barney's,

311

of course. We were always transferring money back and over and had built a great trust and friendship with each other.'

O'Malley adds: 'Jack was a brilliant thinker and was never afraid to think big as long as it was aligned to his beliefs. If he saw value in something, he wouldn't be afraid to bet big either.'

After some small talk, Lynch had asked him: 'Do you know why I asked you here?'

O'Malley said: 'I think so – is it to do some work in London?'

'Yes,' retorted Lynch. 'But a different type; it's what I have been discussing with you for years . . .'

O'Malley knew what he meant well enough. 'This was a dream of ours and it often came up for discussion . . . how we would land the big one. My heart starting racing but I tried to stay calm.

'Jack emphasised the importance of silence – not a word to anyone. He told me the date and that this was for Barney. Enough said. I knew the drill. I told Jack I was honoured to be included and to be trusted.'

He adds: 'It was not easy keeping something like this quiet. I had to tell the family I was in London for work, although that couldn't really be described as a lie. I didn't want to check Barney's runners or find out any information about the plans; I just wanted to be focused on what Jack wanted me to do.'

For all the laughter and bonhomie in the St Paul's apartments, it soon dawned on the team that the whole enterprise had been planned with something approaching military precision by Parsons. Though it could be suggested that even Stormin' Norman didn't have to contend with such curses as unpredictable transport in London – works on the Underground – and the ash cloud.

The strategy for most of the group would be to start from areas on the outskirts of London and move back in towards the city as quickly as their form of transport would permit. The trial runs on Sunday were an invaluable exercise. Fold-up bicycles and the Underground combined effectively to enhance speed of movement for many.

Mike Green, the only man provided with a full-sized bicycle, soon discovered it was unsuited to his frame. 'The saddle must have been set for an NBA player, and with no spanners to lower it, I was standing for the duration of the cycle – nice,' he says, laughing at the memory. 'But we loved the military-style attack. My route was to cycle for about ten minutes and then rack the bike, Tube it to an outer suburb, place bets and work back in along the Tube line, stopping off at the different high streets along the way to place bets. Once I returned to the bike, it was a cycle ride to shops in the inner-city area. That evening there were Tube works on-going, so I had to bus the route instead – typical.'

Dara O'Malley was one of the exceptions not to be allocated a small-wheeled fold-up bicycle. 'At fifteen stone, I'm glad it wasn't me . . .' he reflects. He had three areas to cover where there are large clusters of betting offices: Hackney, Bethnal Green and Liverpool Street. 'The only logistical challenge I had was to get a taxi from Bethnal Green to Liverpool Street. We were told to touch the door as we passed each bookie on the pre-run. I actually did this for the first few and then realised that I needed to relax, so I just nodded my head as I passed the others, thinking, "I'll be back . . .""

CHAPTER 32

8 p.m., Sunday, 9 May

Martin Parsons called for silence. The laughter and banter immediately ceased. It was time for the details to be fully revealed. Well, not quite everything. Not even then. All the majority needed to know about was the London shop operation of which they were part.

The scheme, as will become apparent, had been orchestrated down to extraordinarily fine detail. To create the perfect symphony there could not be a discordant note.

Even that briefing had been meticulously prepared. There had been a rehearsal, with discussions about the best way to present information to an audience some of whom had even less experience of serious gambling than Patrick McGovern. 'As a teacher, my own experiences of learning were of some use here in deciding content and how best to structure the presentation,' he says.

Both Parsons and Lynch knew it was vital to make an impression on the group, which stood now in subdued but questioning silence. The pair gave an impassioned explanation of what lay behind the scheme.

The team knew and trusted Lynch. But Parsons was a stranger, and he was clearly the ringleader of the betting operation. He knew he had to be convincing enough to satisfy the group's curiosity. His message had to be sufficient to reassure any of the team who might have been harbouring residual doubts because of the covert nature of the operation. 'You can't treat people as idiots when they are giving up two days for you out of their lives,' explains Parsons, for whom it seemed strange to finally discuss the scheme openly. He recalls: 'I felt as though I was handing over a baby I had single-handedly been looking after for months to strangers for the first time.'

There had to be a *raison d'être*, a principle at stake. It was crucial to explain what had inspired and lay behind the scheme. Yes, big money was involved, he told them, but he stressed that none of those partici-pating would make a fortune. This was about more than lucre.

Parsons elaborated on the character behind the scheme. 'Only two or three of them would have met or spoken to Barney,' he explains. 'So I just told them a bit about how he operated. How he had spent most of his life in combat with the firms who owned the shops they were to go in. It was important to impress on them that this was not just a tourist looking to get lucky by chancing his arm.

'I told them that what we had planned shouldn't be possible, but we were going to try to do it. All they were being asked to do was put on a bet. Several bets.

'We spoke about all the work that had gone into getting to that point. I referred to it as a gun that had been loaded and aimed at the shops, and all that was left for them to do was to pull the trigger – but crucially without knocking the gun out of its stand.'

'I went through Barney's autobiography. I spoke of the annual costs of running operation, of buying the horses. I stressed that any winnings were not going to change anyone's lifestyle – Barney wasn't going to go off and buy a yacht or a Ferrari – though maybe some would ultimately end up improving education and health in Africa.

'This would be a one-off attempt at making a part of racing history. They were told that it was not illegal, or against any rules within racing, for a third party to place bets for someone else in a betting shop.

'Jack and I stressed to them, "Once you bring the dockets back and hand them in, that's you finished. Job done." That would be the last they heard of it. Collection of winnings would be carried out by others. If disputes did arise afterwards, this was not something they were going to have to be involved in – or, worst of all, appear in court over.'

Lynch had recruited the team and felt an added responsibility to ensure that all his men were completely on-side. He explains: 'The last thing we wanted was anyone going to bed that night thinking, "What the hell are we getting ourselves into here?" – and wobbling at the last moment.'

Lynch likened those few hours to a sports team pep talk. 'We did go on a bit – we were there until two the next morning,' he says. 'But remember, it meant so much to us. To be honest, most people would have said, "Let them off at twelve o'clock." But to my mind, if they had been in London for any other reason, they'd be in a nightclub till two or three anyway. There'd be plenty of time for that afterwards.'

Their audience focused intently on what they were

told. No one wanted to be guilty of jeopardising the whole plan. Most vital was the guidance to the uninitiated amongst them about the behaviour of the regular betting man. It was a short course in betting-shop etiquette. Maybe it wasn't from the RADA guide to method acting but it was good enough.

Some may well consider this absurdly melodramatic. Placing a bet? How difficult could that be, even for those unfamiliar with the process, for heaven's sake? But this was different. These were the kind of bets that were liable to arouse suspicion if any staff bothered to scrutinise them. And one injudicious move could scupper the whole plan. They weren't punters; some were not even the types to have an occasional flutter. They would be well out of their comfort zone.

'We went through all the possible scenarios they could be faced with at the counter,' says Parsons. 'Whatever the response was, they had to know what to say.'

When a stranger walks into a betting shop, he is assessed, sized up by staff and other punters, especially if his visit is only brief. It's human nature. Many betting shop punters work out their bets on the premises. It's an unusual form of transaction, almost ritualistic at times. Punters tend to survey the form on the *Racing Post* pages, check the latest betting, identify whether their selection is fancied. Maybe even watch another race first, as those around them suffer – or savour the moment. Quite probably hang around to look for other opportunities if their bet goes down. In general, a visit to a betting shop is a leisurely affair. Few dash in and watch one race. Most linger. It can be almost hypnotic.

'Depending on the circumstances, we told them to walk

in, evaluate the scene, have a couple of quid on the dogs maybe, if necessary watch a race,' says Parsons. 'They were told to be as fast as they could between shops, but once inside to make it look as if this was the first one they had been in all day – the opposite of what they were actually doing.

'If a dog race or virtual race was about to go off as they entered a shop, they were to have a few pounds on the favourite. If there was a member of staff in a suit or wearing a badge with a more senior role on it than shop manager, then they were told to leave without placing a bet.'

Don't look suspicious. That was a priority. Parsons impressed on the team that they should enjoy the experience. They shouldn't walk into an empty shop looking as though they had the weight of the world on their shoulders. They had to perform the part of an ordinary punter hoping to get lucky with an unlikely-looking multiple bet. One recruit who had worked in a betting shop for a short time, explained how it felt from the other side of the counter. He did some role-playing with those who had never placed a bet, to help put their minds at ease before they retired to bed: a rehearsal for the following day's live performance.

THERE'S NO OTHER atmosphere quite like the betting Colosseum, on the racecourse or in the offices; so many Christians prepared to perish for their beliefs, surrounded by other kindred spirits. We're all in this together: man – the majority are men – versus bookie.

As Al Alvarez, poet, critic, poker aficionado and novelist, once reflected on the typical gambler: 'He basically believes in luck. He's not an optimist. He thinks he has a special relationship with fate. There are moments when he's chosen. One of the select. The moments may be few and far between; some kind of wonderful run happens and he feels blessed.'

Alvarez's words formed part of one of the richest insights into the psyche of the betting man: *The Gambler*, Channel 4's compelling programme, which followed the exploits of Jonathan Rendall, the award-winning author who back in 2000 was given £12,000 to bet on a series of events worldwide. Viewers lived vicariously through his pain and sporadic joy. One of the most evocative pieces of film-making laid bare his emotions as his fancy, Flagship Uberalles, contested the 2000 Queen Mother Champion Chase. He had on £1,000, at 11–10 on – the biggest bet he'd had in his life. You see nothing of the race, just a close-up of his taut, tormented features as he inhales deeply from a cigarette – and it wasn't even his own money.

Paul Nicholls' splendid chaser blunders at the second last fence and finishes third. The crowd disperses around Rendall. 'I'm not the only one to have done my money,' he says, taking some consolation from that, as all losing gamblers do, but then adds: 'It's ridiculous, this gambling lark. It's a cliché, but it's a bloody lonely place when you lose.'

Another clip sees Rendall at Lingfield. 'Going to put a Yankee on,' he explains. '. . . bit of a mug's bet. You're not supposed to do 'em, but I love 'em. Yankees are where bookies earn their money.' He adds: 'Fifty pounds laid out, and if they all come in, several thousand pounds.'

Inevitably, his don't.

On 10 May, Curley, the antithesis of such a backer, and his allies were determined to demonstrate that the Yankee and the treble could be anything but a futile exercise – provided this unlikely team of individuals could convince staff they were nothing more than regular punters intent on getting lucky.

Staff normally give only a cursory glance to a bet, particularly if the stake is low. But in this situation it would require the team to take prices on a four-horse accumulator. Low stakes, but still . . . The inherent danger was that it would trip the alarm in the minds of staff if any of them bothered to calculate, even roughly, what those four horses could collectively win.

Based on his extensive research, Parsons told the group which shop personnel to target and which to avoid. He wouldn't win any prizes for political correctness. 'Middle-aged women are generally fairly conscientious staff, afraid of doing anything wrong,' he said. 'But against that, women are less likely to follow racing. Male staff are more likely to be racing fans who might even keep an eye on Curley runners.'

The team were told to target younger women where possible. 'They are generally inattentive, often reading magazines or texting. Many of the staff of the big chains, you might as well be dealing with machines. They're just robotic. No interest in what's on the slip. Just take it, take the money, bang. Just want you away from the counter as quickly as possible to get back to what they're doing. That's a result of accountants running the show.'

However, there were exceptions. 'Paddy Power still has a family business ethos to it. Their staff are trained to have their eyes open. They're sharp. We reduced what we were doing with Power's on the back of that. We didn't want them to give the game away.'

The psyche of the staff member who was to accept the bet was at the forefront of the planning of the operation. The fact that they were trained to contact higher powers upon being presented with anything they were unsure about meant that one phone call at the start of the operation could be the beginning of the end.

Requested stakes for the operation would deliberately be kept below researched referral limits for the various firms. But it would have been an oversight to assume that all of the hundreds of shop staff were going to act according to general unwritten and written rules. The reaction of one over-eager or suspicious employee had to be considered: the worst-case scenario.

Parsons knew that when staff did make general calls to managers or trading departments to confirm stakes allowed, they were routinely asked, 'Is the customer a stranger?' That would therefore be in the forefront of the shop assistants' minds.

The team were left in no doubt: if things got tricky in any shape or form, they were to bale out and make sure they took their betting slips with them. It was made clear to them that individuals weren't going to receive a tongue-lashing if they didn't get many shops done.

The reality was that most of the time the bets were going to be accepted without demur, but it was the one time they were not that could jeopardise the effectiveness of the whole plan. Parsons explains: 'It should be remembered that not placing a bet in one shop where we could have been rumbled could potentially have meant bets could be placed in fifty others. It was emphasised that this was not a competition between them to see who could get the most bets on.'

Henry MacCormack, the man at the Dorchester, reflects: 'Both Martin and Barney had shown great trust in Jack's choice of "reliable" men. Martin showed his complete faith in us and guided us through all of our fears. He gave us tips to calm us down if we suspected that a member of staff in any of the shops were suspicious.

'"Back a dog or something," he said. "Sit back and watch it run. Take your time and relax. If you feel that there is a problem, just move on and get the bet on in the next shop."'

It was not until late on that the horses and races were revealed.

All the blank betting shop slips to be written out were in their destination envelopes to ensure that as much cash could be placed as quickly as possible. On a large table there were piles of every bookmaker's range of dockets for Yankee and treble bets. One of each type of bet was to be placed in all the designated shops.

The Yankee bets involved all four horses. That was straightforward enough. The trebles, though, had required more thought – in consultation with Curley. Four horses meant four possible permutations.

The horses were identified in the order they would run, as follows: A (Agapanthus), B (Savaronola), C (Sommersturm) and D (Jeu De Roseau). The four possible trebles were therefore: ABC, ABD, ACD, BCD.

All of these trebles were placed, not just ABC, although the trio of horses from the Curley stable were considered the strongest contenders. That was the trainer's call. The final decision had been to heavily weight the treble ABC and distribute the rest evenly between ABD, ACD and BCD.

'We wanted to make sure each treble was covered as we wanted as time progressed,' explains Parsons. 'If markets for the races were suspended at any point in the afternoon, we wanted the trebles to be distributed as evenly as possible both numerically and across the different firms in order to maximise profits.'

The team set to work. It was a scene somehow reminiscent of pupils staying in after school and told to write 100 lines. Mike Green recalls: 'As Martin called out the names of the horses, race meeting and race times, you could sense the man was tense – this was months, years, in the making and he and Jack were delivering for their friend and mentor.'

It was an irksome task. 'Jesus,' Dara O'Malley thought to himself. 'Barney Curley could have chosen horses with easier names to spell.'

It was well gone midnight before the boys were released and finally allowed to lay their heads, minds buzzing and exhilarated by what was ahead, on their pillows.

FROM THE MOMENT the team dispersed, any details could have been divulged to friends and relatives. 'It showed the trust in the group,' says Mike Green. 'Anyone not fully on board at that point could have brought the whole plan down by leaking the information.'

No one did.

For some, though, sleep didn't come easy, or immediately. Indeed, some couldn't sleep at all, and headed out in the dead of night to walk their route once more.

Not all the boys' accommodation was quite so luxurious as that offered by the apartments, or the Dorchester. Mike Green and Dara O'Malley were staying in a nearby hostel. 'We had a great laugh at that, comparing the Dorchester to our hostel,' says O'Malley. 'The beds had high wooden partitions on the side. I told Mike at one stage that if I died, he could just put a lid on the bed and it would do as a coffin.'

He adds: 'We spoke for a few hours about our day and the day we would have tomorrow. How could a trainer with twelve horses get four of them to peak on one day? We agreed that two winners would be a great achievement.'

Green remembers chuckling to himself as he drifted off: 'Here we were in the middle of London, ready to be runners for Barney Curley, though as far as the outside world was aware, I was enjoying a visit to Reading Football Club, and I was sleeping in some sort of a coffin bed. You couldn't make it up.'

IN THE REAL WORLD, politics still dominated the news schedules. There was still no clear blue sky for the Tories as they negotiated with the Lib Dems, and Gordon Brown clung on to office tenaciously. Meanwhile, in the stratosphere, that accursed ash cloud was still affecting flights throughout Europe.

It left one man, Sean Fallon, an accountant, stranded in Barcelona. At mid afternoon on the Saturday, Spanish air traffic control had closed seven airports. It meant that Fallon, a key player, was still stuck in Spain at 10 p.m. the night before he was pencilled in to start placing bets in Finchley. He was the only member of the team absent from the Sunday-night briefing.

Patrick McGovern's organisational prowess came into its own. He arranged an escape plan for Fallon, involving a late-night train journey west to Madrid, followed by a bus journey out to an airport hotel. That ensured that Fallon was on an early-morning flight into Heathrow, where he disembarked at 10.15 a.m. He placed his luggage in an airport locker and, printing off his itinerary for the day in the airport business centre, took a taxi that delivered him to Finchley for 11.55. He arrived in position five minutes before the team got the call to go to work.

Sean Fallon had barely had a bet in a bookmaker's beforehand – and certainly not a multiple – and has not had a bet since that time. But Lynch explains: 'He was the model student, if you like. He was in awe of the experience. This was his dream come true. In my head he was crucial to the operation, and I wanted him to be part of it, no matter what.'

Meanwhile, in the early hours of Monday morning, Henry MacCormack prepared to head back across the metropolis from the St Paul's base to Park Lane. He recalls: 'Laden down by envelopes stuffed with cash and hundreds of betting slips, I walked out on to a deserted street outside St Paul's. It was 3 a.m. and the city was deserted – no buses, taxis or even minicabs. Here I was, carrying about £5K in cash, with only a few dodgy-looking characters for company. With no other method of transport apart from my feet, I started the long walk to Mayfair. Not the glamour I expected from my weekend. Eventually I managed to flag down what I thought was a minicab and negotiated a rate back to the hotel. I had a very uneasy feeling in the car, given my cargo. But on getting back to the hotel I was high as a kite. I recall laying out all my envelopes and betting slips on the floor and starting to organise each bet and destination. It felt like the night before a major heist.'

It was perhaps just as well that neither Henry MacCormack nor any of his fellow punters were aware that up in Newmarket there was serious concern about one of the runners. It would have seriously punctured the positive vibes.

The whole plot had threatened to unravel when one horse was found to be lame. Two days before he was scheduled to race in the first division of the amateur riders' handicap at Wolverhampton, and having already completed his last piece of work, Savaronola, who was regarded as one of the soundest horses in the yard, having not missed a day's training in his life, emerged from his box in a sorry state. 'He was as lame as a duck,' says Curley.

For trainers, it's a perennial curse. Noble and graceful they may be, but horses are extraordinarily fragile creatures. You have to question whether a designer would construct one like it if asked to start afresh and build an ultra-reliable, fleet-footed, human-bearing animal to race at speeds in excess of 30 m.p.h.

Equipped with absurdly slender limbs supporting half a ton, they place enormous stresses on them. They are prone to injury – with tendon injuries particularly commonplace – illness and infection. No trainer can feel totally confident about any runner on any day, let alone four of them.

Savaronola's problem was not serious. A vet, Neil,

Steven and a blacksmith, Andrew Skinner, were consulted. The gelding had an infection in his hoof which was full of pus. The pressure on the foot was relieved. Normally, seven days' rest would have been advisable.

'I told the blacksmith, "This horse is running on Monday. What are his chances?" recalls Curley. He told me there was a chance he could be fit to race in forty-eight hours. "Maybe fifty-fifty to be sound."

'If he wasn't running, the whole thing was up the creek. It was a blow, but there was no shouting or roaring. At quarter to ten, I went up to Mass, thinking, "If it's going to come, it's going to come."'

Parsons, kept informed, waited anxiously for news from the yard as Savaronola came out of his box the next two mornings. The horse was not sound enough to run on the Sunday, but there was improvement.

CHAPTER 33

8 a.m., Monday, 10 May

An early inspection of Savaronola at Barney Curley's Newmarket yard didn't completely assuage concerns over his well-being. The five-year-old still did not appear entirely right, but his condition improved considerably the more he was walked and trotted by Curley's assistant, Andrew Stringer.

It was decided that Savaronola would travel to Wolverhampton. However, there was a caveat. 'That morning, we had trotted him up and he seemed to be sound,' recalls Curley. 'But I gave Declan Queally clear instructions: "Ride him down to the start, but if you have any doubts about the horse's soundness for one stride on the way to post, even at the start, dismount him and withdraw the horse." He should not have any compunction about doing that.'

Curley's feeling was that once the horse was at the racecourse, the adrenalin kicking in through the preliminaries would overcome any discomfort he might have been feeling. If he hadn't been a constituent of something so significant that was so close to fruition, he would have been declared a non-runner and saved for another day.

The implications would be far from ideal, however 'If Savaronola was a non-runner then everything would have been down to three horses, which reduced the potential payout,' says Parsons. 'By then, the money would have been down and the bookmakers' cards marked for all time.'

Even with Savaronola's participation, the quartet in pursuit of a multimillion-pound purse hardly inspired overwhelming confidence. To anyone not involved, it looked about as promising as challenging Arnie Schwarzenegger to an arm-wrestling competition.

It bears repetition that only one of the horses, Agapanthus, had won a race of any kind in this country, and according to his trainer he 'wasn't easy – he could pack it in'. Savaronola could possibly pull up lame, and Jeu De Roseau hadn't been on a racecourse for more than two years. His ability to put his best hoof forward had to be taken on trust. There was only one, Sommersturm, about whom there were no worries.

In London, the shop troops had their own anxieties with which to contend. Henry MacCormack, the guest of the Dorchester, for one.

So pumped up the previous night, he experienced a transformation in his mood the next morning as reality struck him hard. He felt ill at the prospect of what was expected of him. The would-be James Bond figure was both shaken and stirred.

He had been tasked to place a bet ten times greater than elsewhere. It was possibly as well that he was unaware that if all went as Martin Parsons had planned, winnings from that bet alone would be into the hundreds of thousands, depending on prices obtained.

'After a bad night's sleep, I was up early as I had calls

to make,' MacCormack recalls. 'It was a regular Monday back in Dublin and business went on. I ate a good break-fast and waited for the call from St Paul's.

'As time went on, I got more and more tense. I sat in the lobby, went back up to the room and down again. There seemed to be a delay in getting started which just blew my nerves to bits.

'To be honest, I didn't really fully grasp the operation and was therefore apprehensive about making a mistake that would destroy it for Jack and Martin. I had a cup of tea and watched the wealthy of the world congregate. Sir Alex Ferguson and an entourage arrived. I was aware he had a horse running in one of our races that day that was the likely favourite. I thought, "Little does he know . . ."'

Noon, Monday, 10 May

Martin Parsons had checked the prices of the quartet on the exchanges every hour through the night and into the following morning. He was satisfied with what he observed.

By late morning, they were mostly priced up as follows: 11–2 Agapanthus, 4–1 Savaronola, 9–4 Sommersturm and 25–1 Jeu De Roseau. Parsons knew that eventually these odds would take a dive. But by then, all bets should have been in place.

St Paul's Great Tom had tolled 12 noon when, in one of the nearby apartments, Parsons, Lynch and Patrick McGovern sent out texts to the team of bet-placers who earlier had been dispersed throughout London and told to wait for further instructions. All knew what was expected of them. Not only had the members of the group been well schooled the night before, but each had been issued with a one-page briefing sheet:

OPERATION CHAINSAW 10 05 2013
You wouldn't be getting this sheet if you didn't know the rules!

The relevant horses tomorrow are as follows. It will be handy to have this with you:
A Agapanthus – 4.10 Brighton
B Savaronola – 5.00 Wolverhampton
C Sommersturm – 5.30 Wolverhampton
D Jeu De Roseau – 7.30 Towcester

Before you leave:
- Phones charged, primary phone (use primary phone for texting out on vibrate/silent – you are effectively going to be in a quiet meeting for three hours and after that you will be free to do what you like)
- Bring slips
- Bring cash
- Bring your sheet
- If applicable bring your bag, spare top, glasses, cap, lock for bike and key
- Have your system for what goes in what pocket clear in your head

Entering shop:
- Is the manager/cashier sharp? Target young females most likely to ignore
- A punter doesn't normally know what he is going to back entering (do your homework)
- If in doubt head out casually/back some greyhounds as well? Remember you are a punter not a messenger

- Locate the slips in the shop. The shop staff must think you wrote them out
- They must be the same slips that are in the shop

Approaching counter:
- Relax and be confident
- Is the cashier smart?
- If in doubt pull the treble out or pull out completely
- If in any doubt with Power's – pull out
- 'How are you, can I take prices on these please?'
- Don't let them ring back to HQ, take docket (you've to get the train!), bolt
- Be ready to explain why they have never seen you if needed – just new to the area
- Why you've backed it in multiple shops – 'my father just called and he wants the same bet as well'/'I have lost fortunes on Curley over past three years, he hasn't so many horses running without a coup being imminent, it was a long time since he landed one'
- Stay relaxed

Exiting shop:
- Have a message, keep it simple. Is there anyone that might see you?
- Remember you're a punter and if there is a finish of a race, watch it

Outside shop:
- Make sure pockets are OK and in order
- Write down the bets done on your sheet but don't be obvious, it can wait

ONE SHOP LOST IS NO HARM, ONE ALARM BELL TRIGGERED IS GAME OVER. RELAX. BE CONFIDENT. DON'T HURRY. IF IN DOUBT, SHOUT.

Parsons recalls: 'The atmosphere that morning had been subdued, but everyone was in good spirits. No one was really larking about or cracking jokes but I think that was more them wanting to show they were taking the job seriously.'

Exposed nerves provoked some black humour.

'Hey, what happens if one of us is involved in some sort of accident?' someone piped up. It was actually a serious question. No flippancy was intended.

'Just don't get blood on the slips,' was Parsons' typically droll response. It provoked laughter and relieved any tension, though he would later stress: 'Obviously we didn't want anyone taking chances with their lives, especially on the bicycles and moped on the busy roads.'

The texts from HQ directed the team to start working their way through a good proportion of the capital's betting shops, particularly in the clusters that had been identified; areas like Edgware Road, Liverpool Street, Chinatown and Camden.

'I would have loved to have been going out there with the boys to complete a route of forty shops I now knew so well,' says Parsons of the office routine he had organised. 'I could tell them off the top of my head that the twenty-seventh shop one of them was going in was down the side of a Boots chemist and had a black and white sign instead of the usual coloured one, and would probably have one woman in it when they got there called Brenda who wore far too much perfume to try and mask the fact she was a heavy smoker.'

Parsons was also aware that some shop staff would have their wits about them. 'I remember the previous week walking with Jack into a Jennings bet shop in Camden. A twenty-something guy behind the counter immediately said to us, "What do you boys want?" and questioned who we were. It was a bit weird, almost like he had been waiting for us. Jack told him we were looking at the shops on the street with a view to renting an empty unit.

'We had clearly stood out on that occasion, as people he didn't know. Perhaps we were being paranoid, but we didn't want too many possible cute individuals like that on the day itself.'

Those involved would later draw parallels between certain aspects of events on 10 May and those contained in that classic caper film *The Italian Job* – the original sixties version. Together, the talents and characters of Curley and Martin Parsons formed a powerful blend. They could be likened to Michael Caine's Charlie Croker and Noël Coward's Mr Bridger.

Remember that memorable line? (No, not the one about 'You were only supposed to blow the bloody doors off.') The one that had Mr Bridger, masterminding from his prison cell a complex heist of gold bullion in Turin, emphasising to Charlie Croker: 'If you go through with this, you've got to win. If you muck it up, don't ever think of coming back – except in your coffin.' Parsons and Lynch weren't quite as exacting team leaders. Instead of those iconic Minis, these guys had bikes, including fold-ups, a moped, the Tube network and, if necessary, taxis and a good deal of legwork, all dependent on the itinerary they were given. With this variety of transport they could hit two or three clusters of shops around Tube stations on the lines into central London before ending up in the heart of the city where bookmakers' shops are most densely distributed.

Each man was allocated a starting point where several different bookmakers had shops close together. A good example was Acton, where seven bookmaking firms were represented within a few hundred yards of each other on the main high street.

Though speed was of the essence and Parsons had planned for as many betting shops to be hit as possible, this was no ad hoc undertaking. It wasn't a case of strewing confetti in a churchyard and seeing which way the breeze took it. It was all carefully targeted. Bets were strategically varied with firms and their different shops. Team members were instructed to visit only the specific locations on the mapped itinerary they were given, passing many others without stopping. Bets were placed in only one of each firm's offices where two of the same were close together.

'This was far from a case of get everything you can as quick as you can,' says Parsons. 'It was aimed at steadily building stakes across the board while keeping prices from being shortened for as long as possible.'

They might hit ten shops and then leave for another cluster fifteen minutes away; the rationale, according to Parsons, being that no single area manager was going to see too much action early on that afternoon in the shops they covered.

The level of stakes on trebles and Yankees had been carefully calculated. Parsons' analysis suggested that

Ladbrokes requested staff to refer upwards any Yankees of £5 or bigger – 11 lines with a total stake of £55. Hence in that firm's shops, the team put a lot of £4 Yankees through (11 bets, meaning a £44 total outlay). And that became the norm elsewhere too. 'The big firms pretty much operate at roughly the same levels,' says Parsons. 'Betfred probably get more multiples traffic due to their bonuses on such bets, so run them through slightly easier if anything.' He adds: 'Bets as small as a £4 Yankee sailed under the bar, but were potentially each worth five figures.' Similarly, it was believed that £16 trebles would be accepted without challenge. It meant the total outlay per shop would start at £60.

Parsons monitored prices from HQ and staking was stepped up when he thought it necessary as prices shortened.

Members of the team had had varied tasks allotted to them. A number had pre-planned specific tasks. They were instructed to turn off their phones for the day and were given new ones along with detailed itineraries. As the afternoon progressed, all did as they were instructed. But that was nothing more than expected by Lynch when he had recruited them.

The initial period of waiting with everyone ready in position had been tense for Parsons and Lynch. A careless word can spread like a virus. One leak from anyone involved or another blog post like that of the *Guardian*'s Chris Cook in April 2009 and the whole thing was potentially ruined. 'A forest fire where prices disappear across the board about a Curley runner, which we have seen so many times before, would have been a devastating blow so close to kick-off,' says Parsons. 'Anyone who thought they could win a few quid for themselves on the side would be the ultimate threat to success. A stray £50 bet in the morning could have cost hundreds of thousands.'

Once they began to hit the betting shops, authenticity as well as speed was key. 'It was a tricky balance. We were asking them to take the typical journey of the regular backer – but to keep the exercise short,' Parsons explains.

His greater fear was not the human element, but technology. He admits: 'The machine they process bets into and automated controls within this were a much bigger potential threat than the individual shop staff. The traders in head office have access to the feed of bets coming through from all their shops combined. The scheme was aimed at them having to physically look for our bets on their systems after they were placed rather than the bets triggering alarms and flashing lights on their screens.

He adds: 'By the time the bets were struck, it was too late for them to do anything. The prices were taken. They now had trading decisions to make – if they even noticed the bets. Shorten prices and lay off where they could. Not easy to do when all the other firms are trying to do the same thing.'

No singles, even as part of multiple bets, were placed. This ruled out Lucky 15s, which are the 11 lines of a Yankee with the four win singles also included. Most firms offer bonuses on Lucky 15s and advertise such incentives heavily. 'Although it would have been sweet for firms to pay a further 10 per cent on top of winnings, this was sacrificed so that the magnitude of the operation could stay under the radar for longer,' says Parsons. 'This meant all liabilities were contingent; they would only start showing up or being acted upon more heavily after one of the selections had won.'

Two horses had to win for any payout with the multiple bets. This helped to keep the bigger prices up for longer, meaning more bets could be placed at greater value.

As has been explained, it went against all bookmaker trading experience for a strongly fancied horse not to be backed as a single. Why would anyone jeopardise a payout by including it in a double or a treble with other horses? It just doesn't happen. Those early-morning smaller single bets that invariably act as an early-warning system for bookmakers on a daily basis did not exist that day.

Any price changes were relayed to the team from HQ and their progress monitored. If staking changes were required, or different weighting of the multiples, this was communicated through internet software via grouped texts with delivery reports. The men called with any relevant information they had as they progressed, but this was minimal until the last half-hour, when some began to receive knock-backs.

The fact that the first runner was not until 4.10 was a great advantage. Although many firms had priced up the races in the morning, Parsons' ploy was to wait until everyone was offering odds so that no bookmaker missed out on the action. According to Parsons, some of the major chains do not price up until they have studied market movers with the smaller operators and scrutinised the action on the exchanges. That activity marks their cards for them. 'We were able to get more on with these bigger layers who have more shops – so we waited for them,' he says. 'The prices sat unchanged for three hours with many firms before any bets were placed.'

CHAPTER 34

Early afternoon, Monday 10, May

Unlike the suave playboy adopting his temporary lifestyle at the Dorchester, some of the team dressed down for the part. The idea was that, as far as possible, they should attempt to blend in with the locality they were visiting.

In east London, one fellow wore a replica West Ham football shirt. He also had a Chelsea one on underneath in order to transform himself into a Blues supporter when he headed west.

Coincidentally, Sunday, 9 May, had been the final day of the Premier League season. Arsenal, Chelsea and Manchester United had all been considered certainties to win their games, and they duly obliged. Together with their itineraries, the 'punters' carried winning slips from the football played the day before, the bets placed in certain shops at some point in the preceding week. So Arsenal (beating Fulham 4–0), Chelsea (thrashing Wigan 8–0) and Manchester United (overcoming Stoke 4–0) all contributed to the agenda by winning their matches. The fact that the trio were short-priced didn't matter. It simply gave the team an excuse to collect winnings, and tactically this was important.

For example, £50 staked to win, say, £10 on Arsenal at 5–1 on returned a total of £60. The profit wasn't important. The winning slip could be presented, and fully reinvested immediately on the operation of the day's horse racing. Psychologically, as far as even highly vigilant shop staff are concerned, a guy who has £50 on the football then ploughs all his returns on to the horses is not a threat – despite being a stranger. It immediately created a relationship between shop staff and team member.

The shop assistant possibly did not even have to hand any money over the counter in this scenario, just exchange a winning docket for a fresh live one. They could see that the stakes of the multiple bets on the horses had been calculated by the customer to match the winning returns of the football bet.

The difference in the handwriting on the slip of the football bet and the new bet going on was there to be seen but was not an issue – if it was even noticed. The automated scanning of the barcode was all the staff had to deal with. The winning football docket was instead evidence that our man had previously placed a bet in the shop over the last few days, and with this assumption made, it was job done. This was merely a returning punter, the kind of customer the shops thrived on, having bets on football teams at short prices – presumably as a fan – then putting the lot back on horses in multiples. It was not the face of what was potentially the biggest organised gamble in racing history.

'It was important when the boys set out at twelve,' explains Parsons. 'We didn't want any early knock-backs while the big prices were still there. They were to start with four or five shops close together, then have a short journey to the next cluster. If they all got on in this first wave it looked good for the remainder of their routes.'

That was how it proved. Between 12.01 p.m. and 4.08 p.m., just before the off of the first race targeted, well over a thousand Yankees and trebles were placed in offices throughout Greater London and various parts of the UK and Ireland.

Dara O'Malley recalls from his diary of the day:

> Mike and I woke early, had a shower and left the hostel. The sun greeted us when we left, thankfully. I headed to Hackney, had my breakfast and waited, and waited.
>
> I spent my time lying on the grass in a churchyard, resting my head on my rucksack, which contained £2,000. I constantly watched my phone. It seemed like I was waiting forever but eventually the text came, and we were all systems go.
>
> I headed into my first shop, Betterbet, at 12 p.m. In truth, I had been in there earlier in the day surveying the shop and making sure I knew where I would be going. Shops are quiet at that time and very few bets are placed. I spent some time moving around the walls, studying form, before writing out my docket for a £4 Yankee and £16 treble.
>
> I had one pre-written docket but did not use it as this was not a time to raise suspicion. I handed over the docket and said: 'Can I take prices on those?'
>
> She never looked up, marked down the prices and I moved quickly to the next shop. This was

a different story. It was obvious when I went to the counter that there was a new staff member being trained by a shop manager. 'Great,' I thought, 'extra scrutiny on my docket is just what I need.' To avoid this, I swiftly left.

It was onwards and upwards from there. Although Hackney and Bethnal Green were quieter betting shops, I felt like I was becoming a professional. I would slip the docket in my *Racing Post* before entering, quickly survey the counter to observe the staff and locate a seat out of sight of the counter.

At the seat, I pretended to write the docket, got up, placed my bet and calmly asked, 'Can I take prices on those?' I found you quickly get to read staff in a betting shop. Younger workers in general were soft prey; they were disengaged, on the phone, reading magazines and totally uninterested. I always tried to hand my docket to these members and tried to avoid a staff member who engaged with customers or was surveying the punters.

I headed back into London down the Central Line, as far as Liverpool Street. Everywhere there were betting shops. How they could fit 10 in such a small area was beyond me – and all seemed to be Hill's or Coral's.

It was approaching 2.00 p.m. and the shops were a lot busier than previously. The odds on our horses had started to shorten so there was little time left. I was sprinting between shops and the hot weather was taking its toll on my appearance. I was wiping the sweat from my brow before entering shops and in some instances I was walking straight to the counter and putting on a bet.

In some shops, it was so busy, I was getting two bets on at different sides of the counter. I knew the game would soon be up, so I was taking more risks but it was working.

During this time I had two guys back in Ireland organised, doing the same in local towns. Jack texted me, and I sent it straight on, followed by a call. I could not tell them what was happening but they were used to getting on for me so they knew the score.

They phoned me during the process: some bookies were not giving them prices and they wondered what the hell was going on. I told them to keep trying and all would become apparent in time.

At one point of my journey, I stopped to organise myself. I had separate compartments for cash, new dockets and old dockets. I was fumbling with the cash in my bag when two police officers passed. I quickly hid it. Guilt, I suppose, but no reason for it.

In one of the William Hill shops, I was about to put my bet on when I noticed a message on the screen behind the counter. It simply said to avoid taking any multiple bets with the following horses: Agapanthus, Savaronola, Sommersturm and Jeu De Roseau. I had the docket on the counter; the staff member looked at me curiously, wondering why I had not handed it over. I looked at her and said, 'I don't think you will be accepting this . . .' and left as quickly as I'd entered. I phoned back to Jack and told him.

Within seconds we had a text to avoid all Hill's shops but there were plenty more shops to hit, although the odds were disintegrating at that stage.

I was one of the first back to the apartment and just in time for the first race. Martin met me and congratulated me for my efforts. 'How many shops did you get?' he asked.

I replied: 'Around twenty-seven – but I didn't get a price in one of them.'

He was delighted. So was I. I should have been exhausted as I had never run so much in my life, but there was such an adrenalin rush. I started to tally up and balance my dockets and my job was done.

When we were all back in the apartment, Martin made a passing comment that the prices were solid all morning, which meant that none of the team had said a word. This was the highlight for me.

While relatively small bets that would go unnoticed were placed throughout London and parts of Ireland, Henry MacCormack was charged with a more onerous responsibility – to place a £50 Yankee, which meant a total stake of £550. That was a sizeable wager even in this particular office. If he could get the prices and the horses prevailed, it meant a possible payout of more than £300,000 in one shop alone.

The man at the Dorchester takes up the story . . .

'Eventually the text came to get started. I felt like throwing up outside Victor Chandler's shop. My story was that I had winnings to collect and was leaving town that day but wanted one last bet. The staff had gotten to know me the day before. I spent about half an hour there, then wrote out my bet and prepared to hand in the killer slip. I knew my bet was about ten times that of the regular bets that we would be placing for the rest of the day.

'I handed in the slip. The girl at the desk took it, started to look at it, and then called the manager. He surveyed me long and hard. I really thought the game was up. He started tapping on his computer and, after what seemed like twenty minutes, returned and said that he would take the bet – but only on the basis of Jeu De Roseau at SP as it was a big price at 25–1. If this move earned him a bonus he deserved it.

'I strode out into the bright light. It was like being released from a cell after an interrogation. I felt sick. It took me a few minutes to gather myself. I made the call back to HQ and explained that they had only given me the SP on Jeu De Roseau. I got a few words of encouragement and set off on my way through the bookies of Mayfair.

'My next stop was Ladbrokes. I entered a very busy shop and again was very nervous. I felt that all the staff were watching me and knew that I was up to no good. I heard

Martin's words in my head: "If you suspect something, back a greyhound." So I did. The dog lost and I walked up and placed my Yankee. No problems, and on to the next bookie.

'A text came through which I will never forget. It simply read: "It's working – keep going."

'It was lunchtime and the crowds really started to come out of the surrounding offices. As a non-gambler I couldn't believe how many people were rushing to place bets in Coral's Mayfair office. In hindsight, I realise I could have gone back and placed the same bet ten times and it wouldn't have aroused any suspicion.

'You could really see the difference in staff quality and motivation in the other shops when compared to the Victor Chandler manager. But that was a testimony to Martin's planning. The system he had devised was set up to exploit the bookies' weakness and reliance on low-paid staff and standardised software systems. I completed about six or seven shops in Mayfair, exited at Piccadilly and took a taxi through Hyde Park and past Buckingham Palace to my next target location.

'Victoria was equally busy until the lunch-hour rush had ended. I had shops on the street as well as in Victoria station. There were a couple of pretty rough shops. I decided now would be a good time to ditch the handkerchief and tie that I had worn for Mayfair.

'Again, these shops were a lesson to a non-gambler. What appeared to be alcoholics and addicted gamblers staring into lines of fruit machines. The biggest surprise of all was virtual racing. The idea just seemed insane to me. Skill or knowledge surely has no role to play. It just seemed so desperate.

'Once I was done in Victoria it was off to my next stop – Pimlico. This was a real treat. I was much more relaxed about the process and was able to enjoy the area. It was a lovely area, with its trendy shops set in front of the backdrop of Battersea Power Station. On completing three or four bookies in Pimlico I came back in a circle towards Victoria along Vauxhall Bridge Road. Success was in the air. We had done our bit. Now it was down to the horses.

'I returned to the Dorchester, took the lift, went straight into the bathroom and pulled my shoes off as quickly as I could. I will never forget the sight of the blisters.

'I lay flat on the bed for about ten minutes, laughing out loud at what had just happened. It was an incredible experience. I had a cup of tea, returned about ten calls and packed my bag. We were called back to St Paul's to watch the races.'

By now, just before 4 p.m., virtually all the trebles and Yankees had been placed in the offices and the runners were lining up for the 4.10 at Brighton. The betting operation was complete. The shop troops could relax, sit back and wait for events on the racecourse to complete the equation. In their ignorance, a number believed it would be as simple as that.

CHAPTER 35

4 p.m., Monday, 10 May

'The races start tomorrow and I'm not going to have any mob fighting in Brighton. I don't give a cuss for your worthless skin, but people who matter may get hurt.'

'Meaning who?'

'Meaning decent, innocent people, poor people, out to put a shilling on the Tote.'

It is approaching seven decades since the local police chief delivered his warning to Richard Attenborough's pathologically malevolent character 'Pinkie' Brown in the original film adaptation of Graham Greene's *Brighton Rock*.

A sense of gentility has long replaced Brighton's seedy dirty-weekend ambience and the reputation of its race-course as a brutal battleground for warring razor gangs. Yet a visit to the track still stirs the imagination; still somehow evokes the slightly decadent spirit of the place in those immediate post-war years, captured so memorably by John Boulting's film.

Even on a Monday in late spring, relatively early in

the Flat season, the crowds thronged in to place their 'shilling on the Tote' at the marvellously distinctive course laid out high on the Sussex Downs.

It's hard not to suspect that the creator of the left-handed horseshoe-shaped switchback track, which finishes with a steep descent, followed by a final stamina-sapping ascent to the line, was having a bit of mischief. That creator had royal connections. In 1779, King George III's brother, Henry Frederick, Duke of Cumberland, who was renting a house in Brighton (then Brighthelmstone), was instrumental, with his gambling friends, in establishing a racecourse on the turf above what is today the Whitehawk Estate.

Some horses thrive there. Some don't. Back in the seventies, the horses run by trainer Richmond Chartres Sturdy seemingly had an affinity with the place. A fascinating fellow, whose nickname was 'Two-sausages Sturdy' – on account of the fact that that was unvaryingly his lads' daily ration – he was based at Shrewton on Salisbury Plain. He became notorious for selling race touches at Brighton, frequently with Lester Piggott in the saddle. Questioned by stewards, Sturdy explained that his horses 'enjoyed the sea air'.

Would Agapanthus similarly relish it? Although Tom Queally had long been familiar with the contours of the course, this was his mount's first experience of them. As he steered Agapanthus to the start of the 4.10, the Whoopsadaisy Charity Handicap, over 1m 2f, you couldn't have blamed him for pondering what glories lay ahead at rather more illustrious venues and in rather grander company than this.

It was three months away from Frankel's first appearance, and the beginning of his projection like a shooting star before the racing public. Queally had already been conscious of his striking potential when he partnered Khalid Abdullah's colt at home. On this day, Agapanthus would be one of four rides for Sir Henry Cecil's retained jockey, though none was for the respected and much-loved Newmarket trainer. These were all spare rides.

In his first race, Queally had finished fourth. Now he was infused with confidence. 'It really does help when you can trust Barney as a trainer to have the horse spot on,' he says. And he had more than a notion that this was the case today. 'I had a little idea about what was supposed to happen,' he agrees. 'Though there was nothing said.'

The race was worth £3,238 to the winner. As an owner, you'd have to win seven such races a year just to cover your costs. Highly unlikely with a moderate handicapper, but it was of no concern to Curley this day.

Joe Fanning had been aboard the gelding when he had won at Yarmouth 13 months earlier – Agapanthus' only victory in Britain – but Queally was well aware of the horse's traits. 'Tom would have been in and about at the yard all the time, and he would have had an idea that he was a bit of a two-timer; that you had to get stuck into him,' says Curley. 'Tom doesn't jump about on horses normally, but he's very strong if required.'

The trainer had no need to issue instructions. 'I'm not a man that gives the gospel in the parade ring,' he explains. 'I remember Timmy Murphy riding Zabeel Palace for me at Ascot in October 2009, a handicap hurdle. He'd never ridden for me in his life. The horse had won the previous time at Plumpton (and had gone up 7lb in the weights for it).

'He says to me, "I suppose you want me to come late, like Plumpton?" I just nodded and said: "Come later . . ." That was all. And that's what he did. You'd think he had done it by computer he was so precise in his timing – took it up halfway up the run-in.' And won smoothly, by just under two lengths.

That's the kind of initiative Curley demands from all his jockeys. 'It was a lesson from Charlie Whittingham way back when I started. I give hardly any instructions to them,' he says. 'I might have said "should win, stays well" or "he might be a short runner", or "he's a gutsy beggar, this". But I employ good riders who should know what they're doing, and who've done their homework before they come to the races. Most good professional jockeys look up everything in The Form Book.' He adds: 'Anyway [if he said too much], you'd just get these fellas flustered . . . my reputation being that I'd be having a few pounds on.'

Ostensibly Agapanthus' race was a tight affair, with just half a stone separating the top- and bottom-weighted horses, and the betting reflected that. Parsons had analysed the race, looking for possible dangers, and had added his own notes on the runners. Next to the jockeys' names are each horse's handicap rating, which determines the weight carried in that race.

Blue Tango Amanda Perrett Neil Callan 69: ran C&D (course and distance)last twice, beaten short head as 5–2 fav latest, just caught. Goose Green hd back in 3rd. Up 4lb for that. Consistent.

What's Up Doc Lawney Hill Ian Mongan 67: consistent handicapper in 70s in last three years.

Won selling hurdle 9–4 Fakenham Tuesday, ran
to 108. Leads, game, stays well.

Goose Green Ron Hodges Daryll Holland 66: ran
3rd behind Blue Tango last week. Won twice
over C&D last summer, off 46 and 58, running
to 69. Up 4lb for 3rd last time.

Inspirina Richard Ford J.-P. Guillambert 66: wants
further, stays on well. Consistent.

Agapanthus B. J. Curley Tom Queally 63.

Freedom Fire G. L. Moore Liam Keniry 62:
consistent, runs to 69.

Parsons' conclusion was this: 'All consistent but
exposed types who stay quite well. What's Up Doc
wouldn't want giving too much rope in front. Often kicks
off steady pace fair way out. Inspirina will be running
on.' Only 7lb covered the six-runner field on official
ratings, and on paper, 5 lengths would cover the five of
them. But Parsons also knew that his boss had a fair idea
Agapanthus was at peak fitness, and on exceptionally
good terms with himself.

That spin over hurdles could prove vital. To any unconnected observer, it was an inauspicious performance, but
Curley put a positive interpretation on his thirteenth of
14 at Fakenham. 'Agapanthus turned nasty in 2009,' he
recalls. 'We rested him, and he loved his day out hurdling,
and just began to shine.'

This was one intended runner he hadn't taken to Lingfield
for that informal trial. Curley explains: 'He was a bit of a
law unto himself. He'd have just been a nuisance. He didn't
need a trial. I knew what he'd run up to. Also that trial
was a gruelling mile and a half while the Brighton race was
one mile two furlongs. I wanted to leave him fresh.'

That confidence looked utterly misplaced when the runners bounced out of the stalls. Agapanthus didn't have the appearance of a hot favourite. Certainly the bookies would have been heartened in the early stages by the sight of the gelding last of the six, and Tom Queally already having to give him some encouragement.

For a moment it looked as though the entire plan would fall apart before it had even begun. The betting team, which had by now returned to base, had expected four comfortable winners. Surely this wasn't in the synopsis for the day?

'. . . Agapanthus being stoked along, trying to improve . . .,' observed racecourse commentator Simon Holt. Queally stayed cool and maintained his driving rhythm. No panic. Half a mile from home, Agapanthus began to make progress.

'Out wide, Agapanthus is now staying on with a bit of purpose. They meet the rising ground . . . Agapanthus on the wide outside.'

'Inside the last furlong, Inspirina looks easy meat now for Agapanthus . . . Agapanthus draws alongside Inspirina in the run to the line . . . . and Agapanthus wins well in the hands of Tom Queally for Barney Curley. Inspirina second. Goose Green third.'

Slowly, inexorably, Curley's charge had gathered in his rivals, and relishing the rising ground, had stayed on to lead inside the final furlong, winning comfortably by two lengths. 'I had to use a little gentle persuasion,' says the rider. 'It wasn't a two-year-old filly first-time-out type of ride, anyway.'

It had been anxious watching for those involved, though. Punters on Betfair, who can bet 'in running', could have got 10–1 on him at one point, before he asserted himself in the closing stages.

All concerned could breathe easily again. Only Curley was oblivious to the drama, having been delayed at Cambridge's Addenbrooke's Hospital. 'I'd just said to Martin, "Any problems, ring me." You have to do that. You can't be interfering with everything. We had a plan. Do it. Something goes wrong, ring me. I never got any phone calls.'

He arrived home a few minutes after the race, and called Parsons. 'Well?' he asked with typical brevity.

Parsons put his mind at rest. 'It was just like chatting to him on any other day. In fact Barney was quieter than normal,' recalls his aide. 'He called a couple of times in the morning to see how the books [on his runners] had priced up, but that was it.'

The first winner up – and the early prices Parsons and his team had taken as part of their multiples were as long as 11–2. It represented a nice first leg of the gamble – though there was nothing actually won from the mammoth multiple bet operation. Not yet.

There was one guarantee, however. When Agapanthus flashed across the line, it confirmed that the outlay for the operation, around £100,000, had been recouped. When the opening betting show on-course for Agapanthus' race at Brighton came in at just before 4.00, the horse had been backed separately by Parsons and his associates – but not before then – as a single to win the opening race. The opening price with the on-course bookmakers was 7–4. He drifted out to 5–2 and started at 2–1 favourite. 'We averaged out about 9–4. Great trading, but fairly irrelevant at the time as we sat on the edge of something potentially so big,' reflects Parsons.

Whatever happened next, the winnings from that

single covered the outlay on all the trebles and Yankees. It was now, effectively, a bet to nothing.

The major strength of the whole operation was that no money was shown as win singles, other than that late money on Agapanthus. This stratagem meant that liabilities on the other runners wouldn't appear on the books until Agapanthus won.

According to Parsons, it is very hard for bookmakers to physically monitor all their multiple liabilities, however large. Only after Agapanthus had won would the liabilities for the pending second legs of the doubles become apparent. If Agapanthus had been the only winner, all the multiple bets would have gone down. Two of the quartet had to win for any return.

The first liabilities after Agapanthus had won appeared as three doubles on the Yankee bets: A and B, A and C, and A and D. It meant that prices on the other three horses collapsed across the board of the entire industry after the first winner, but by then early prices had been taken in the shops.

Tom Queally, oblivious to such concerns, would ride another winner (this time for Eve Johnson Houghton) in the next race to complete a double on the day. It all depended now on what quality his brother Declan could entice from his two runners at Wolverhampton, neither of which had won a race in this country, and one of which was possibly still suffering the effects of a hoof problem.

CHAPTER 36

4.55 p.m., Monday, 10 May

The runners made their way to post for the 5.00 at Wolverhampton, a track that has never been noted for its charm. Author James Gill, in his book *Racecourses of Great Britain*, wrote rather unkindly of 'the unlikely event of anyone making a voluntary trip to Wolverhampton'.

Dunstall Park has rarely featured high-grade sport in its calendar, other than the Midlands Cesarewitch and the Midlands Cambridgeshire. But the last 20 years has seen the track's development as an all-weather venue, with floodlights installed. Saturday nights are particularly popular with local racegoers, who bet and dine, hopefully financed by their winnings.

Monday afternoons are considerably quieter.

Declan Queally, riding Savaronola in the 5.00, had had the chance to familiarise himself with the course a couple of weeks earlier when Curley had asked him to partner his runner Sir Mozart. The partnership had finished third in an amateur riders' handicap over six furlongs, at 14–1, but what was more important was that young Queally now had experience of the one-mile track and its Polytrack surface.

'It's a big thing to come from the point-to-point field to ride at Wolverhampton,' explains Curley.

Queally was not intimidated by the challenge. 'All I knew about my horses was what I'd read in The Form Book, and I'd watched a couple of videos. I just turned up and rode them,' he says. 'Barney didn't say much – just told me to keep it simple. Don't complicate things.'

His brother Tom had every confidence in him completing the job on the Curley duo. 'You'd give him a run-down of particular traits of the horses, and I obviously informed him of his chances. Declan had a claim [a 5lb allowance based on the number of Flat winners he'd ridden], but that wouldn't indicate the wealth of experience he would have brought to an amateur race.'

Division I of the Sportingbet Stan Cullis Amateur Riders' Handicap, over 1m 4f, worth a few pence over £1,384 to the winner, was a distinctly low-grade event, for horses aged four and over, rated 0–55. Races are classified between 1 (elite) and 7 This was class 6.

Again Martin Parsons had looked closely at Savaronola's opposition. This is the field, with handicap ratings (jockeys' weight allowances are in parentheses) and Parsons' comments:

Magic Warrior Jimmy Fox Mrs Sarah-Jane Fox (5) 55: off since Aug 09 when returned at Kempton on Monday, beaten 27 lengths over 10f, 66–1. Light of former days.

Savaronola Barney Curley Mr D. L. Queally (5) 55.

Snowberry Hill Lucinda Featherstone Mr J. P. Featherstone (5) 53: off since Sept 09. Exposed stayer – wants 2m.

Highland River Aytach Sadik Miss E. J. Jones 52: exposed runs to 61. Pulled up over hurdles before 2 out, 28–1 handicap off 99 two weeks ago, 2m5f Ludlow.

Laura Land Mark Brisbourne Mr Ben Brisbourne (3) 52: just 4 runs, last run Oct 09, first hcap off 52, not yet justified mark. Could be anything.

Call Of Duty Dianne Sayer Miss E. C. Sayer (5) 52: decent 2 yr old for Mark Johnston rated 75 but off for 18 months and never regained form in 12 months. Beaten 15 and 31 lengths last 2 recent runs after another 7-month break.

Haka Dancer Philip Kirby Mr A. T. Brook (7) 51: very moderate, only 3 runs on flat, shown nothing.

If I Had Him George Baker Mr S. Walker 50: 6 hurdle runs since Sept 09, off since February. Maiden after 20 runs all codes. (Exposed as hurdler 113 2½–3 miles.) Hard to assess Flat form, but best hurdle form would put him in at 60–65.

Darfour Martin Hill Miss E. J. Jones 49: another decent M. Johnston 2 yr old, over 7f, once rated 82 but rapid decline and exposed as 95-rated hurdler. Off since Jan. Never run further than 10f.

Anasy Gay Kelleway Mr R. Birkett (3) 48: just 4 runs, last Oct 09. 3 x 7f maidens never showed. Beaten 9 lengths over 9f Wolv only handicap. Run off 48 latest at 40–1. Poor form so far, would have to improve significantly after 7 months off.

Bedarra Boy David Arbuthnot Mr T. P. Finn (5)
48: paceless on form shown.
Cemgraft Paddy Butler Miss Zoe Lilly (3) 47: off
since Dec 08. Paceless.

'Poor race,' opined Parsons in his analysis of a contest
in which 9lb separated top and bottom weight, adding:
'Will say revolves around betting. If I Had Him could
have 10–15lb in hand. Laura Land and Anasy being
persevered with, shown nothing yet in only runs each,
but could be better than that.' The majority of the runners
had little to commend them. A couple had shown some
form as juveniles when trained by Mark Johnston, but
had declined since. There were two veterans, Magic
Warrior and Cemgraft, aged 10 and 9 respectively, at
either end of the handicap.

One horse, the principal threat to the Curley runner,
was of particular interest, though. Fortuitously for Curley,
the field of 12 included the George Baker-trained If I
Had Him, running for the first time in the red silks,
appropriately, of the Manchester United manager Sir
Alex Ferguson. He had moved from the Gowran, County
Kilkenny, yard of James Morrissey to Baker's stables in
Whitsbury, Hampshire, less than a month earlier.
Significantly, he was partnered by top amateur Simon
Walker. In amateur riders' events an experienced jockey
with a good record tends to be an even more crucial factor
than in professional races.

Ferguson's gelding was still a maiden after 20 runs under
both codes, but Curley believed that If I Had Him's
National Hunt form in Ireland, where he had been placed,
made him the obvious threat. The trainer had emphasised
that fact to his jockey. 'I told him that Sir Alex Ferguson

had a horse in the race. I said, "He's your danger – watch him."'

First time out for his new trainer, If I Had Him was well fancied in the market, and that suited Curley down to the ground. Though Savaronola started at 11–10 favourite, money for the Ferguson horse ensured he could still be backed at relatively remunerative odds early in the day.

'This was a great help to the prices we were able to take in what was overall a weak race,' says Parsons. 'If he hadn't been in there, Savaronola would have been priced up a much shorter favourite himself. The difference in half a point in price made such a vast impact on the potential payouts of the multiples.'

But still that worry about Savaronola's well-being persisted. 'If I had to have a bet, I would have bet that he wouldn't be sound,' says Curley. Declan Queally, however, arrived at the start satisfied that his mount was suffering no ill effects from that hoof infection. That confidence was not misplaced.

'*Plenty in with chances with three left to run,*' racecourse commentator Derek Thompson called them home . . . '*Here comes Barney Curley's Savaronola on the outside. Trying to get through on the outside Bedarra Boy and the red and white colours of If I Had Him. Into the home straight, the white face of the favourite Savaronola kicks and has gone three clear. Three lengths clear, Savaronola. Here comes the chasing group, Sir Alex Ferguson's If I Had Him is coming down in seond. Third place is Darfour . . . . it's a one-horse race. Savaronola five clear with half a furlong left to run, the Barney Curley colours . . . the favourite wins. Second If I had Him for Sir Alex Ferguson, third Bedarra Boy.*'

Curley's representative had the race won by the two-furlong pole, and surged clear for the first victory of his career at the twelfth time of trying in both Flat and jump codes. He won by six lengths from Ferguson's charge.

'Declan Queally was excellent,' says Curley. 'He kept in Sir Alex Ferguson's horse, If I Had Him, ridden by the best amateur in Britain, and made sure he didn't see daylight, which was important. He had him covered. Very few amateurs could have done that. For a young fella, it was very good race-riding to do what he did. It wouldn't have done his riding reputation any harm.'

Some time later, Curley recalls, he was in conversation with Ferguson. 'He told me: "I backed that bloody horse that day . . ."'

The *Racing Post* reviewed the race thus:

> [Savaronola] was gambled on and ran out a most decisive winner. He had yet to win a race and had shown little over hurdles the last twice, but as ever with this yard the money talked and it was clear at the top of the home straight he was going to complete the task. He obviously had plenty in hand, but horses from the stable rarely follow up, and he is probably more of one to keep an eye out for back over jumps down the line.

He didn't win again, under either code.

On this day, though, it was two from two. The betting team at St Paul's could scarcely believe what they were witnessing. This was all proceeding so smoothly.

Meanwhile, Curley sat in his chair and watched from afar. 'I got back from hospital and one of them had won. The one I'd had worries about won six lengths. I'm in clover now. And I haven't any doubts about Sommersturm.'

After that easy victory of Curley's representative in the first division of the amateurs' handicap, the on-course bookmakers took no chances with his runner in the second half an hour later.

5.25 p.m., Monday, 10 May

From an opening show of 6–4 on, Sommersturm was hammered in to an SP of 3–1 on favourite. Not that it was of concern to Curley and his team. They had already obtained early prices as big as 7–2 included in the trebles and Yankees. They were, by far, the shortest odds of any of the quartet. The SP was the kind of price that doesn't countenance failure.

This was the banker; a shoo-in. For all concerned, even Curley, the horse was unbeatable. After the first two had gone in, the third, Sommersturm, according to Curley, 'was like a penalty kick'. But as England's Stuart Pearce and Chris Waddle can attest, penalties don't always hit the back of the net.

Sommersturm was joint top weight in what was again a poor handicap. This was the field, with handicap ratings, and Parsons' comments:

Sommersturm Barney Curley Mr D. L. Queally (5) 55.

Kristopher James Mark Brisbourne Mr Ben Brisbourne (3) 55: last run Oct 09, won 9½f 0–55 handicap off 52 Wolv. First win in 16 runs. Never run over 1m 4f.

Lisbon Lion James Moffat Miss Rebecca Sparkes (7) 53: maiden. Beaten 8 lengths 5th of 9 C&D

365

2 weeks ago. Travels well, not finishing.

Wee Ziggy Michael Mullineaux Miss M. Mullineaux (5) 52: maiden after 31 runs.

Blackstone Vegas Derek Shaw Mr S. Walker 52: consistent, up 2lb for fair 2nd to Sworn Tigress 4 weeks ago C&D.

Wabbraan Martin Hill Miss E. J. Jones 51: stays well. Won well off 65 last March, up to 74. Ran up to 58 two weeks ago, staying on over 11f Kempton off 5lb higher.

Bright Sparky Michael Easterby Mr O. Greenall 50: won similar race C&D 22 Feb 9–4 fav off 46, up 4lb. Since beaten 55 lengths 2 mile handicap chase Southwell. Very limitd.

Schinken Otto Malcolm Jefferson Miss R. Jefferson (3) 48: very limited, outsider.

Naledi Richard Price Mr M. Price (3) 48: won desperate 9½f Wolv 0–55 off 47 in March. Exposed, limited.

Prickles Karen George Mr C. D. Thompson (5) 48: poor, paceless.

Barbirolli William Stone Miss C. Scott (7) 46: exposed, limited, runs to 55, consistent.

Parsons had adjudged that the contest was, even for its class, distinctly weak. He commented that Blackstone Vegas and Wabbraan offered the best form, and that whatever beat the former would win.

NOTHING DID BEAT Blackstone Vegas.

Half a mile to run, and doubts were already dampening

all the heavy expectancy surrounding Sommersturm as commentator Derek Thompson announced: '. . . *I'm looking for the favourite . . . the favourite's got it to do . . . . the favourite's under pressure . . . here they come back towards us . . . two left to run . . . the favourites's only got three behind, got no chance. Blackstone Vegas hits the front under Simon Walker. He wins it.'*

Back at the St Paul's base, there was silence. Disbelief. The party had been crashed by an unwanted stranger.

Henry MacCormack encapsulates that moment: 'When I arrived back to the apartment there was a great feeling of triumphalism. The plan had been executed to perfection and Martin and Jack were buzzing. For the next hour the team started to arrive back, tired but pumped with adrenalin. We all gathered around to watch the third race on a laptop screen. This was not in the script. The energy was zapped from the room.'

Lynch emphasises: 'The fact that the third got beaten hammered home to them that there's no certainty in racing. We'd pretty much told them that there was no doubt about the outcome.'

Parsons was dumbfounded. 'I'd sat there and watched Savaronola win that Wolverhampton race half an hour before by an easy six lengths,' he says. 'A month earlier, I'd seen Sommersturm account for him comfortably at Lingfield in that serious gallop. It was clear from the piece of work Sommersturm was the superior horse. I said: "this is going to win a furlong. I could ride this."'

He adds: 'When he got beat, it was "work that one out". I was so desperately disappointed purely because I knew we would never get another chance at backing four horses to win on the same day in this way ever again. The main aim had been to relieve most bookmakers on

367

the high street of their maximum pay-outs and this was not now possible.

'That was final leg of the treble we'd had a lot of the money on. We worked on the basis that the first three would win, easily, and then we could relax and hopefully cheer Jeu De Roseau home as well.'

There could be no escaping the harsh reality: Derek Shaw's four-year-old had defied joint top weight, with Sommersturm eventually finishing well to be a four-lengths sixth.

Curley was to recall later: 'If my best friend had said which horse would be a definite winner today, I'd have said Sommersturm, judging by the way he'd done that racecourse gallop for me at Lingfield. He'd devoured Savaronola.'

Declan Queally could offer no explanation. 'He got a bit boxed in, and didn't pick up. He just didn't perform as they thought he was going to.'

Curley, however, was unruffled. 'Barney just called and asked "Well?" again, same as he had after the two winners,' says Parsons. 'He was more concerned that his St Bernard hadn't been taken out because of his hospital visit so he took him out on the gallops for a walk.'

That left the fourth horse, Chris Grant's runner Jeu De Roseau. With all the doubts about his fitness, he had been merely 'intended to add a little cream at the end'. Now his participation acquired a new significance.

CHAPTER 37

6 p.m., Monday, 10 May

It was a typical British spring evening, by now overcast with a chill in the air, as Denis O'Regan arrived at Towcester racecourse a good hour and a half before his one race of the evening. It gave him sufficient time for a spell in the course sauna. His horse had been allotted 10st 6lb in the Niftylift Handicap Hurdle, and he would have to 'maybe sweat off 1lb' to 'do' that weight. The Irishman would have half a ton of horse under him, but even a pound can be decisive.

Jeu De Roseau's projected SP in the morning papers would have suggested a no-hoper who would benefit from the run, although some might have suspected that it was an awfully long journey down from County Durham for no return.

Though O'Regan had ridden work for Curley, he had not made the connection between Jeu De Roseau and the man who had originally trained him. However, en route from his home at Hungerford, O'Regan had received a cryptic text from his then agent, Sam Stronge, who'd been following the racing during the day. It read to the effect: *Is there something you haven't told me? Do you know something I don't?*

O'Regan texted back: *I don't know what's going on. How would I know?*

He recalls Stronge responding: *Your horse has just gone from 25–1 to 6–4 favourite.*

On arrival, O'Regan immediately had it confirmed that something was indeed in the air. He says, with a laugh: 'You have to pass the bookies on the way in; they're parked in front of the weighing room, and I remember them staring at me curiously walking in – though I had no idea what it was all about.

'I just remember when I weighed out, I said to Chris, "What's happening here?" He just gave me the nod, to say, "This has a chance." That's all I needed really.'

So just why was Jeu De Roseau available for several hours to back at 22–1 (indeed, as big as 25–1 and 28–1 in places early on), a price that would normally condemn a runner to the ranks of also-rans?

The facts were that on the morning of the race Jeu De Roseau had been priced appropriately for a horse from a small stable in County Durham returning from over two years off the racecourse, even accepting that he had been dropped 13lb since his last run – coincidentally on the same course – when he finished eleventh of 12, beaten 54 lengths.

This was a horse that had never won over Flat or jumps and since arriving from Ireland had started at prices up to 66–1. In the five races he finished he had been beaten an aggregate 251 lengths.

Given that background, the betting patterns involving Jeu De Roseau had been extraordinary. Before Sommersturm ran, Jeu De Roseau was odds on. When

Sommersturm was beaten, the firms relaxed a little, and he drifted out to 2–1 before returning at 6–4. Few 22–1 chances in the morning are returned at those odds.

The dramatic contraction of the horse's odds might not have appeared such a mysterious phenomenon once the Curley connection was brought into the equation. No one would argue that Jeu De Roseau was a much longer early-morning price running under the care of a new trainer than he would have been if he was appearing on the card in Barney Curley's colours.

With the greatest respect to Chris Grant, one of his runners would not automatically strike fear into the book-making industry. By his own admission, he is not a betting man. Even Jeu De Roseau's history with Curley would not have been considered particularly relevant – not until late in the afternoon, by which time two of Curley's three runners had prevailed.

The sponsors of the race are manufacturers of cherry-pickers, amongst other products. In his quest for a crucial third winner, Curley himself couldn't have picked the jockey for the last representative of the quartet more expertly. O'Regan's career had been going through a transitional period. He had undergone that split with Howard Johnson, and had been out of the saddle for three months after breaking his fibula in a fall at Kempton in October. He had also suffered from a dearth of winners, and from whip bans, probably from trying too hard to ride winners on what were maybe not the highest calibre of horses.

He was here for one ride, for a fee of £141.21 and a percentage for a win or place in the event, which was worth £4,119.05 to the winning owner. But freelance jockeys rarely turn down any ride. Out of sight, out of trainers' calculations. 'I'll tell you exactly how I felt,' says O'Regan. 'I felt Chris'd come a long way to Towcester for one runner for me to tip up and not give him much of a ride.'

O'Regan knew what Grant expected of him. 'I'm too young to have seen him ride, of course, but I've seen videos,' says the jockey, who was born in 1982. 'Chris was very strong, that's why they called him Rambo, wasn't it? He likes them drilled, he likes them ridden hard. You watch the rides I've given some of his horses over the years, and I've ridden them very aggressively. I think that really played a big part in the kind of ride I gave the horse.'

He adds: 'At that time in my career, I was very angry too. I had no job, and I was hungry, as a person, and as a jockey, even though my style of riding wouldn't always suggest that. It's a fact. I do feel when I ride for Chris, I seem to ride with more aggression and anger than I would for other trainers because other trainers like me to sit quiet and give them a chance.'

Towcester, located in the parkland of chairman Lord Hesketh's Easton Neston estate, off the A5 between Northampton and Milton Keynes, isn't generally host to the highest-quality racing. But a generous crowd had been attracted to the day's only jump meeting – a number no doubt drawn there by the free basic admission policy for all but the track's two big meetings. The 1m 6f course is noted for a punishing uphill finish that is liable to find out any horse less than stout-hearted.

By the time the starter sent the 13 runners (there were two non-runners) – on its way, Den Maschine, the horse so feared in the seller an hour earlier, had already vindicated Grant's decision to swerve that contest, having won easily.

As Jeu De Roseau set off, there was no hint of what was to follow. Tony McCoy dictated the pace early on with a searching gallop on his mount Manjam. Racecourse commentator John Hunt takes it up: *'Tony McCoy's gone straight into the lead here on Manjam at what looks to be a good clip . . . Jeu De Roseau, the favourite, heavily backed, is three from the rear in these early stages . . . the pace looks pretty strong . . . Jeu De Roseau's supporters will be watching him like an absolute hawk over the next couple . . . but he's well in touch towards the inside and jumped that very neatly indeed.*

'The favourite in sixth place, just nudged along there as they approach the next flight. But still Manjam with the advantage from Midnight Spirit travelling pretty well. Witch of the Wave in fourth. Fifth Jeu De Roseau, but being ridden to stay in touch with them at the moment.'

From the stands, it had appeared that O'Regan's horse had cleared the first of the eight hurdles with a degree of deliberation, and, to the casual onlooker, was struggling. His rider could have been forgiven for taking the same view.

The jockey had to get serious with him from some way out, and that 6-4 favouritism suddenly appeared ridiculously short. His supporters had surely got it spectacularly wrong. Anyone unaware of the horse's background could be forgiven for suspecting that he would undoubtedly benefit from the run, but make his way home in his own time.

With that relentless early pace forced by McCoy, Jeu De Roseau touched 11-2 in running with Betfair, having been off the bridle a long way out. Some jockeys would have downed tools.

Chris Grant concedes: 'Going away from the stands, you're thinking "this ain't winning nothing".'

With many other jockeys, perhaps not. But that evening, he was in the right hands. O'Regan's experience told him that the early pace would tell on the leaders and, despite having plenty of ground to make up, had him bearing down on the leaders by the straight.

John Hunt again: *'The third last, and there's a bad mistake by Witch of the Wave, and that gave a lovely run up the inside for Jeu De Roseau. He's into third, but being ridden. The two in front of him going better at the moment as they begin the turn for home. A long way to go still.*

'Manjam out in front from Midnight Spirit. Jeu De Roseau, bidding to land this huge gamble, is in third place, but still two lengths to find on the front pair. They head towards the second last. Midnight Spirit crashed through that, landed, though in front from Manjam. Jeu De Roseau still having everything thrown at him. Ruby Crown coming hard over on the far side. One flight left to take. We've got a great finish on our hands here. Midnight Spirit, Ruby Crown, Jeu De Roseau – it all depends on the jumping here at the last. Ruby Crown jumped well, so too did Jeu De Roseau. Jeu De Roseau noses to the front here, LANDING A COLOSSAL GAMBLE . . .'

The jockey takes up the story: 'I knew they'd gone too quick up front. It was a 0–105 race, all were rated less than 100, and were horses of mostly modest quality, and they do not stay going at that pace. They're just limited horses. They cannot keep going at that gallop around Towcester. That's what kept playing at the back of my mind . . . just hang on in there, and have a bit of luck and a run down the inner, and I would get there.

'After the second hurdle, although he was a bit high,

he came down and he got a lot slicker in his jumping and he actually started gaining ground, and I was away.

'I just needed the race to come to me a little bit rather than me to go and get it. They slowed down coming to the hill, and I got a good jump at the third last, and a great run up the inside. All of that helped. But by no means did I think I was on a horse with 20lb in hand.'

This was where his sheer bloody-minded desire to get the horse home took over as he drove his mount to lead over the last and maintain that momentum to the line. O'Regan's performance was an inspired one, irrespective of the circumstances.

'I'm not a cocky person, but in the last furlong I really had to lift him,' he says. 'It's amazing really. Never at any stage did he give the feeling that he was going to pick up and win half the track or anything. He was all out, with nothing left.'

Back in the betting HQ, a roar went up that was not quite the done thing in such an upmarket locale. It had at least one fellow resident of the apartments knocking on the door to demand that the occupants keep the noise down.

Just over seven and a half hours after the elaborate scheme had been set in motion, it was all over.

Gambles are just as likely to come unstuck as to reap rewards. There was no doubt Sommersturm's defeat was a significant blow. But Curley and his betting team – Mr Cool and the gang, if you prefer – had been blessed by good fortune in so many respects. It was the day when the banker failed to deliver, but the outsider came to the rescue.

Parsons recalls: 'I was in a separate room with Jack, and on the phone talking to Barney. I left a laptop running with a streaming feed from ATR [the satellite racing service] in the room next door. The other boys' picture had cut out. They didn't even see it. But the commotion from next door told them what they wanted to know. They all started celebrating despite not even seeing him win. I still listen to the commentary once a month in the car. I get an incredible buzz from hearing it.'

He adds: 'For my age, I've watched as much racing as anybody, and I wouldn't have shouted at the TV five times. Because Denis's horse had been outpaced in the early part of the race, you just wondered, "What's this all about?" But he was coming and coming. The hill at Towcester is the stiffest in the country. I knew it was going to be close. In the last two furlongs you just had to shout him home, didn't you?'

Lynch adds: 'I would have hopped on a few horses when I was younger, though I was like a bag of sand. Useless. But that last hurdle, I jumped it with him. I'll never forget that stride at that last hurdle. It will live with me for ever.'

For Parsons, it provided a telling response to those who could never understand why he had not gone the conventional route of many of his fellow students at university. They'd say to him: 'Martin, why don't you get a proper job – not just sitting there at the computer?' Amongst them was Curley's wife Maureen. She still couldn't understand either why someone with a degree was doing this. When Jeu De Roseau struck the front, the normally placid Parsons could be heard yelling in mock self-censure: 'Why don't you get a proper job?'

In Newmarket, it was all rather more subdued. As Jeu De Roseau cleared that last hurdle, the solitary figure of Barney Curley in his usual position in his red chair drew quietly on his cigarette. 'I was sitting here, watched all the races on TV, but was not the least bit excited,' he says in the phlegmatic tone of an occasional racegoer who'd got a decent return from a £2 placepot. 'My attitude was, "If it comes it comes; if not, I'm not troubled."'

Parsons attempts to explain Curley's apparent insouciance. 'One of the reasons Barney has stood the test of time is that there is very little emotion involved,' he says. 'It keeps his judgement unclouded. He gets a buzz out of the planning and execution but he is never going to let one race change his mood or life no matter what is materially at stake. This day was really no different.'

That evening, Curley says, he may have passed a comment to Maureen that the day's proceedings had been successful. Though he couldn't guarantee it.

Wouldn't most husbands think it relevant to inform their wives that a scheme they'd devised had just won a fortune?

He looks bemused. 'Would you expect me to tell her if I lost several million? No, I never put her in the frame. She would never know what I was doing. I thought that was always best. I wouldn't have said much.'

Maureen must have had a fair idea of the scale of the scheme that had been instigated from her home, however.

'The highlight for me was that shortly after Jeu De Roseau won, she called me on my mobile to congratulate me,' recalls Parsons. 'In light of her well-intentioned criticism of my chosen path in life, I found this touching.'

Within racing, the details soon spread. That night, the *Racing Post* had a report on its online site under the headline 'Jeu De Roseau Lands Huge Punt At Towcester'.

Punters landed an extraordinary gamble on
Monday when the Chris Grant-trained Jeu De
Roseau scored a narrow victory at Towcester,
after being backed down to an SP of 6–4 from
25–1 in the morning.

The winner, formerly trained by Andrew
Stringer – renowned punter Barney Curley's
ex-assistant – and before that by Curley himself,
had been heavily backed all day, and the victory
followed gambles on three Curley-trained
runners earlier in the day.

Bookmakers, keen to downplay the outcome,
estimated losses of £1m.

The report hopelessly understated the reality, and even
that could have been so much worse.

Jeu De Roseau was one of Denis O'Regan's 402 rides
in 2010, which included major events at Cheltenham
and Aintree, amid scenes of feverish excitement. A month
earlier, he had finished runner-up on Black Apalachi in
the Grand National in front of more than 70,000 racegoers.

The 7.30 at Towcester on that May evening was a
considerably quieter affair. Yet for O'Regan it remains a
graphic memory. Though the race was insignificant in
itself, the context was important. 'I felt great. It was like
having a major victory at a big meeting, though it was
only a poxy little winner at a Towcester night meeting.
If it hadn't been for Barney's part, no one would have
noticed it.

'When I went back and watched everything and looked
at how it all took place, what happened throughout the
day, I was just blown away. My confidence was sky-high

after what people said about it. It made the front page of the *Racing Post*. It was as good as a Cheltenham winner, nearly.'

He adds: 'There was no pressure going into the ride because I didn't know what was happening. Sam Stronge would have heard during the day that there was a connection with the Barney Curley gamble. He knew that I was involved with Barney along the way. I had ridden out for him, and got quite close to him. But it was phenomenal: having known him and been so close to him, Barney never said a word to me about anything. Not even a word. Had I known what was happening I suppose I would have felt more relief. When I read everything, I felt very happy that I was the one who'd delivered the gold.'

The official Form Book verdict said it all: 'Jumped deliberately 1st, towards rear, ridden and headway before 3 out, still 4th and struggling to pick up before 2 out, driven and sustained run to lead last, soon asserted flat, fine ride (op 9–4 tchd 5–4).'

The *Racing Post* commented:

> The six-year-old showed very little when last seen, but bits and pieces of earlier form, not least when just 3l behind Won In The Dark, entitled him to huge respect off this lowly mark of 82. Although his hurdling was not entirely fluent early, it improved as the race progressed as he made headway up the inside and produced upsides at the last, he pinged it before staying on strongly to land the plunge under a fine ride.

Curley reflects: 'Chris Grant was right. The horse wasn't fit. But he was a good horse and he's improved a lot since.

And no jockey in the world would have won on that horse that day other than Denis O'Regan. I don't care what anyone says. He kept at him. We were also lucky that they went too fast at the beginning.'

He believes he had the multiple National Hunt champion jockey Tony McCoy to thank, in large part. 'The way the race was run with Tony McCoy setting such a fast pace early on, and maintaining it, was crucial. If they had gone slow it would have turned into a sprint for home. Over an inadequate trip, Jeu De Roseau would surely have been beaten.'

Chris Grant adds: 'I didn't even realise Curley had that many runners that day – until I got to the races. But Barney, knowing the horse of old, and knowing his form, [obviously felt] if he did come back would be worth putting in with his own horses.

'I never backed him. I'm not a gambling man at all. But we thought he'd run a big race if things went right. I was surprised when I got to the races and he was backed into favouritism. I got there, and someone said, "By 'eck, there's some money for your horse." I was a bit gobsmacked then. But then I thought they'd have a little bit on him down there, with Andrew having seen him work the week before.

'But Denis O'Regan gave him a proper ride. Things just worked out all right on the day. He got a tune out of him.'

Both Grant and Curley could be thankful that Jeu De Roseau hadn't been confined to the seller. After both horses had run that evening, Den Maschine would be assessed by the handicapper as no less than 33lb superior to Grant's charge.

Nevertheless, the trainer had clearly cracked his horse's

enigma code. At the time of writing, Jeu De Roseau is rated 38lb higher over hurdles than on 10 May, having won twice more and been placed several times. He has won three times on the Flat in between as well and could be considered a decent investment for owner Bill Raw and trainer Chris Grant, whose yard has continued to prosper. He certainly came good at the right time for Curley.

'He's done really well, the horse,' says Grant. 'When you thought what he was rated then, you could see why Barney backed him – if he thought he was anywhere near.'

As for Jeu De Roseau's jockey, O'Regan has made up the lost ground in his career. The upwards trajectory has continued where it left off after Howard Johnson. He now rides for John Ferguson, manager of Sheikh Mohammed's Darley operation and also a highly successful trainer.

CHAPTER 38

11 May 2010: the fallout (Part I)

The scale of the coup would require time to become fully apparent. Curiously, most of the layers, normally so vocal, had seemingly undergone a collective removal of the larynx in the immediate aftermath.

Their reticence was telling. As Brian O'Connor, racing correspondent of the *Irish Times*, emphasised in a blog, 'It's when you can't move for quotes from bookmakers reporting how they have been slain by colossal gambles and that it had been a bloodbath that they have, of course, in truth barely been grazed. Contrast this rush to play the media game with the reticence that accompanied Barney Curley's latest coup. It got name-rank-and-serial-number awful quick then.'

A one-off six- or seven-figure jackpot victory by a guy who gets lucky by picking numbers on the basis of birth dates, or selects horses' names after friends and relations, is feted by the bookmakers – a wonderful example to the remainder of punterland.

This was an entirely different matter. One horse – the nap of the day – had saved them from a serious flaying, but 10 May remained an embarrassment. Flaws in their systems had been exposed, not at the hands of some anonymous player, but by the nation's best-known backer.

All those hundreds of £4 Yankees went on to return winnings of up to £4,706 each. That figure would have risen to over £26,000 if Sommersturm had also won.

Parsons says: 'Bookmakers love to broadcast how much a big-race favourite has cost them. This, though, displayed a lack of vigilance in their trading departments, and they were at pains to suppress the reality.'

Normally, as we have seen, they take no chances with Curley's runners. The plan succeeded because bookmakers didn't take sufficient account of multiple bets, the horses didn't have much obvious form and, as Curley adds: 'If you've been quiet for quite a time . . .'

The bookies with a few exceptions remained, Trappist-like. 'Those hit the hardest kept quietest,' says Parsons. David Hood, the former conditional jockey who was then William Hill's PR director, contended that 'we will never know' how much had been won.

Curley soon knew precisely. The previous night, Parsons and Lynch had done a final audit of the figures. Parsons' calculations confirmed that it was the most won on horse racing in a single day. The total winnings amounted to £3.9 million, nearly twice as much as today's equivalent of what was won on Yellow Sam in 1975. It prompted Curley, not given to hyperbole where his betting is concerned, to tell the *Independent*'s Chris McCrrath: 'No one will ever win as much money again on horse racing this century.'

In fact, the loss to the layers was probably considerably greater. 'There must have been some betting shop managers who will have copped on and told their friends (to join in the action) . . .' declares Curley mischievously.

David Hood, interviewed the next morning as ATR reported on the events of 10 May, claimed that his firm had been on to the operation from 'very early' on the Monday morning. Because of this they had been able to manage their liabilities very carefully and wouldn't have lost six figures on the day.

According to Parsons, at 11.50 a.m. on the day itself, not one bet had been placed at a William Hill office. At 12 noon the horses were priced up at 11–2 Agapanthus, 4–1 Savaronola, 9–4 Sommersturm and 22–1 Jeu De Roseau. The only change by 12.32 p.m. was that they had pushed Savaronola out from 4–1 to 9–2.

Parsons claims, 'We took ninety grand off them from the shops around our base alone, with all bets placed after twelve noon. At three p.m., some three hours after we started placing bets with them, they were still laying £4 Yankees to lose five grand. Does that sound like a firm who were "on to the operation from very early that morning"?'

Parsons adds that at 2.32 p.m. Hill's were still laying bets such as £26 trebles that won £4,654 throughout their UK shops. He still has a copy of the dockets to confirm it.

The contrast in bookmakers' responses to 'May 10' with the day when Frankie Derttori went through the card, the partner of seven winners at Ascot in September 1996 could not have been more striking. Chris McGrath of the *Independent* described the latter occasion as "The Mug Punter's Revenge" adding how "the young Italian was the natural focus of any impulsive bet."

McGrath tells of one couple who had come up to London from Somerset to celebrate their wedding anniversary. He had gone racing at Ascot. She had gone shopping. To give his wife an interest, the husband made her a present of a bet at Ladbrokes in Mayfair. They included a £5 each-way accumulator on Dettori's mounts, She simply loved his personality.

Even with £900,000 win capped at the maximum £500,000, the couple, according to McGrath, were not too despondent, having originally calculated their winnings at £300,000. There were numerous similar stories that day, but whatever the layers' immediate costs, they would have had to pay many times that for the advertising it yielded them.

The reality was that any losses were recouped many times over by the big firms through multiple bets which handicap the regular punter before they even start.

On 10 May 2010, Curley took a little of it back from them.

BOOKMAKERS HAD BEEN attacked precisely where they felt safest and in an area that was profitable. Parsons says: 'Inspiration was drawn by the industry's excessive promotion of multiples. If they promote it, they think you'll lose, and that is where they are weakest.'

Afterwards, Curley stressed the overriding importance of getting the equine details right. Without that, it was a powerful army of men marching without weaponry. 'The important part was getting the four horses. No doubt about it. That was the nightmare,' he reflects drily.

However, he was in debt to a highly disciplined group who had placed hundreds of bets. Curley, through his lieutenants, had demanded trust, and they had responded impeccably. 'Let's just say that none of these people broke the line,' says Curley, just as he had applauded his own men who had contributed to the Yellow Sam coup all those years before. 'Jeu De Roseau was 25–1 for three hours and didn't move. That was a big achievement. I told them they'd be part of history – something they'd be able to tell their grandchildren.'

He laughs at the vision of fold-up bicycles taken on the Tube to expedite the operation. 'The synchronisation of the bets was brilliantly executed, but I don't take much credit for it. The most difficult aspect was keeping things quiet. Fifty pounds in the wrong place at the wrong time – that's all it would have needed. Most people are untrustworthy when it comes to money. But no one told tales out of school.'

Parsons confirms: 'There wasn't any kind of leak, and Barney thinks we performed a miracle finding a team who all kept it so quiet. But these were proper people who thrived under the responsibility of the trust placed in them.'

His only slight regret, in hindsight, was that the plans may have been over-cautious. Parsons believes that 95 per cent of the time, members of the team could have dashed in, placed the bet and been out the door again in a few seconds, and it would have made no difference. Few would have been as sharp as the manager of Victor Chandler who stymied the attempted high-stakes bet.

As has been already testified by Henry MacCormack, when he presented his £50 Yankee (a total of £550), the manager would only give SP (which turned out to be 6–4) on Jeu De Roseau when his price was as long as 28–1 in places at the time. If he had been able to obtain the early price, that slip would have paid £65,425. The manager was smart enough only to let him take the three shorter-priced horses. As it was, with Jeu De Roseau at an SP of 6–4, the bet paid just £7,125.

One final thought on that subject worth contemplating. If Henry MacCormack had been able to take that early price on Jeu De Roseau, and Sommersturm had also won, that one Yankee would have returned £358,000

Fortunately for Victor Chandler, his staff were more attuned to possible dangers than most betting office employees. The majority accepted the bets without question. It would only have taken one clued-up staff member or manager of a large chain to think: 'Hang on a minute – that's strange . . .' and alert head office. That was what had concerned Parsons: 'We were maybe a little paranoid ourselves because of that reaction from the Jenningsbet manager in Camden.'

The betting team returned home to lives where no one knew what they had been involved in; back to their everyday routines, but now, as Parsons puts it, with an invisible feather in their caps. Somehow the fact that no one else was aware how they had spent their weekend made it all the more satisfying.

The following morning, Patrick McGovern tidied up the apartments and used a cab to drop the fold-up bikes back to their rental base. For some reason, he was still twitchy, still as wary as when he had first arrived. By now it was ingrained in him not to give the game away. 'The cab driver said he used to like a bet, but it was a mug's game. I was so nervous as to where this line of conversation had come from that when he asked what I did for a living, I told him I was a transport economist; that I'd used the bikes to check cycle routes for the Olympics! Anything to avoid the real reason.'

He walked all the way to Westminster to soak up the

post-election atmosphere, and saw Iain Duncan Smith strut his way into Coalition negotiations before finally making his way home, and back to a life mundane in comparison.

Parsons had dinner with his parents, who were quite unaware of his unorthodox occupation, let alone the special operation he'd been engaged in. 'They asked me how my week had been. "Oh, quiet," I said. "Fairly quiet."'

CHAPTER 39

11 May 2010 (Part II)

Barely had the third victor of the day, Jeu De Roseau, been loaded into his horsebox for the journey back to Durham than the question began to be asked: how had the most fancied of the quartet been beaten? And well beaten at that?

There were some perverse conspiracy theories suggesting that it had never been part of the plan for Sommersturm to win that day, but such conjecture doesn't bear scrutiny. It would have achieved nothing. Withdrawing the horse before the race would have been more beneficial.

Parsons explains: 'A straightforward answer to this would point out that if Sommersturm was a non-runner and had been withdrawn, instead of running and being beaten, and the three others won as they did, the returns from the operation would have been over £8 million – over £4 million more. There would have been no losing lines in any of the bets placed. Similarly, if Sommersturm had run and won, total winnings, even with maximum payouts capped, would have been over £15 million.'

The defeat of that horse had brutally exposed the belief

that there are certainties in racing. Just as had happened in April the previous year, when Curley had targeted a treble, the 'nap' on 10 May had gone down.

Sommersturm had clearly been expected to do the business. Parsons still retains as a keepsake and permanent reminder of the one downside of that day a collection of betting slip counterfoils naming Agapanthus, Savaronola and Sommersturm for the treble. The trio had been considered the solid bets.

The reality was this: if there had been anything un-toward in the horses' running either in April 2009 or on this day 13 months on, it can be guaranteed that the BHA would have descended upon Curley from a great height.

When he conceived the plan, Curley was determined that the bookmakers should be able to offer no just cause, or even a trumped-up one, to evade their liabilities, nor should there be any legal comebacks. 'That was very important for us. We didn't want any "ifs" after winning and not get paid. We got paid (eventually) every dollar. When you're going to do a scheme like this, you've got to make sure it's legal. People don't. That was my first thought.'

In fact the BHA declared – after studying videos of the four horses' past performances, reviewing betting patterns and interviewing Curley – that no rules of racing had been breached. In addition, the Independent Betting Arbitration Service (an impartial adjudicator on disputes that arise between betting/gambling operators and their customers) directed the firms in the UK to pay out their winnings.

That acceptance, particularly by the BHA, didn't satisfy certain critics. For approaching four decades, Barney

Curley's gambling enterprises had been met with the full gamut of responses, but very rarely indifference. This one was no exception. The *Racing Post*'s Alan Sweetman wrote: 'As the drama unfolded on the track and in the offices on Monday, it was hard not be seduced by the thrill, with anticipation building to the moment where Denis O'Regan delivered Jeu De Roseau to victory. So much of the fascination of racing lies in episodes such as this.'

The same paper's Review of the Year reflected: 'Rather like Halley's Comet, Barney Curley is unseen for protracted periods, but bookmakers never forget he is out there plotting quietly. In May, Curley came from out of the blue to blitz across the racing horizon, scorching bookmakers in Britain and Ireland with an expertly orchestrated coup.'

Not everyone was so moved. Eddie Freemantle, presenter on the satellite channel Racing UK, and also a punter, suggested that Curley was exploiting a major failing of the handicap system, 'that these horses had fallen so readily in the weights'. He called on the BHA to 'ban horses widely regarded as uncompetitive following a string of defeats, but just the type Curley has made his reputation with, often bringing them back to win following a lengthy lay-off', adding: 'It makes a mockery of the handicap system . . . Barney is playing the game, but the game is making it easy for him.'

The BHA's head of handicapping Phil Smith issued a staunch rebuttal, analysing the performances of the quartet, including Chris Grant's Jeu De Roseau, and arguing that the descent down the handicap of all the runners was correct, and would have applied whatever the identity of the trainer concerned. He concluded pointedly: 'The reality is that nobody ever complains when we drop a horse by however large an amount unless it wins, unless it is gambled on, and unless it is trained by someone of whom they are suspicious.'

Curley was gratified by Smith's response. 'The handicappers have the hardest job in racing and they are nobody's fools,' he declared.

The Irishman was a master at working within the handicapping system, without transgressing the rules of racing, but so are many others. Certain rather more public trainers are lionised over their capability to 'lay out' a horse for a major handicap. The difference is that Curley operates alone, and information is kept in-house. It all goes back to that adage that the successful gambler knows something that nobody else does.

As has been stressed in previous pages, today there is precious little scope for chicanery. Certainly, in recent years, the racing authorities have been exceptionally vigilant. Stewards observe runners closely. Previous races are reviewed. Betting patterns are scrutinised. Inquiries are held. Action can be draconian, with the guilty handed lengthy suspensions.

For all the opprobrium that certain of Curley's critics heap on him, in four decades as gambler, owner and trainer he has never faced serious sanction for the running of his horses.

One critic, Sean Boyce, who formerly worked for Ladbrokes and is a presenter on the satellite racing channel At the Races, said that Curley was the poker equivalent of a 'mechanic', claiming: 'A card mechanic, provided he holds the deck in his hands and it's his deal, can choose which cards fall where and when.'

Curley scoffs at such barbs.

Much of the success of 10 May was attributable to providence as much as to judgement. He insists that confidence about his own trio had never been total – and he had to take Chris Grant's estimation of Jeu De Roseau on trust. 'He wasn't fit, really. But he stays well. It's Tony McCoy I can thank for going a good pace. Chris's horse had a very low weight and was lucky to get a run at all. Twenty-two horses came out so that he got into the race. Even then, no other jump jockey would have won on the horse. Some may have given him a doodle round, given him a blow after so long off the track.'

The trainer-gambler adds: 'They weren't good races, none of them, but it wasn't a case of stones up their sleeve or anything. At Brighton, Agapanthus was first off the bridle.' Ultimately, however, he believed the gelding was showing his optimum at home, and that his faith had been justified. Just to confirm it, Agapanthus won at Sandown for him the following month, despite the burden of an additional 8lb. He later moved on to Neil Mulholland's Wiltshire stables.

'You never know,' Curley states defiantly. 'Savaronola on Sunday morning was on three legs. The blacksmith did a great job. Yes, he trotted up here in the yard. Running them in a race is a different matter. He could have gone lame after two furlongs. Not too many people except myself would have taken the chance. Declan Queally was brilliant on him. He closed Sir Alex's horse in there on the second last bend. Kept him on the rails and he couldn't get out. By the time he did, the race was over.'

Savaronola turned out to be the most impressive winner of the day. At the time of writing, that has remained his only victory. He moved on to Des Donovan's yard at Exning. (Sir Alex Ferguson's If I Had Him, incidentally, went on to win his next two races, over longer distances, before the end of the month.) Curley adds: 'It's no good me pretending I'm the "great I am" because there was an awful lot of luck involved there.'

The beaten Sommersturm did finally win a race for him, at Wolverhampton of all places, 20 months later, at the nineteenth time of trying in this country. He was backed in from 8–1 to 7–2 joint favourite. The horse moved on to Monmouthshire trainer David Evans and has been successful three times since.

The Sommersturm setback was a rare reversal on a day when Curley was blessed in so many ways. He concedes: 'That gallop at Lingfield led me astray.' His defeat meant the difference between a massive coup, and one which, as Lynch put it later, would have made it on to the front of the *FT* because of the probable fallout within the bookmaking industry.

All of the tens of hundreds of Yankee bets staked in the shops were winning slips, with four winning lines from 11 (three doubles and a treble). But Sommersturm's defeat meant that only the ABD (Agapanthus, Savaronola and Jeu De Roseau) trebles were winners. 'In consequence, 87 per cent of trebles placed in shops lost,' says Parsons. 'It would have been a colossal payout if Sommersturm had won.'

Curley, though, is phlegmatic about it all. If ever an extra £10m could be superfluous to a man's thinking, this was a case in point. A few weeks later, on an evening tour of his stables, Curley halted at Sommersturm's box, gently stroked the horse's head and said: 'You're the fella that cost us ten million, aren't you . . .'

Suggest to him that it was maybe for the best, that it was fortuitous that only three won, and he responds with a world-weary chuckle. 'I'd say the bookies would all have got together . . .' The words trail off. He adds: 'I often think about that, and I'm coming to the conclusion that it's a good job the fourth one didn't win – because we'd have had even more problems getting the money than we did. Throw in the other one, and you're talking over £15 million. We had the power and money to get solicitors and lawyers. Not everybody would.'

Virtually all bookmakers paid the winnings due. But two online bookmaking operations, Betfred.com – Betfred's online operation – withheld payments totalling £823,000. Another firm, 888sport, refused to pay out £23,000. Other Gibraltar-based online operators had paid out – as had Betfred's betting shop division.

It led to a legal stand-off in Gibraltar. Betfred eventually paid out, but only after a protracted and expensive legal case in the self-governing British territory, once known primarily as an important strategic naval base, but increasingly in recent years as an offshore location for financial interests and, of late, internet gaming operators.

Since 1999, there has been a steady migration of online betting companies and it is easy to see why such entities have flocked to the Rock. The benefits include just 1 per cent gaming tax on turnover, capped at £425,000, compared with 15 per cent on profits in the UK. Offshore companies also do not have to pay UK levels of VAT on costs like advertising and are not paying corporation tax to the UK government. Most crucially, offshore operations do not have to pay the 10.75 per cent betting levy on profits – although some do so voluntarily. This is income which is vital to the health of British racing.

Conservative MP Matthew Hancock, whose constituency includes Newmarket, told the Commons in July 2011 that 'in the past few years, levy had fallen from

£110m a year to £59m'. He added: 'Funding for horseracing has been in crisis and the problem has been in part that those [bookmakers] who make a profit from the sport through gambling have gone offshore to escape contributing to the sport on which they rely.'

It should be emphasised that Curley wasn't owed the Betfred winnings himself. Four relatives of Curley's, and a friend of one of them, were owed the money.

Betfred's online operation decision to withhold payment was made pending an investigation, on the advice of the Gibraltar Regulatory Authority, as it was then known, headed by Phill Brear, an ex-Deputy Chief Constable of the West Yorkshire police and formerly the UK Gambling Commission's operations chief. Betfred nullified the bets under a rule stating: 'Any person or group of persons acting in an attempt to defraud Betred.com will have their bets voided'.

The affair became a cause célèbre, not least because it provoked accusations that winnings on bets placed with the online operations of familiar British bookmaking names, based on the Rock, would not necessarily be paid.

Phill Brear denied this was the case when I put it to him for an article which appeared in the *Independent*, claiming 'Millions of bets a week are placed through Gibraltar operators and the winnings are paid out very quickly . . . but a small number find themselves subject to review and examination by the operator and sometimes by ourselves.'

Nevertheless, the stance taken by Betfred was not well timed by a firm which had expanded from one betting shop in Fred Done's home town of Salford in 1967 – mostly funded by a substantial wager on England to win the World Cup in the previous year – to 840 offices by the time it paid £265 million to take over that government-owned

British betting institution, the Tote, created in 1928. It was not the kind of PR Betfred would have desired at that moment. Others in the bookmaking industry were not enamoured by this running dispute, either.

Significantly, Ralph Topping, the chief executive of William Hill, said the new owner of the Tote was setting a 'poor example'. Writing in his blog, Topping said the case was 'not reflecting well on some elements of the betting industry'.

He added: 'Whatever the moral arguments about Curley's approach, the fact is these were legal bets and should be paid out. There was no cheating. The British Horseracing Authority has ruled horses ran according to official rating. There was no reason to disqualify the runners and so no reason not to pay out. The idea that a licensed bookmaker could consider treating high street and online UK customers differently isn't just a slippery slope, it's positively precipitous.'

Phill Brear, the GRA's head of gambling regulation, was unrepentant as relations between his body and the BHA became increasingly strained. He remained adamant that his was the only agency to have conducted 'a meaningful and proportionate' investigation into the coup.

Writing to the *Racing Post*, Brear added: 'Over a period of 12 months we accumulated detailed factual information that no other single party has access to. As a public authority we are not able to release this information, but it has been reviewed by UK counsel and this confirms our view that the coup was a fraudulent enterprise based on deceptions and the systematic misuse of inside information.'

The BHA were having none of it. Its then spokesman Paul Struthers retorted: 'It is not for the GRA to tell us that we are wrong in our interpretation of the rules. This highlights our concerns in relation to offshore betting operators being outside British gambling legislation.'

According to a *Racing Post* report in August 2011, BHA director of Integrity Services Paul Scotney reminded Brear in an email that: 'Barney Curley has used inside information (which he will legitimately have as a trainer) to place a series of bets directly (or indirectly through other parties) on horses to win.

'This in itself is not a breach of our rules as he has not been communicating inside information directly or indirectly to any other person for material reward, gift, favour, or benefit of any kind.

'The reality is that this type of behaviour happens on a daily basis . . . I have no doubt had the betting organisations in Gibraltar (and for that matter in this country) known Barney Curley was behind this, they would not have taken his bets, which is what they have done in the past.'

Brear's handling of the affair led to legal representatives for the five punters applying to the Supreme Court of Gibraltar for a judicial review of the actions and decisions of the GRA. As the row became increasingly acrimonious, lawyers for the claimants even hired a firm of private detectives to follow Brear. Solicitor for the punters, Andrew Montague, maintained: 'My clients instruct me that they are determined to get justice in Gibraltar no matter how long it takes. Who could blame them? After all, they are owed an awful lot of money – almost 1m Euros.'

In Spain, where, it could be suggested, any discomfort caused to the administration of the Gibraltar government is relished, the contrasting positions of the BHA and GRA were observed with a certain fascination. It was presumably purely by coincidence that, during this period, a racecourse in southern Spain, the Hipodromo Costa del Sol at Mijas, not too far from Gibraltar, staged a race named the Premio Barney Curley Stakes?

This 'special race night', as it was branded, included 'a visit from the UK legend of the Turf, renowned gambler and trainer, Barney Curley'.

Then, suddenly, early in 2012, came a declaration that hostilities had ceased. Twenty-one months after it had all started, a joint statement issued by all the participants announced that, after detailed investigations concerning betting activities on 10 May 2010, Gibraltar's Gambling Commissioner had 'decided to pursue the matter no further'. The precise background to this is unknown as all the parties have signed a confidentiality clause.

Betfred paid out under the settlement terms. 888sport followed suit, although not a party to the agreement. Legal action against the Gibraltar Gambling Commissioner – by then Brear's title – was discontinued.

Belatedly, the sabres were sheathed as it became a triumph for rationality, though Brear, apparently could not let the matter rest.

In written evidence to a House of Commons Culture, Media & Sport Select Committee in 2013, he stated: 'The BHA undermined a major investigation by my office by making a decision, in isolation, in favour of its licence holder, then declining on data protection grounds to provide us with anything other than a cursory and legally incoherent explanation, despite the licence holder giving a contradictory version of events to the media. The BHA has subsequently overtly supported the right of BHA licence holders to manipulate races, share inside information and bet on themselves "en masse", by way of using the identities of related third parties.'

CHAPTER 40

Postscript

A little over three years on, and a fatigued Barney Curley, just returned from the overwhelming heat of Zambia, is seated under a tree at his Newmarket stud to recover from the trip, attended by his sleeping St Bernard, Arnie.

Around the turn of the year, a *Racing Post* front page had announced: 'It's farewell Curley – trainer and legendary gambler hangs up his racing and betting boots.'

The bare statistics reveal that in his final season, he finished 271th in the Flat trainers' standings, of 498. He had six winners, from 61 races, and won £17,903 prize money. If you had a pound on all his runners, you'd be £27.87 down for your trouble. Yet right up until the end of 2012, when he declined to renew his licence, Curley continued to confound the bookies, and anyone else who attempted to read him.

In the summer of that year, his gelding Sir Mozart won by eight lengths at Wolverhampton, under Joe Fanning. The horse hadn't won for nearly two years and started at 9–2. An on-course bookmaker, Peter Mace, observed: 'Sir Mozart opened at 12–1 then went down to 5–1, then drifted out to 11–1, then came all the way back. It was weird, but it's Barney Curley – everyone's a bit frightened of him.'

But now, finally, the Irishman was unfettered from the demands of turning a profit from racing. 'The buzz has gone from the game,' he says. 'I don't miss betting in the least.'

Meanwhile, his 10 May team leaders have moved on with their lives. Martin Parsons says he has 'taken up a number of short-term consultancy positions. But I still follow the racing and betting industry closely.'

Jack Lynch, bailed out of the City in the wake of the global financial crisis, disillusioned with the hedonistic champagne existence, and says he has now adopted a slower pace of life back in the countryside in Ireland with the love of his life. He has established a start-up business.

For Curley, habits die hard, his old routine is not readily discarded. The gambler, trainer, crusader and charity founder still wakes at 5.45. But these days there's no cacophony from horses being prepared for their work outside.

The *Guardian*'s racing correspondent Greg Wood juxtaposed Curley's retirement with the enforced exit from Channel 4 racing of his old antagonist John McCririck. The latter would refuse to depart quietly, accusing the TV channel of age discrimination at an industrial tribunal – a case he lost. Wood suggested that they were men who prospered in a different time, and argued that modern racing would not offer the same opportunities for a younger version of Curley starting out in the game. The form of the horses, he wrote, is more reliable these days. But with Curley's departure, 'a little of the colour has been bleached away too'.

Unlike McCririck, Curley had no intention of fighting the passage of the years. 'I had that kick up the arse [his illness], and was probably lucky to get out of it.' He picks up a battered phone book. 'I've had this since I was forty. When I glance through it, so many people are dead.' (Before the year was out, he would be grieving the news that his great friend and owner Patsy Byrne had passed away, aged 64.)

'I regard myself as lucky to still be able to do this,' Curley adds. He means his work in Africa. 'Just had call from a Kenyan priest. We'd given him £27,000 to build a three-classroom school. He told me, "It's started."' Curley has also overseen the launch of an ambitious 'Virtual Learning Africa', with an online link between Omagh College and the schools DAFA supports in Zambia.

'In no way am I a religious buff, but those who can do it should help others. Those people in Zambia can't help themselves. I've learnt so much. I can talk now with knowledge about charity in Africa.

'My philosophy in life is simply to have peace of mind and be ready to meet your Maker. I believe there's a God. We'll meet him some day. He'll be our judge. The big thing he'll be looking for is how did we treat our fellow human beings?

'I've always said I'll die penniless. So I will – bar something comes along again; if I have a touch at something. But if I have enough time to get rid of it, I will.'

It prompts the multimillion-pound question: so why set out to storm the bookies' citadel on 10 May 2010?

It is simply this: the concept, the planning, the subterfuge – it all fires him. Not so the rewards. 'I don't have much regard for money,' he says. 'I had planned that coup every waking hour for so long. A couple of days afterwards, I was empty. It was always the challenge – nothing else.'

And yet in his time he paid a fortune for a stately home, Middleton Park, and Terry Ramsden's mansion.

'A mistake. All mistakes. If I had my life over again, I wouldn't have done that. That's why I always had in mind: if I win a race, fine; if I lose, it's not important. Even on 10 May. I have no interest in building up monuments to my life's work, or wealth for its own sake. There's no pocket in the dead man's shroud.

'I don't want to depart this world with people saying, "He did well, didn't he? He was the man who pulled off a bit of a coup in 2010, or who skinned the bookmakers alive with an audacious plot at Bellewstown." I want to leave this world thinking I'd done a bit of good.

'All I am certain is that I am the only man who could have pulled it off that day. You have to think outside the box. I think differently from other people in racing.'

Back in his office, we watch a race together on TV: the Group 3 Bahrain Trophy at Newmarket's July meeting. For a moment, old instincts kick in. He analyses the contest in fine detail. Tells you why the favourite was beaten. What could improve. Comments on the jockeys. It is purely academic, though.

'I haven't backed for ages – I'd look at them on the TV. That's about it. Do you know, people ask me: "Would you try it again [10 May]?" No. No chance.'

And yet. There's the odd cryptic reference, relating to 'a touch'. He talks about the possibility of a permit to train 'a few of my own horses'.

Just cold turkey? The words of a man whose desire for

combat with the layers of odds will never be quelled? Where this character, the embodiment of unpredictability, is concerned, you simply don't know.

It is a fair bet to say that until the day they carry him out, the bookmakers won't truly rest easy.